How NGOs React

.4574

The book documents OSI Open Society Institute's (OSI) contributions to education change in the Caucasus, Central Asia, and Mongolia which are the results of the project submitted by the coalition of the Open Society Institute/Soros Foundation and spin-off NGOs from Armenia, Azerbaijan, Georgia, Kazakhstan, Kyrgyzstan, Mongolia, Tajikistan, and Uzbekistan. The project has been administered by the International Institute for Education Policy, Planning and Management (EPPM) and supported by the Open Society Institute (OSI) with the contribution of the Education Support Program of OSI Budapest.

How NGOs React

*Globalization and Education Reform
in the Caucasus, Central Asia, and Mongolia*

EDITED BY
IVETA SILOVA AND GITA STEINER-KHAMSI

Kumarian
Press, Inc.

How NGOs React: Globalization and Education Reform in the Caucasus, Central Asia, and Mongolia
Published in 2008 in the United States of America by Kumarian Press, Inc., 1294 Blue Hills Avenue, Bloomfield, CT 06002 USA

The text of this book is set in 10.5.13 Esprit Book.

Production and design by Joan Weber Laflamme, jml ediset
Proofread by Beth Richards
Index by Robert Swanson
Cover design by Sina McCants Mossayeb
Cover photograph by Maryam Borjian

Printed in the United States of America by Thomson-Shore, Inc. Text printed with vegetable oil-based ink.

∞The paper used in this publication meets the minimum requirements of the American National Standard for Information Sciences—Permanence of Paper for printed Library Materials, ANSI Z39.48–1984

Library of Congress Cataloging-in-Publication Data

How NGOs react : globalization and education reform in the Caucasus, Central Asia and Mongolia / edited by Iveta Silova and Gita Steiner-Khamsi.
    p. cm.
    Includes bibliographical references and index.
    ISBN 978-1-56549-257-8 (pbk. : alk. paper)
1. Educational change—Caucasus. 2. Educational change—Mongolia. 3. Educational change—Asia, Central. 4. Non-governmental organizations—Caucasus. 5. Non-governmental organizations—Mongolia. 6. Non-governmental organizations—Asia, Central. 7. Education and globalization. I. Silova, Iveta. II. Steiner-Khamsi, Gita.
  L624.H69 2008
  370'.958—dc22
                2007043514

Contents

Illustrations

Tables

Figures

Preface

Seldom do organizations open their books to a wider audience, revealing the internal strategies and debates that shape their policymaking. Either they print a few copies of self-assessment and evaluation studies for internal use, or they publish thousands of glossy annual reports and brochures for public dissemination. Now is an opportune moment for the national foundations of the Soros Network in the Caucasus, Central Asia, and Mongolia to engage in a critical retrospective of their own work. Several of them have been spun off into national NGOs, and one of them (Open Society Institute Assistance Foundation–Uzbekistan) was shut down by the government. Philanthropist George Soros believes in the limited lifespan of projects and national foundations and continuously reinvents his foundation in ways to scale up social, economic, and political impact. The remaining national foundations in the region realize that their days are numbered because they must eventually phase out, spin off, or leave.

This is not a book on the history of the Soros Network in the post-socialist region. Although historical details are inevitable in a retrospective, they serve to address the broader issues: How do NGOs function in a centralist government environment? What are their roles, challenges, and strategies in influencing educational reform? How do they interface with multilateral aid agencies? The authors of these case studies on Armenia, Azerbaijan, Georgia, Kazakhstan, Kyrgyzstan, Mongolia, Tajikistan, Turkmenistan, and Uzbekistan are former or current educational experts of the Soros Network based in the region. They have given an honest descriptive and analytical account of what worked and what did not in the educational programs that they coordinated and confronted.

The idea to write this book dates back to a hot summer day in Tbilisi, in the Republic of Georgia. In July 2004, the authors attended a memorable meeting of NGOs, mostly staff members of policy centers, representing over fifteen post-socialist countries, organized by the Education Support Program of the Open Society Institute. The Georgian deputy minister of education's keynote address listed all the accomplishments of her government over the past decade: extension of schooling to twelve years, reduction of the number of subjects in the curriculum, introduction of new subjects (for example, civic education and computer literacy), student-centered learning, electives in upper secondary schools, standardized student assessment, reorganization of schools by either closing them down or merging them with ones that were larger and better equipped, decentralization of educational finance and governance, liberalized regulations for textbook publishing, and private-sector involvement in higher education.

The members of the audience nodded in unison. What was unfolding in front of their eyes was the *post-socialist education reform package,* which had traveled across the entire region of Central, Eastern, and Southeastern Europe, the Caucasus, Central Asia, and Mongolia. During the ensuing coffee break, a few of us commented on how interesting it would be to examine what role NGOs, and in particular the Soros Network—the largest and most influential educational NGO in the region during the post-socialist era—have played in supporting, complementing, or correcting reforms with their own educational projects.

Thus, the book was born. But how were we to manage collaboratively a project with twelve authors residing in different countries? The two co-editors approached the Education Support Program of the Open Society Institute (OSI) in Budapest for a grant that would enable the authors to meet and discuss their drafts. The International Institute for Educational Policy, Planning, and Management in Georgia agreed to act as a project implementation agency and coordinate meetings of the authors. The team met twice during the annual conventions of the Comparative and International Education Society (CIES). We were able to present early versions of the chapters at the CIES conferences in Stanford (2005) and Hawaii (2006) and to integrate feedback from researchers and practitioners working in NGOs, universities, and development agencies. The first co-editor, Iveta Silova, took the lead in all these efforts, from securing the grant, to coordinating the team of authors, to ultimately editing the chapters you see here.

As individuals who are semi-peripheral to the NGO world and the Soros Network, we feel compelled to explain in more detail our own role and "location" as co-editors. Iveta Silova was a member of an early cohort of Muskie fellows from Latvia (1995–97), completing her M.A. and M.Ed. degrees at Teachers College, Columbia University. During her studies in New York, she worked as a consultant for the Children and Youth Programs at the OSI, under the remarkable leadership of Liz Lorant. Upon her return to Latvia, she worked for two years as a program coordinator at the Soros Foundation–Latvia. After completing her Ph.D. at Columbia University in 2002, she continued to work as an education consultant and adviser for the OSI's Children and Youth Programs in New York and the Education Support Program in Budapest. In addition, she worked as a researcher and visiting professor in Almaty (Kazakhstan) and Baku (Azerbaijan) for over five years. Over the past few years she has continued to work as an education consultant, adviser, and researcher for UNICEF, the Organization for Security and Co-operation in Europe (OSCE), and the World Bank in the countries of the former socialist bloc, including Southeast Europe (Macedonia and Bosnia and Herzegovina), the Baltic states (Latvia), the Caucasus (Azerbaijan and Georgia), Central Asia (Kazakhstan, Kyrgyzstan, Tajikistan, Turkmenistan, and Uzbekistan), and Russia.

As with many professors, Gita Steiner-Khamsi owes most of her applied work experience in development to her students. Her former students, Iveta Silova and Ami Talkow (Golden), recommended her to OSI New York as a consultant. What started with a recommendation turned out to be a major professional and personal bond with the Mongolian Foundation for Open Society in Ulaanbaatar. A three-year project (School 2001) continued with another three-year project (Teacher 2005) and eventually spanned a ten-year period in which she has been actively involved as an analyst and adviser for educational reform in Mongolia. She also served for a short time (2002–5) as a member of the General Education Sub-Board of the OSI. In addition to her consultancies for the Soros Network, she has conducted several analytical studies for DANIDA (Danish International Development Agency) and UNESCO in Mongolia, the World Bank in Mongolia and Tajikistan, and for the United States Agency for International Development (USAID) in Tajikistan and Kyrgyzstan.

Having worked extensively in this part of the world and being semi-peripherally involved with the Soros Network, we felt honored that the authors, education experts based in the region, entrusted us with co-editing a volume that included their case studies. They moved beyond merely describing what worked and what did not in their respective countries. As authors and co-editors we reserved the right to express our opinions freely, including the possibility that our analyses and interpretations would not always reflect the views held by the Soros Network. For safeguarding this publishing freedom, we have a person of great integrity and visionary leadership, Hugh McLean, director of the Education Support Program of OSI (now based in London), to thank.

Beyond the utility of having two co-editors, this collaboration has strengthened an intellectual partnership that began years ago. We are also grateful for having worked so closely with colleagues based in the Caucasus, Central Asia, and Mongolia. In a period that has seen great social, political, and economic upheaval, we deeply respect them for having stayed in the turbulent NGO sector over this long decade. For the Soros Network, an era of great effort and accomplishment in the region is coming to an end. It is not without distress that individuals and institutions have taken note of the Soros Network's decision to move on to other parts of the world. What is left behind, however, is more than this book: it is a network of educational experts that now work in other NGOs, development agencies, and, in some cases, government structures. Ultimately, our thanks and hopes are with them.

Abbreviations and Acronyms

ACCELS	American Councils for International Education
ADB	Asian Development Bank
CIDA	Canadian International Development Agency
CIES	Comparative and International Education Society
CMEA	Council for Mutual Economic Assistance
DANIDA	Danish International Development Agency
EBRD	European Bank for Reconstruction and Development
EDMD	Education Decentralization and Management Development project
EFA	Education for All
EMIS	Education Management Information System
EPSU	Education Program Support Unit
ERSU	Education Reform Support Unit (Tajikistan)
ESP	Education Support Program (formerly the IEP and before that the EPSU)
EU	European Union
FTI	Fast-Track Initiative
GDP	gross domestic product
GDR	German Democratic Republic
GNI	gross national income
GTZ	die Deutsche Gesellschaft für Technische Zusammenarbeit
ICT	information and communication technology
IDEA	International Debate Education Association
IEP	Institute for Educational Policy (formerly the EPSU)
IMF	International Monetary Fund
IREX	International Research and Exchanges Board

ISSA	International Step by Step Association
JICA	Japanese International Cooperation Agency
KOICA	Korea International Cooperation Agency
MDGs	Millennium Development Goals
MEA	Mongolian Education Alliance
MFOS	Mongolian Foundation for Open Society
MOECS	Ministry of Education, Culture and Science (Mongolia)
OBE	outcomes-based education
ODA	official development assistance
OECD	Organisation for Economic Co-operation and Development
OSCE	Organization for Security and Co-operation in Europe
OSGF	Open Society Georgia Foundation
OSI	Open Society Institute
OSIAF	Open Society Institute Assistance Foundation
PEAKS	Participation, Education, and Knowledge Strengthening (USAID-funded project)
READ	Rural Education and Development (Mongolia)
RSDP	Rural School Development Project (Mongolia)
RWCT	"Reading and Writing for Critical Thinking" (OSI)
SAP	structural adjustment program
SbS	"Step by Step" (OSI)
SFK	Soros Foundation–Kazakhstan
SIDA	Swedish International Development Cooperation Agency
TAN	transnational advocacy network
TICA	Turkish International Cooperation Agency
UN	United Nations
UNDP	United Nations Development Programme
UNESCO	United Nations Educational, Scientific, and Cultural Organization
USAID	United States Agency for International Development

Introduction

Unwrapping the Post-Socialist Education Reform Package

IVETA SILOVA AND GITA STEINER-KHAMSI

The authors of this book have taken on the ambitious task of examining educational development during a particular historical moment in the Caucasus, Central Asia, and Mongolia. The period under investigation begins in 1992, when new funders—development banks and bilateral donors—entered the region. The organizations of the United Nations system, in particular the United Nations Educational, Scientific, and Cultural Organization (UNESCO) and the United Nations Development Programme (UNDP), had been the only international organizations that bridged both world-systems during the Cold War. Thus, they were not newcomers but rather reinvented themselves in response to the new challenges of the post-Soviet or post-socialist era. In the mid-1990s, shortly after the appearance of international aid in the region, the international NGOs opened field offices or national foundations. By the end of the 1990s, all segments of the donor community were represented, their agendas set, and contours of educational development clearly discernible. The authors end their retrospective with the year 2007. Because of their past or current professional association with the national foundations of the Soros Network, the authors of this book naturally present their assessment from the perspective of NGOs.

In an attempt to identify patterns of educational development in the region, we have taken a step back to reflect on why some educational reforms have emerged only in one or two countries, whereas others have spread rapidly across the region. Globalization only partially explains why educational systems have in some areas converged toward an international model of educational reform. Globalization in the context of donor-dependent countries is not a vaguely defined, faceless "external force." Rather, it is represented by international organizations operating as donors and implementers of reform projects. This "globalization with a face" is the focus of our interest.

Not all educational systems, however, have been reformed in the same manner, and differences persist. An international comparative perspective is needed to identify "traveling reforms" that have been transferred to every corner of the world, including in the Caucasus, Central Asia, and Mongolia. But it is also necessary to use a regional, as well as a national, lens to detect the actual differences that exist with regard to education development. A trifocal perspective—international, regional and national—will bring to light reform areas that had been susceptible to convergence or divergence, respectively, and help us to understand the enacting forces, that is, the agencies and reasons, for educational transfer across the region.

From a regional perspective, it is puzzling to discover what we label a post-socialist education reform package. The package was transferred to the region after the collapse of Soviet Empire. From Baku to Ulaanbaatar, educational policymakers have used remarkably similar education reform rhetoric, consisting of the following package: extension of the curriculum to eleven or twelve years of schooling, introduction of new subjects (for example, English and computer literacy), student-centered learning, electives in upper-secondary schools, introduction of standards and/or outcomes-based education (OBE), decentralization of educational finance and governance, reorganization (or "rationalization") of schools, privatization of higher education, standardization of student assessment, liberalization of textbook publishing, and the establishment of education management and information systems. The package also includes some country-specific features such as emphasis on female education in Muslim countries, and post-conflict education in the areas afflicted by wars and civil unrest.

However, it is important to supplement the regional focus with an international perspective. The emergence of practically identical education reform packages in the Caucasus, Central Asia, and Mongolia has several causes. The most basic has to do with the history these countries share. Not only were their educational systems shaped by Soviet educational policies and, with few exceptions, very similar until the early 1990s, but these countries also experienced structural reform policies administered by the same international donors (World Bank, Asian Development Bank, U.N. organizations) in the early and mid-1990s. In a few cases the post-socialist education reform package was imposed. In most of the countries in the region, however, it was voluntarily borrowed out of fear of "falling behind" internationally (Steiner-Khamsi and Stolpe 2006, 189). In other words, some of the features of the package are not restricted to the region. From an international comparative perspective we can see elements of it in other countries where structural adjustment policies had been imposed.

Finally, a national perspective is necessary to understand how international and regional reforms encounter local realities, as well as how national institutions selectively draw on experiences from other countries. Even though international consultants are sometimes caught mixing up countries, peoples, and currencies, the countries of the region were not a *tabula rasa* when international organizations began to draw attention to them. How the reforms of the 1990s and the new millennium interacted with institutions and practices that had been in place is an important question. Which reforms were resisted, which were enthusiastically embraced, and which were selectively implemented in the varied national contexts are topics of investigation that require area-specific knowledge. This knowledge has helped us to sharpen a national lens on educational development.

In an attempt to capture distinctive voices, unique histories, and local meanings, the chapters in this book pin down the post-socialist education reform package at the country level, reflect on the outcomes of reform, and examine various NGO responses to educational change. We focus on one of the largest and most influential NGOs in the region—the Open Society Institute and Soros Foundation Network. We examine Soros's role in alternatively supporting, complementing, or correcting post-socialist reforms in the education sector. In instances where there is a reform vacuum—such as Uzbekistan and Turkmenistan—we study the network's role in providing a substitution for direct change. This book chronicles the educational interventions of the network of national Soros Foundations by considering the remarkable repertoire of strategies used to build "open societies" in the centralist (in some countries also repressive) post-socialist governance contexts, of the Caucasus, Central Asia, and Mongolia, while also addressing the larger issues of complex relationships among NGOs, state, and donors in international education development.

Agenda-setting by international donors

For the majority of countries in the Caucasus and Central Asia, independence came suddenly and unexpectedly as a consequence of the collapse of the Soviet Union. In fact, some scholars have argued that most of these countries were "forced into independence," whether they wanted it or not (Ibrayeva 2003, 156; Jones Luong 2004; Bremmer and Taras 1996).[1] Since then, the newly independent countries have moved along distinctly different trajectories of post-socialist transformation. To varying degrees, all of them have been affected by unemployment, falling wage levels, increased poverty, and the social problems that have accompanied the post-socialist transformation processes. Some experienced armed conflicts in the early 1990s.[2] Some countries—Armenia, Georgia, the Kyrgyz Republic, and Mongolia—attempted to adopt democratic political reforms with open elections in a multi-party system. The rest of the countries in the region—Azerbaijan, Kazakhstan, Tajikistan, Turkmenistan, and Uzbekistan—have increasingly settled into authoritarian or semi-authoritarian regimes.

For all the diversity to be found in the Caucasus, Central Asia, and Mongolia, these countries share a common story. Not only did they emerge from the same socialist past, but they also have been subject to similar external influences since the collapse of the Soviet Union in 1991. External influences came most visibly in the form of foreign aid, which boomed in the early 1990s, and then escalated further at the start of the millennium. By the beginning of 1992, the largest international agencies—such as the United Nations, World Bank, International Monetary Fund (IMF), European Bank for Reconstruction and Development (EBRD), Asian Development Bank (ADB), and OSCE—had already conducted assessment missions to the Caucasus and Central Asia. They also began preparing for the establishment of a permanent presence (Gleason 1997).

At the same time, bilateral cooperation was launched through national foreign aid agencies such as USAID, the Japanese International Cooperation Agency (JICA), the Canadian International Development Agency (CIDA), Turkish International Cooperation Agency (TICA), DANIDA, die Deutsche Gesellschaft für Technische Zusammenarbeit (GTZ), and many others. In addition, private foundations and philanthropies such as the Open Society Institute and Soros Foundation Network and the Aga Khan Foundation were established in most countries in the region. Finally, an army of international NGOs, including Save the Children, Mercy Corps, Academy for Educational Development, CARE, and others, arrived to assist in democratization efforts.

Each and every international organization has its own country assistance strategy. Where these organizations operate and what they fund reflects, more often than not, organizational logic rather than local needs. There is an established research tradition within international comparative education, started by Brian Holmes, to dissect "donor logic." Written during the era of the Cold War in 1981, Holmes found that, regardless of circumstances, British and American experts almost always favored the introduction of a decentralized system of educational administrators, whereas Soviet and German Democratic Republic experts always recommended the introduction of polytechnical education in countries they advised.

An analysis of donor involvement in Mongolia illustrates this concept. Whereas the donor logic of the ADB and the World Bank is finance driven, the logic of bilateral aid agencies is self-referential in a different way. The bilateral agencies of the German and Danish governments—GTZ and DANIDA—selectively export "best practices" from their own educational systems that are supposedly missing or underrepresented in Mongolia. For example, German consultants have felt compelled—not only in Mongolia but also in many other countries—to contribute to vocational education. Meanwhile, Danish experts focus on small schools and students with special needs. Once the Americans got involved under the auspices of the Millennium Development Fund, their specialists emphasized English-language and information-and-communication technology (ICT) reform in Mongolia. The decision of what to support in the Mongolian educational sector is driven more by what the lender has to offer than what the borrower actually needs. There has been a "gentlemen's agreement" among development banks in Mongolia that has softened over the past three years. Until 2004, the World Bank took the lead, with the support of UNDP and many other donors, in poverty alleviation and other social-sector programs. Meanwhile, it stayed away from educational reform, because the ADB was recognized as the "lead donor" in the educational sector.

Asian donors, particularly JICA and the Korea International Cooperation Agency (KOICA), are infrastructure and resource oriented ("hard-type" aid), but have not yet become involved in "soft-type" aid, such as the reform of content or methods in education. Both have shipped technical equipment for radio, TV, and video-conferencing studios, as well as computers (some of which are secondhand) to educational institutions. Perhaps one of the most fascinating criterion for selecting target countries is the one used by the government of Switzerland: only countries that are mountainous and small (for example, Kyrgyzstan, Tajikistan) receive Swiss aid. As bizarre as this may sound, it is not uncommon for bilateral donors to give aid to countries they perceive as being similar to their own (see Alesina and Dollar 2000).

It is important to bear in mind that despite the massive increase in aid over the past fifteen years, the Caucasus and Central Asian region has been considered a low priority for international donors. An international perspective might be helpful here. An analysis of funding patterns provides a glimpse into the close link between aid and foreign policy. The so-called Greenbook, periodically compiled by USAID for the U.S. Congress, is a valuable source for analyzing funding priorities and target countries of the U.S. government. The Greenbook lists figures on U.S. overseas loans and grants under three categories: economic assistance (USAID grants and loans, Food for Peace, Peace Corps, etc.), military assistance (Military Assistance Program, International Military Education and Training Program, etc.), and other U.S. government loans (export-import bank loans, direct loans, etc.).[3] Judging from the statistical information (USAID 2001), the Middle East has constituted the highest priority for the U.S. government. Israel was by far the largest recipient, followed by Egypt. Israel has received US$81 billion since its creation, and Egypt has received US$53 billion since the early 1970s. Another country regarded as a high priority was South Vietnam. During its short existence it received US$24 billion in the form of U.S. grants and loans. In contrast, the entire sub-Saharan African continent has received only US$31 billion between 1945 and 2001 (Westad 2005, 156).

Alberto Alesina and David Dollar (2000) take their analysis of statistical information on loans and grants a step further, by presenting a multivariate analysis of donor strategy that considers trade openness, democracy, civil liberties, colonial status, direct foreign investment, initial income, and population of the target countries. Their analyses are not restricted to U.S. government loans and grants but include all donors from market economies. They find that former colonial empires (in particular, Portugal, the United Kingdom, France, Australia, Belgium) spend more than half of their external aid on their former colonies. From 1970 to 1994, Portugal channeled 97 percent of its aid to its former colonies. In comparison, the United Kingdom allocated 78 percent, France 57 percent, Australia 56 percent, and Belgium 54 percent of their external funding to former colonies. Another variable, being a "U.N. friend," also proved important for donor selection of target countries. This variable measures whether the target country has voted in line with the donor at U.N. conferences. It accounts for Japanese funding patterns in the post–Cold War period. In the past decade Japan directed funds to poor countries in return for a vote on admitting Japan as an additional member of the U.N. Security Council. Although Alesina and Dollar's regression analyses cover all bilateral donors, their findings confirm the trend reported earlier for the U.S. government. Of all the strategies that bilateral donors employ to select target countries, political and economic interests overshadow all other considerations.

To return to our regional focus and address the donor logic of international organizations, we would like to comment briefly on U.N. organizations. It is necessary to distinguish between the two U.N. players in education, UNICEF and UNESCO. Phillip Jones has scrutinized the donor logic of multilaterals (Jones 1998; 2004) and found great differences, depending upon how they are funded. He points out that UNICEF relies on voluntary donations from governments, private foundations, or individuals, and therefore "its analyses of need tend to be dramatic, its projections tend to be alarmist and its solutions tend to be populist" (Jones 1998, 151). In contrast, UNESCO runs on membership fees that are, unfortunately, more successfully extracted from low-income governments than they are from high-income governments. Given the global scope of UNESCO's operation, supported by minimal funding, little ends up left at the country level. As mentioned before, UNDP and UNESCO are trusted organizations because they have had a presence at times when other international organizations shied away from, or were not given access to, the region. Despite the low budget of UNICEF and UNESCO, they succeed in mobilizing funds from other donors, and in recent years have engaged in more analytical work and policy analysis. In most countries of the Caucasus, Central Asia, and Mongolia, for example, UNESCO's reputation is so great that some projects are erroneously attributed to UNESCO even though they are funded by others.

We conclude this reflection on donor logic with a few observations on NGO logic. NGOs are, in terms of policy studies, "transnational epistemic communities" (Haas 1992; Rose 1993). They believe in a cause and advance it at every opportunity. In organizational terminology the term *mission* is used rather than the terms *episteme, belief,* or *cause.* The mission of the OSI, for example, has been to advance open societies in countries where the founder, George Soros, and his board of directors identify the greatest need. The receptiveness to "open society values," used interchangeably throughout the 1990s with "civil society building," was particularly great in countries with a strong state and a weak public. UNICEF, despite its classification as a multilateral organization, also sometimes presents itself as an international NGO, or an "epistemic community." This is because UNICEF promotes a specific cause or agenda, such as a "rights-based approach" to education. For multilateral and bilateral donors, the need of a government for external financial assistance is sufficient reason to start up operations in a country. Different from these large donors, international NGOs depend on a "policy window" (Kingdon 1984); that is, they rely on an opportunity or a turn of events in which the mission of the NGO is likely to resonate. The political transformations in the early 1990s that demanded a stronger civil society involvement in public affairs represented a window of opportunity for the Soros Network. The next chapter will address in greater detail the donor logic of Soros and demonstrate how it has undergone various manifestations over the course of the past twenty years or so.

Foreign aid to the region increased after the tragic events in New York on September 11, 2001. While a growing number of international donors were primarily interested "to support development, promote democracy and buttress stability" (OSI 2002), others were worried about the potential for Muslim fundamentalism. International development assistance has become so vast and varied that ministries of education in most countries have had to create special units responsible for keeping track of education activities initiated by different international organizations (Silova 2005). As Eugene Rumer, the former Clinton administration official in charge of Eurasian affairs, observed, the events of 9/11 have put Central Asia on the frontlines of the global war on terrorism and produced

> new winners and losers in and around Central Asia: Central Asia itself has been the big winner. The world cares about the region and has focused its attention on it to the degree unimagined in the 1990s. The reason the world cares is not that Central Asia has nuclear weapons left over from the Soviet Union, as it did in the early 1990s, or because of oil and gas, as it did in the mid-1990s, or because of human rights campaigning by NGOs as it did in the late 1990s. The world cares about Central Asia for two reasons: proximity to the South Asian tinderbox; and belated realization on the part of the Western political establishment that failed states cannot be left to their own devices indefinitely, no matter how remote or irrelevant they may be. (Quoted in Rumer and Yee 2002, 8)

Following the flow of foreign aid, a growing numbers of international consultants arrived to the region. Some cynical observers of education reform in the region described these international experts as outsiders who "borrow your watch to tell you the time" (Bassler 2005, 165). Almost unanimously, international experts and agencies insisted educational systems in the region were approaching a "crisis situation." This was clearly expressed in the titles of some of their numerous field reports—*A Generation at Risk: Children in the Central Asian Republics of Kazakhstan and Kyrgyzstan* (ADB 1998), *Youth in Central Asia: Losing the New Generation* (International Crisis Group 2003), and *Public Spending on Education in the CIS-7 Countries: The Hidden Crisis* (World Bank 2003), *Country Analysis Mongolia: Transition from the Second to the Third World?* (SIDA 1998), along with many others.

Practically every education sector review rushed to point out the alarming indicators of crisis: falling expenditures, declining literacy rates, decreasing enrollment, rising student dropout, deteriorating capital infrastructure, outdated textbooks, stagnated curricula, and a lack of qualified teachers. Most reports concluded that educational systems had become less equitable, with students from rural areas and low socioeconomic levels increasingly marginalized. In the case of Turkmenistan, and increasingly Uzbekistan, curricula had become dominated by ideological indoctrination and characterized by cults of personality. Furthermore, educational systems across the region had been corroded by endemic corruption. Combined, the challenges associated with the post-socialist transformation processes made it practically impossible to provide basic education for all children, let alone to undertake a fundamental reform of the national educational systems (Silova, Johnson, and Heyneman 2007).

For the people of the Caucasus, Central Asia, and Mongolia, realization of the impeding "education crisis" was tragic. People felt their educational systems had been better under socialism. As the International Crisis Group (2003, ii) put it, "In a world where many .people expect progress with each generation," most youth in Central Asia and the Caucasus were actually worse off than their parents after the collapse of the Soviet Union. In this context, many people began to talk nostalgically of their educational experiences during the socialist period, often referring to the Soviet system as "the good old" one (Belkanov 2000, 86).

International development assistance has begun systematically to target the educational sectors of the countries in the Caucasus, Central Asia, and Mongolia to solve the educational crises and save "the generation at risk." With the exception of Turkmenistan (which did not allow any international interference in the education sector), every country has been subject to a myriad of international education-assistance projects. Similar to aid relationships in any context, education system reforms have been driven primarily by the agendas and procedures of the funding and technical assistance agencies (Samoff 1999, 249). Notwithstanding the diversity of local contexts and the variety of international agencies funding education reform initiatives, the proposed recommendations for saving "the generation at risk" have been carefully framed within the internationally recognized discourses of Education for All (EFA), Millennium Development Goals (MDGs), and other internationally accepted benchmarks of education development.

Education for All for all countries?

It is striking that the trajectories of educational development, described in the previous section, have remarkably little in common with the directions inscribed in international agreements such as EFA, MDGs, and the Fast-Track Initiative (FTI). The reason is simple. The EFA Agreement, established in 1990, and the international agreements that followed were not meant specifically to address the situation in post-socialist countries. At the time, in fact, the post-socialist region was not on the map of recipient governments. As a corollary, the emphasis of international donor agreements has been on basic education, which, with the exception of a few bilateral aid agencies, is narrowly defined as primary school.[4]

A brief comment on this history of educational development in the post-socialist region illustrates how inappropriate the primary-school focus of EFA has been. EFA, defined as universal access to basic education (eight or nine years of schooling) was declared a priority at the 22nd Congress of the Communist Party of the Soviet Union in 1961. The 25th Congress finally declared basic education, that is eight or nine years of schooling, mandatory for socialist educational systems. Having systematically pursued universal access to education throughout the 1960s, the Communist Party went on to develop a four-year plan for the modernization and quality improvement of basic education for the period from 1971 to 1975. In reviewing the educational research literature from former socialist countries, one finds frequent references to the lack of student motivation and lethargy in schools that should be addressed with more active teaching methods (e.g., Sandshaasüren and Shernossek 1981; see also Steiner-Khamsi and Stolpe 2006, chap. 2). Throughout the region, laboratory schools were established to test new teaching methods. Such schools continue to be affiliated with pre-service teacher-training institutions. The need for more student-centered teaching was a recurrent theme throughout the 1970s and 1980s in the former Soviet region.

There were two features, in particular, that socialist educational systems claimed as their own: universal access to education and lifelong learning. Socialist comparative-education literature abounds with accounts of how these two features are lacking in "bourgeois" education, not only in developing countries but also in the capitalist First World. Perhaps the most graphic illustration of the Marxist-Leninist review style was the edited booklet on the 18th General Assembly Meeting of UNESCO (Gerth 1975). The editor, Ilse Gerth, a government official in charge of international relations in the German Democratic Republic (GDR), selected controversial topics and prepared response essays on four topics:

- The theory of the "world educational crisis"
- The bourgeois conception of lifelong learning
- The terminology and feature of "innovation" in educational planning and activities
- The bourgeois position on "immigrant workers" (Gerth 1975, 3)

For example, Gerth (1976a) dismantled "the world educational crisis" as a bourgeois construct and requested that the imperialist member-states speak for themselves. There was no educational crisis in socialist countries. On the contrary, socialist countries had superior systems in place, because socialism shielded the educational sector from the types of crises to which capitalist countries were exposed. Another vehemently attacked UNESCO term was the concept of permanent or lifelong education. Marxist-Leninist educational researchers (Széchy 1986; Gerth 1975) resented the selective borrowing of a concept that was saturated with socialist conceptions of education. Lifelong learning was quintessentially socialist. Not only did socialist systems deserve to be credited for having successfully implemented the notion of lifelong learning, but it must be acknowledged that high-quality lifelong learning requires a political, economic, and social environment—socialist— where the practice would be truly valued:

> Only the socialist educational system, which includes pre-school, school, after-school, as well as all stages of post-secondary

education, provides the necessary foundation for lifelong learning of high socialist quality. The socialist society implements the teachings of the founders of Marxism-Leninism in practice by conceptualizing learning as a lifelong process. (Gerth 1975, 42)

Research on multilaterals and the U.N. system in particular has only begun to reflect on the Cold War era. With easier access to archival material in both world-systems, past accounts of important historical events are in need of reexamination. As mentioned in previous publications (Steiner-Khamsi 2006; Steiner-Khamsi and deJong-Lambert 2006, 89), the role of socialist countries in leading events such as the 1974 UNESCO Revolution has not been sufficiently investigated. Although Phillip Jones (1998, 2004) and Karen Mundy (1999) report in some detail on the demand for a new international economic order that was put forward during the 18th General Assembly Meeting in 1974, they tend to reduce the Revolution to a shift in power relations between first- and third-world countries. A singular event, the election of Amadou Mahtar M'Bow from a third-world country (Senegal) to secretary general in 1974 has been overemphasized as an explanation for why the United States, the United Kingdom, and Singapore left the organization a decade later.[5] Other events during the 1974 meetings of the General Assembly that hint at the politicization of the organization, such as the UNESCO resolution against the Chilean military junta or against the Israeli occupation of Arab territories, deserve equal consideration. As Gerth, GDR comparative education researcher and government representative for multilateral organizations, noted in her report on thirty years of UNESCO, the 18th General Assembly Meeting was a breakthrough for socialist countries (Gerth 1976b). The majority of member states finally recognized, after years of insistence by the first three socialist members (USSR, Ukraine, Belarus), "the need to understand the political dimension of educational issues" (Gerth 1976b, 356).

Even though the revolutionary changes of the early 1990s were a step forward politically—installing a multi-party system—they also meant two steps back for educational development. Several African countries for which EFA was primarily designed also shifted their priorities to secondary-school development. The education sector strategies of Kenya and Uganda, to provide just two examples, identify lower-secondary school, rather than primary school, as their primary reform goal. Nevertheless, the "Africanization" of aid, reinforced most recently in the EFA FTI, has had major repercussions for the post-socialist region. Since loans and grants are predominantly given for primary-school reform, the ministries of education in the region had to reframe their needs in terms of this particular sub-sector. In a region where gross enrollment ratios for primary school are between 80 and 100 percent (UNICEF 2006), this is easier said than done.

In order to secure a grant or loan, the ministries of education had first to learn to speak the language of the international donors. For example, what the Ministry of Education of Mongolia really needed and demanded was external financial assistance to rehabilitate its deteriorating dormitory-school system and build more school facilities in urban and semi-urban areas. This would curb emigration from rural areas and remedy overcrowding. What it received instead from the ADB were measures to enhance the "quality of education" in schools based in regional centers and towns.

Prior to the EFA FTI, funds were not made readily available for capital investments. Demands had to be phrased in terms of "quality of education" needs.[6] Ministries of education also had to familiarize themselves with the new philosophy of aid; it was necessary to emphasize needs, not accomplishments. They had to convey a graphic sense of educational crisis to attract external funding. Furthermore, it was not sufficient to point to the need for *modernization* of the educational system. Donors wanted to hear the term *reform,* suggesting a revamping of structures that were in place. After years of using ineffective strategies to attract international donors, the ministries of education finally learned to belittle their own accomplishments and instead emphasize how far their system lagged behind other countries. These new tactics were diametrically opposed to what ministries of education had been socialized to do for decades, that is, to proclaim that the goals set for the five-, seven-, or nine-year plan had been accomplished ahead of schedule. Competition among "fraternal" socialist states to accomplish their multi-year educational plans gave way to competition over who was furthest away from "international standards" in education.

Nowadays, ministries of education are socialized to declare their multi-year educational plans or, to use the contemporary term, their *education sector strategy* to have failed in order to legitimize grants or loans. Such tactics have little to do with the actual reality of educational development. A typical communist slogan—We had five years to accomplish the plan, but we did it in four!—and the post-socialist strategy of exaggerating shortcomings are equally misleading. The victory of the laggards nowadays derives from the need of donors to have a grant or a loan approved by their own board of directors. The governments, as beneficiaries of loans and grants, assist the donors in their difficult predicament of having to make a case for funding. The donors must justify their portfolio by emphasizing why a commitment should be made toward one country at the expense of others.

In order to establish a need for external intervention or funding, the ministries of education sometimes tamper with statistics. Dropout statistics in Mongolia provide a good example of how data varies depending on the source. It also shows how ministries of education retroactively manipulate information to match their policy agenda (see Steiner-Khamsi and Stolpe 2006, chap. 9). Similar to other former socialist countries, the official statistics in Mongolia underreport dropouts and perpetuate the myth that the dropout problem, after peaking in the early 1990s, is subsiding. This "statistical eradication" of dropouts from official records, however, is only half the story. The rest is even more intriguing and reveals the retrospective fabrication made possible through the mismatch of figures provided by different government sources. The difference between the figures provided by the Ministry of Education/National Statistical Office (11,953 dropouts), and the Human Rights Commission of Mongolia (68,115) is by far the largest. Surprisingly, there is also a big difference between reports by two departments within the same ministry. The non-formal education department reports 40,000 dropouts, while the department in charge of educational statistics at the Ministry of Education reports only 11,953.

These vast discrepancies suggest that the various government agencies may send different signals to different constituencies. The Ministry of Education and the National Statistical Office are accountable to the general public as well as to international financial institutions that have subsidized educational reform over the past fifteen years. However, the Non-Formal Education Department at the Ministry of Education and UNICEF are seeking additional funds for financing non-formal education programs for dropouts. Their price tag must reflect the large number of potential participants (40,000) who would be served in non-formal education programs. The newest spin on dropout statistics in Mongolia was during the EFA FTI assessment in 2005. International consultants helped "prove" that drop-out during primary school is, especially for poor boys in rural areas, an issue that must be systematically addressed.

Besides tampering with statistical information, the ministries of education also had to learn to become "policy-bilingual": stating one thing to their own political constituency and another to donors. Gender equity in education, one of the MDGs, is a good case in point. In Mongolia, for example, the gender parity index is in favor of girls, yet the MDGs assume that girls are educationally disenfranchised. What to do? In 2004 the Mongolian government used the media to broadcast the need to introduce affirmative action favoring males for teacher education to combat discrimination against young boys. The assumption was that if boys had male teachers as role models, they would do better academically. Yet, the technical reports and recommendations produced by international consultants (see ADB 2004) and approved by the government of Mongolia emphasized the need to combat gender discrimination (of women) at the higher levels of education (M.A. and Ph.D. levels).

This is not to downplay issues of primary-school completion in the post-socialist region. Children who do not enroll in schools (termed "left-outs" by UNICEF) or who drop out after the first grade do exist, and their numbers have increased over the past fifteen years. The reasons for dropout or left-out children are multifold. They relate to the rising cost of private education and the high opportunity cost of attending schools in rural areas where children (especially boys) are used for labor in agriculture or animal husbandry. Last but not least is the lack of provision for children with special needs. It has only been in the last two to three years that ministries of education have been forced to draw more attention to inclusive education. Throughout the 1990s, EFA goals were discussed in the abstract, with very few effective strategies to enhance access for poor children or children with special needs.

We are not alone in pointing out the absurdity of universal benchmarking and target-setting. Individual governments must comply in order to receive external assistance, no matter how irrelevant the standards are. Jonathan Jansen (2005) provides a detailed policy analysis of the fallacies embedded in target-setting, and Michael Clemens, Charles Kenny, and Todd Moss (2007) criticize the MDG framework for using the same yardstick to measure "development success" across a wide variety of national contexts. But the difference between what international benchmarks determine in terms of educational development and what the actual realities are is perhaps nowhere as great as in the post-socialist region.

As mentioned before, the post-socialist region did not exist when EFA was conceived in 1990. As latecomers to the EFA world-system, the thirty-plus governments in the region perhaps never took these international plans and agreements seriously enough to criticize them. They simply reframed their needs in terms of the agreements and spoke the language of the donors to obtain the necessary financial support. More analytical support by international NGOs would have helped steer international agreements in a direction that would have benefited, or at least not harmed, educational development in the post-socialist region. It is only in the last few years that international NGOs and U.N. organizations have started to get involved in more comprehensive strategic and analytical work and to leave behind their exclusive concentration on single issues, such as civil society building (OSI), child-friendly schools (UNICEF), or inclusive education (Save the Children U.K.).

In sum, there is a huge gap between the goals of EFA and MDG, and the reform package that was implemented during the early stages of the post-socialist period. The gap is a result of the policy bilingualism mentioned earlier; the ministries learned to speak the language of the donors to secure a loan or a grant for reforms. But once the funding was secured, the money was channeled into other "modernization" projects, which, as the following description of the post-socialist reform package will illustrate, were quite similar across the region.

The post-socialist education reform package

In our review of reforms in the Caucasus, Central Asia, and Mongolia, we were inspired by Joel Samoff's astute observation of education sector reviews in African countries (Samoff 1999). He noticed that most education sector reviews start out with a statement that education in Africa is in crisis. Even though the reviews deal with different educational systems, they are "remarkably similar" in their analysis as well as in the presentation of the solution to the problem (Samoff 1999, 249). The analyses are written in a diagnostic style, provoking associations with a sick body that needs to be remedied, and the policy solutions are prescriptive, conveying a sense of uncontested authority. In concert with Samoff's observation, we find the education sector review in the countries of this particular region also strikingly similar. They are diagnostic in their analyses and prescriptive with regard to recommendations. Similarly, most education sector reviews start out with statements such as "progress has been made," but "efforts need to be re-doubled" to achieve the goals set out in the education sector strategy.

We draw on Samoff's observations and propose taking his analysis a step further by scratching at the surface of the reform package, which only initially appears to be homogeneous. Upon unwrapping the package, regional and national differences surface. A closer examination requires use of a trifocal lens: an international, regional, and national focus. The features of the post-socialist education reform package are unique in that they combine (1) elements common to any low-income, developing country that implements the structural adjustment programs (SAPs) recommended by the international financial institutions, (2) education reform aspects specific to the entire former socialist region, and (3) country- or region-specific components (see Table 1). Although these features vary from place to place, they do exist (at least discursively) in most countries of the region. As mentioned earlier, the only exception is Turkmenistan, which, until the death of President Niyazov in 2007, did not allow any international cooperation in the area of education and was completely isolated from international influence.

Features related to the structural adjustment programs

The first part of the post-socialist education reform package consists of features related to the implementation of SAPs initiated by international financial institutions. There are typical not only of the Caucasus, Central Asia, and Mongolia, but also of many other developing countries. Since the mid-1990s, all countries in the region (with the exception of Turkmenistan) accepted large loans for the restructuring of the educational sector and subsequently became subject to certain terms and conditions. For example, the World

Table 1.
Features of the post-socialist education reform package

FEATURES RELATED TO THE STRUCTURAL ADJUSTMENT PROGRAMS

- **Reduction of public expenditure on education**
  Lowering public expenditures for education in terms of educational spending as a percentage of total public spending and in terms of educational spending as a percentage of the GDP.

- **Increase of private spending on education**
  Introduction of formal fees in private schools, universities, and noncompulsory levels of education, encouraging community contributions towards financing of school facilities, introducing payments for textbooks, school meals, and extracurricular activities.

- **Decentralization of education finance and governance**
  Increasing cost effectiveness and efficiency by decentralizing education finance (including financial autonomy at school level by introducing per capita financing) and by enhancing social accountability and participation.

- **Rationalization of school staff and reorganization of schools**
  Rationalization (or optimization) of school staff and buildings to increase the efficiency of spending in the education sector. Rationalization reforms usually include improvement in teacher-to-student ratios, rationalization of school staff (for example, firing "redundant" auxiliary teachers and technical support staff), reorganization of schools (for example, closure of small rural schools and merging of several smaller schools in cities and regions into large, complex schools).

- **Increase of internal efficiency by reducing "wastages" and leakages**
  Detailed analyses of public expenditures and tracking expenditures at the various levels of government in order to identify areas where money is inefficiently used, misallocated, or lost (leakage).

FEATURES RELATED TO THE INHERITED SOCIALIST LEGACIES IN EDUCATION

- **Education extension to eleven or twelve years**
  Extension of general education curriculum—from ten to eleven or twelve years of schooling—has been generally undertaken in order to realign the former socialist educational systems with the Western education standards. Most countries referenced the Declaration of the Council of Europe (1992),

which stated that twelve-year education was the most widely used worldwide and was necessary for the international recognition of secondary education certificates by universities abroad.

- **Curriculum standards (OBE)**
  Introduction of curriculum standards has been generally associated with a new approach to curriculum reform. Moving away from an exclusive focus on knowledge acquisition prevalent during the Soviet period, new curriculum standards have been introduced to redistribute subject matter among competencies and learning areas. In short, the reform involves a shift from remembering facts to understanding and applying the learned material. Introduction of curriculum standards is often perceived as a tool for quality enhancement in education.

- **Standardized assessment systems (centralized university entrance examinations)**
  The introduction of standardized testing for school-leaving and/or university admissions has been primarily used as a measure to curb corruption in education. It marks a shift from the traditional practice of oral examinations administered by individual educational institutions to a more transparent assessment of students' knowledge and skills.

- **Market-driven textbook provision**
  Issues surrounding textbook reform generally concern breaking away from the old, centralized system of textbook provision to a more open, fair, and competitive publishing market. The goal is to increase the quality of textbooks by de-monopolizing authorship, stimulating competition among publishers, and providing a choice of textbooks and teaching/learning materials for students, teachers, and schools.

- **Increased educational choice (private schools)**
  To signal a retreat from a state monopoly over education, the post-socialist governments have widely advocated for increased choice in educational provision. This has involved the establishment of private schools across the former socialist region.

- **Student-centered learning**
  Introduction of student-centered learning is a prototypical example of a reform that has been implemented to signal "democratization" of teaching and learning at the classroom level. The introduction of these "new technologies"—cooperative learning, group work, individualized learning—have aimed to soften the traditional teacher-led approaches common to Soviet education practice.

- **Community schools**
  The concept of community schools has been introduced as a measure to increase community participation in education. Activities may also include service provision for the community offered by the school, turning community-participation projects into income-generating activities.

FEATURES RELATED TO COUNTRY-SPECIFIC OR REGION-SPECIFIC NEEDS

- **Girls' education**
  Several Muslim countries of Central Asia (Uzbekistan, Tajikistan) and the Caucasus (Azerbaijan) have experienced decreasing enrollment rates for female students since the collapse of the Soviet Union. This has resulted in the introduction of various initiatives aimed at improving girls' access to education.

- **Conflict resolution/peace education**
  In the early 1990s, conflict resolution and peace education were among the most typical components of the education-reform packages in countries experiencing civil unrest and/or war (for example, Armenia, Azerbaijan, Tajikistan). By the end of the 1990s, however, this reform component had lost its urgency and now has been entirely displaced in some countries.

- **Turkish schools**
  Signaling the importance of new geopolitical alliances, a network of Turkish schools has emerged in the Turkic-speaking countries of Central Asia (Kazakhstan, Kyrgyzstan, Turkmenistan, and Uzbekistan) and the Caucasus (Azerbaijan). These are usually private schools that have been established by the Turkish government and/or the Gülen community.

Bank and the ADB loans for education sector development projects constituted, on average, US$40 million to US$60 million in each country during the 1990s and 2000s. The exception was Uzbekistan, which borrowed over US$200 million, and Turkmenistan, which did not received any loans for education sector reform (see Table 2).

It is important to note that the most recent allocations made from the Catalytic Fund of the EFA FTI are not listed in Table 2. The EFA FTI grants were assessed, approved, and disbursed at breathtaking speed. The sums allocated to governments as part of the EFA FTI grants are mind-boggling. The EFA FTI marks the beginning of a new era in international cooperation, in which donors contribute to operational costs, downplay earlier concerns regarding sustainability of externally funded provisions, and fail to reflect on the risks of donor dependency. The EFA FTI also advances "international knowledge banks" that are fed with educational statistics

**Table 2. World Bank and ADB education sector loans
to the countries of the Caucasus and Central Asia**

INTER-NATIONAL AGENCY	EDUCATION SECTOR LOAN	TIME SPAN	LOAN AMOUNT (in US millions)
ARMENIA			
World Bank	Education Management and Finance Reform Project	1998–2002	$15
World Bank	Education Quality and Relevance Project (three phase education sector reform loan)	2004–2013	$44 (est.)
AZERBAIJAN			
World Bank	Education Sector Reform Project	1999–2004	$5
World Bank	Education Sector Development Project (three phase education sector reform loan)	2003–2012	$63 (est.)
GEORGIA			
World Bank	Education System Realignment and Strengthening Project (three phase education sector reform loan)	2001–2013	$60 (est.)
KAZAKHSTAN			
ADB	Basic Education Project	1998–2002	$35
ADB	Education Rehabilitation and Management Improvement	1995–2001	$20
KYRGYZSTAN			
World Bank	Rural Education Project	2004–2010	$15
ADB	Community-based Early Childhood Development	2004–2009	$10
ADB	Education Sector Development Program	1998–2004	$37

INTER-NATIONAL AGENCY	EDUCATION SECTOR LOAN	TIME SPAN	LOAN AMOUNT (in US millions)
	UZBEKISTAN		
World Bank	Basic Education Project	2006–2010	$40 (est.)
ADB	Second Textbook Development	2004–2010	$25
ADB	Education Sector Development Project	2003–2008	$38.5
ADB	Education Sector Development Program	2003–2007	$70
ADB	Information and Communication Technology in Basic Education	2006–2011	$30
ADB	Basic Education Textbook Development	1998–2003	$20
	TAJIKISTAN		
World Bank	Education Reform Project	1999–2003	$5
World Bank	Education Modernization Project	2003–2008	$24
ADB	Education Sector Reform	2003–2009	$7.5
	MONGOLIA		
World Bank	Rural Education and Development Project	2007–2012	$4
ADB	Education Sector Development Program	1997–2002	$15.5
ADB	Second Education Development Project	2002–2008	$14
ADB	Third Education Development Project	2007–2012	$13

provided by ministries of education. Statistical information is collected for the baseline year in which the grant is being disbursed and for each subsequent year until it expires. Statistical information is gathered in order to monitor progress globally by comparing educational development in a country with internationally prescribed benchmarks of the EFA FTI Indicative Framework. Bilateral donors are placed in an interesting bind: on the one hand, they fund projects that pursue their country-specific "logic," and on the other hand, they co-finance projects funded by the development banks and multilateral organizations such as the EFA FTI. The volume of the EFA FTI grants ultimately calls into question the use of direct bilateral aid.

Arguably, the debt burden and structural adjustment policies are inextricably linked. Among other goals, the implementation of structural reforms in the education sector aimed to increase efficiency in the use of public funding as well as to reform financing and management of educational institutions. The rationale behind these reforms was to increase the chances of loan repayment through the introduction of "appropriate policies" or conditionalities (IMF 2004, 1). For the education sector this meant cutting down public expenditures, increasing private spending, decentralizing finance and governance, and increasing system efficiency (see Table 1).

For the past decade, international financial institutions in the region powered the generic two-pronged structural adjustment formula: one, generating income by charging fees or tuition; and two, reducing expenditures by privatizing educational provisions (especially in the preschool and higher-education sector) and by reducing waste. For example, Arvo Kuddo (2004) reported that the Ministry of Education in Armenia established "annual rationalization plans" to reduce the number of teachers from 46,800 in 2003, to 31,100 in 2006 (a decline of 34 percent), and non-teacher staff from 24,200 in 2003 to 21,300 in 2006 (a reduction of 12 percent). Rationalization, or downsizing of the education work force, has undoubtedly been a big success politically, even as it provokes the greatest social opposition (Kuddo 2004, 2). In Kazakhstan the school rationalization reform has resulted in the closure of 3,667 preschools (from 5,226 to 1,558) and the shutting down of 590 general education schools (from 8,694 to 8,104) during four years of reform (ADB

2004). The reform has led to a mass-scale closure of preschools and small rural schools, leaving thousands of children without any access to education.

Clearly, educational spending dramatically dropped in all post-socialist countries in the early to mid-1990s. This applies whether we use the percentage of gross domestic product (GDP) allocated to education as a measure or educational spending as a percentage of public expenditures (UNICEF 1999, 5). The picture of rapidly falling public expenditures for education is especially grim in the Republic of Georgia, where educational spending previously accounted for almost 36 percent of all government spending but within only four years (1993–97) was slashed by more than half. In 1997, the government of Georgia was able to commit less than 15 percent of its public spending to education (UNICEF 1999, 5). Despite the pressure to curb educational spending significantly, several governments succeeded in increasing the percentage of GDP allocated to it in the first few years of the new millennium (Armenia, Azerbaijan, Mongolia, and Tajikistan).

Features related to the inherited socialist legacies in education

In addition to the structural adjustment reforms, most countries also experienced education reforms that were specific to the region, and not necessarily applicable in other parts of the world. These specifically post-socialist education reform features included adaptation of the existing educational systems to the new free-market environment as well as appropriation of "international" or "Western" standards. In particular, these reforms included the extension of the curriculum from ten to eleven or twelve years of study, introduction of electives to increase the flexibility and relevance of the curriculum, introduction of choice and free-market mechanisms in education, and others (see Table 1). In most countries these reforms were introduced for the purpose of not falling behind internationally or, in the case of Kazakhstan and the Caucasus (Armenia, Azerbaijan, Georgia), to signal commitment to joining the "European education space" (Nóvoa and Lawn 2002).

For example, Heyneman (2004) outlines some reforms that were typical of the entire post-socialist region due to the uniform educational structures inherited from the Soviet Union. In particular, he explained that some reforms included reorganization of the education governance structures in higher and vocational education to remove unnecessary bureaucratic layers within these systems and to improve flexibility of educational institutions in order to respond to rapidly changing market needs. Other reforms focused on the necessity of overcoming outdated mechanisms of university entrance—previously based on oral examinations and subject to corrupt practices in the post-Soviet environment—by introducing "more modern systems of examinations and standardized testing" (Heyneman 2004, 5). Furthermore, some reforms (especially of curriculum and textbooks) were specifically designed to substitute the "old" Soviet values with new ones, to address "the need for cultural rejuvenation and renewal" in recently established democracies (Heyneman 2004, 5).

In addition to the reforms directly related to dismantling Soviet structures, practices, and values, some education reforms were driven by the desire of some countries in the region to join the European education space. For Kazakhstan and the Caucasus, for example, European educational assistance was, perhaps, most influential in affecting education reform rhetoric. This is particularly true in relation to the introduction of such concepts as *knowledge society, accountability,* and *democratization* (Lawn and Lingard 2002, 299). Furthermore, European Union (EU) policies triggered the structural adjustment of the educational systems in Kazakhstan and the Caucasus, as illustrated in the extension of the school year from ten to eleven or twelve years of study, and structural changes within the higher education systems known as the Bologna Process (that is, introducing a three-level higher education program including bachelor, master, and doctoral degree programs).

Country-specific variations

In addition to the structural adjustment reforms, which development banks indiscriminately transfer to donor-dependent countries on whichever continent the country is situated, and the regional reform initiatives (post-socialist reform package) that address educational development in this part of the world, there is a long list of reforms that are country specific. More often than not, these are not funded from external sources unless they are seen as having international significance, such as supporting a secularized version of Islamic education in Kazakhstan, Kyrgyzstan, and Tajikistan (funded by the Turkish International Development Agency and the Gülen community).

Often country-specific reforms are prematurely dismissed as an internal issue and fail to secure external funding. In Mongolia, for example, education for children from herder families was neglected for more than a decade. Even though one-third of the population consists of nomadic pastoralists, the boarding-school system—ensuring access to children from nomadic herder families— collapsed partly because there were no best practices in nomadic education international organizations could draw upon to legitimize their own involvement. Another puzzle arises when the country-specific context is diametrically opposed to what international agreements presuppose. For example, what should international donors do if there is an "inverse gender gap" favoring girls over boys? Should they revise the international agreement or ignore the issue as an anomaly? As mentioned earlier, international donors found a niche in education where they could reinforce their theory of universal discrimination against girls. Females are outperforming males throughout the educational system in Mongolia, and educational attainment is higher for females than males. Yet, the gender gap closes in higher education. Another way of dealing with the inverse gender gap was to focus on dropouts in rural areas, who are mostly poor males.

There is a misconception among international donors that all reforms in the region are externally funded. There are numerous reforms that are designed in-country, funded from government sources, and implemented by government officials. In fact, such nationally initiated reforms are inscribed in action programs of political parties and periodically surface during election season. Just because no documentation is available in English or because no external funding has been sought does not mean these national programs or action plans do not exist.

What is left out of the package

Any researcher who attempts to unwrap the reform packages that were transferred from one country or context to another should pause and ask what was *not* included. For international NGOs, in particular, it has been tremendously important to identify areas of reforms that are underserved. These areas fall through the cracks because they are not given attention by governments or by large international donors. There are three areas, in particular, that have been neglected: education for children with special needs, in-service training for teachers, and participatory education governance.

For example, education for children with special needs has been strongly advanced first by Save the Children U.K. and later on by other NGOs and UNICEF. Save the Children U.K. developed and disseminated teaching material, as well as training modules on inclusive education, throughout the region. There is, in general, little government and donor interest in catering to children who are "left out" of formal education unless they fall into officially defined categories such as rural poor or orphans. Other groups of children who are entirely dependent upon NGO support include street children as well as children who lack residential registration due to rural-urban migration or internal displacement of their parents.

In-service training was identified first by national foundations of the Soros Network as a neglected area of reform. It was customary for teachers in the region to be entitled to "upgrading" or professional-development courses every five years. After the universal in-service training system collapsed only select teachers and administrators were enrolled. Priority was given to those who were immediately affected by ongoing reforms, such as primary-school teachers (extension of schooling from ten to eleven years) and school administrators (decentralization of educational finance). Funds were absorbed for these special groups, and regular teachers lost their entitlement to continuous professional development. It is striking to see that international agreements (EFA, MDG, EFA FTI) mostly focus on the recipients (students), thus neglecting the supply side in education (teachers). It is this vacuum that first the Soros Network, and then other NGOs, filled.

It is worth mentioning that some reforms were part of the package but only selectively implemented. As several of the case studies in this book (especially the case studies of Armenia and Georgia) point out, the decentralization reforms were conceived to cover both financial and governance issues. In reality, however, development banks only promoted decentralization of finance, again leaving decentralization of governance, in the form of community participation, wide open for NGOs. In the area of decentralization reforms, the Soros Network corrected or complemented ongoing reform by funding projects that enhanced civic involvement and community participation.

What do reforms do?

The literature on development and education addresses important questions presented in this book: Who gives aid to whom? Who deserves aid? What does aid do? The first question deals with the logic of donors as well as their mission and their target countries (see Alesina and Dollar 2000; Easterly 2002). The second question deals with conditionalities of aid, which in recent years have placed an emphasis on "good governance" (for the most recent discussion, see Dollar and Levin, 2006). The third question forces us to examine the impact of external assistance on existing practices and structures. We have tailored the third question to match the focus of this book by asking what (imported) reforms do.

Different from what is commonly assumed, reforms that are imported with the financial support of international organizations, governmental or nongovernmental, do not simply replace existing practices and structures. As the chapters in this book will illustrate, the educational reforms in the region are—despite coming from the same socialist past and having received an identical education reform "package" since independence—quite distinct. Today, fifteen years after reform packages began being transferred to the region, they have had different outcomes in different countries. Some have remained, others were reversed, and yet others moved back and forth. What is needed is a long-term perspective to evaluate how a reform was actually implemented, if it was implemented at all, and how it affected what was already in place. Only by evaluating a reform a few years after it has been in place can we see whether it has replaced, added to, or modified existing practices and structures. Our approach is to examine how elements of the post-socialist reform package have been implemented differently.

We are not the only ones who are curious about how and why the same reforms play out differently in separate national contexts. Anthropological studies also draw attention to local or national differences. Kathryn Anderson-Levitt (2003), for example, gathered a group of cultural anthropologists to reflect on whether national systems in different parts of the world are indeed converging toward an international model of education. Different from world culture theory, associated with neo-institutionalism advanced by sociologists at Stanford University (for example, John Meyer, Francisco Ramirez), anthropologists reject such a claim and instead emphasize how global reforms are interpreted differently once they are imported or borrowed. The case studies in Anderson-Levitt's edited volume, as remarkable as they are, focus exclusively on how a global reform such as, for example, OBE, takes on different meanings in various contexts. The destiny of existing policies in light of global forces is not explicitly addressed.

It is no small feat to examine how the same reform is interpreted differently, as this tells us something about culture, particularly the culture of reform, in the various policy contexts. However, hybridization resulting from the encounter between imported and already existing policies is but one of several conceivable outcomes. Others include a replacement of previous policies or, at the other extreme, a reinforcement of what had already been in place. Again, hybridization has been amply documented (for example, Anderson-Levitt 2003), and replacement as an outcome of borrowing has also been extensively studied in societies that have undergone revolutionary changes (for example, Spreen 2004). Both strands of research view policy borrowing, or more broadly speaking, globalization, as a form of external intervention that inevitably triggers change.

For a variety of political and economic reasons, so-called external interventions are frequently internally induced when politicians and policymakers utilize the semantics of globalization to generate reform pressure. However, we are still left with cases where imported policy exclusively served to reinforce existing policies. Other than Silova's study on bilingual education policies in post-Soviet Latvia (Silova 2005) and another, smaller comparative study on OBE in Central Asia (Steiner-Khamsi, Silova, Johnson 2006), there is little in the way of empirical evidence to suggest that policy borrowing is sometimes used to legitimize and reinforce existing practices. In our small comparative study of OBE in Central Asia we confirmed Silova's earlier findings (Silova 2005) and presented an additional case (Mongolia) where the introduction of OBE merely reinforced an elaborate monitoring system by adding yet another element of teacher accountability to what had been in place for the past thirty years (Steiner-Khamsi, Silova, Johnson 2006).

The few studies that have been conducted to date focus on reforms that have been transferred by multilateral donors, that is, development banks and the U.N. system. Several international NGOs also engage in transnational reform transfer due to their dual capacity as donor and implementer. In the Caucasus and Central Asia, the network of national Soros Foundations, Save the Children U.K., the Aga Khan Foundation, and World Vision—to name just a few—also deserve closer scrutiny with regard to their reform impact. The proposed classification into reforms that augmented, corrected, replaced, or modified existing practices can therefore be extended to an analysis of reforms supported by NGOs in the region.

Complementing existing reforms

Some of the reforms that NGOs advanced were simply added, either permanently or temporarily, and then ultimately dropped because they did not fit an existing structure. Civic education is a good example to illustrate an NGO-supported reform that was devoid of considerations regarding curricular constraints. What decentralization of finance is to development banks, civic education is to NGOs: a panacea to cure every problem in the educational system. OSI, USAID (Civitas), the EU and a host of other international organizations developed modules and trained teachers for civic education. The OSI package "Democracy for All," adopted from a progressive post-apartheid program, was very popular in the region because of its interactive and skills-based approach. Yet in many countries OSI civic education was competing with similar programs developed by other NGOs because, to date, there is either very limited or no curricular space for this type of initiative. In some countries civic education is part of social sciences, an area already filled by prescribed curricular content. In other countries, such as Tajikistan, civic education was squeezed into law/government studies that only allotted one hour per week of instructional time during grades eight and nine. This is far too little to accommodate one civic-education package, let alone selectively implement components from others. In fact, instructional time for law/government studies, previously occupied by subject matter that dealt with historical materialism or Marxist-Leninist theory, was drastically reduced in the 1990s, despite the efforts of NGOs to have civic education as a separate subject included in the curriculum. Ten years later, civic-education textbooks added to the regular curriculum are used only in abbreviated versions, if at all. By competing to implement various forms of civic education into a curriculum that was already cluttered with too many subjects and too little time for instruction, NGOs undermined one another in a goal they all shared.

Correcting the existing reforms

We can only speculate about why governments and large international donors have ignored in-service teacher training, because few studies have been carried out on this subject. Salaries for teachers are low, and the prestige of the profession has suffered visibly. This has resulted in tremendous teacher recruitment and retention problems. The outcome in some countries (for example, Kyrgyzstan and Tajikistan) has been a dramatic teacher shortage. Another indication of the unattractiveness of the teaching profession is the demographics of teachers: one-third to one-quarter of teachers have been in public service for more than twenty years and thus are eligible for retirement. We found a disturbing attitude toward the teaching corps in the region. Some large donors considered teachers to be a "lost generation," not worth investing in. Donors believed teachers had been "indoctrinated" for decades by socialist methods of thinking and teaching. Intervention in the "future generation," that is, in students at pre-service teacher education, was also considered off limits for large donors, for two reasons: first, higher-education reform is not a priority of international aid; and second, there is too much "wastage" in teacher education, given that fewer than half of the graduates in teacher education ever enter the teaching profession. As mentioned previously, this gap was first filled by the Soros Network and then by other NGOs.

Replacing existing reforms

There are numerous examples of reforms that were funded and supported by NGOs that replaced previous education practices. Typically, these projects were in compliance with government plans to replace the inherited socialist educational provisions with new ones. The development of English language textbooks or world history textbooks, advanced in several national Soros Foundations, is an example of a reform that was sustained. Even in the most authoritarian countries in the region (such as Uzbekistan and Turkmenistan), government officials allowed international NGOs to develop new textbooks and teacher-training modules to substitute for outdated teaching materials.

Hybridizing existing reforms

The fourth type of policy impact is perhaps the most intriguing: NGO projects that hybridized or modified existing practices. Student-centered learning is a prototypical example of a reform that was forcefully advanced by all NGOs in the region and locally adapted to the cultural context. It did not replace teacher-led instruction but rather "softened up" traditional ways of teaching by including elements of student-centered learning. Teachers who participated in the numerous in-service teacher training workshops on student-centered, interactive, or cooperative learning—or the OSI versions of it, Reading and Writing for Critical Thinking (RWCT), Debate, or Step by Step (SbS)—embraced these so-called new technologies. They reported that their students were more engaged as a result of these methods and that they themselves had learned about individual students' needs and abilities. They subsequently implemented methods of student-centered learning in their teaching and student assessment, but only selectively.

For cultural, environmental, and structural reasons, student-centered learning means something different in the context of Caucasus and Central Asia. Culturally, teachers are respected for their knowledge. Situations in which students might ask questions the teacher cannot answer are carefully avoided. In our classroom observations in Mongolia, for example, we noticed that student-led group work was used only to consolidate knowledge that had already been transmitted by the teacher. Environmentally, student-centered learning in the form of student independent research or student project work played out differently in a context where there is very limited access to books or other sources of written information. Finally, there are structural reasons that constrain the systematic implementation of student-centered learning. The two main obstacles are the current student assessment methods and the current teacher-salary structure.

These two constraints are explained in greater detail here, because they are indicative of valuable project work, funded and implemented by NGOs, that lacks systematic integration into broader policy-related issues. First, individual student progress, as advanced in student-centered learning, is not part of the government-approved assessment repertoire. Students are exposed to quizzes and, at the end of each cycle, to standardized tests. Group work or individual student progress is not evaluated, especially in lower- and upper-secondary school.

Exceptions are worth mentioning here. The National Scholarship Test (university entrance exam) in Kyrgyzstan—funded by USAID and directed by a former trainer in RWCT—measures student skills rather than just student knowledge. The test attempts to expand the emphasis on student skills into the lower levels of secondary schooling. Another example is OBE in Mongolia. In principle, teachers are supposed to measure individual student progress throughout the year and take notes on each student. Yet this principle is not enforced because teachers lack the time, commitment, and knowledge to do so. The salary structure for teachers also undermines student-centered learning. Teacher salaries are, as outlined in greater detail in the concluding chapter, below the national average. Teachers need to work additional hours or take on additional jobs to make a living, leaving them with very little time for lesson preparation and student feedback.

To make things worse, salary contracts are structured in a way that confines the salary of a teacher to his or her actual teaching hours. All additional pedagogical activities (such as grading student notebooks) are reimbursed separately. During Soviet times the statutory teaching hours for teachers (stavka) was twenty-four hours for primary-school teachers, and eighteen hours for lower- and upper-secondary school teachers. The two core features of the *stavka* system—base salary based on the hours taught, with supplements for additional pedagogical activities—were the defining characteristic of the Soviet teacher-salary system that has been in effect since 1948. The peculiarities of the *stavka* system have always been a topic of great academic curiosity and professional interest in nonsocialist countries. They were well-documented in English, especially during the Cold War (see, for example, Bereday and Schlesinger 1963). Not much has changed over the past sixty years except for a gradual decrease of the statutory teaching hours (in the past fifteen years) to accommodate the necessity of having a second job or teaching additional hours. Any other pedagogical activity, including grading student notebooks or providing feedback on written assignments, is still paid additionally. Not only is formative student evaluation not seen as part of the teacher's job (and compensated for financially), but not all teachers are entitled to this supplement. In the post-Soviet region only teachers of language, math, physics, and technical drawing are entitled to the notebook-checking supplement (Steiner-Khamsi 2007). The assumption is that other subjects, such as history, geography, biology, etc., are "soft subjects," with little preparation required by students or formative evaluation required by teachers. In Tajikistan, the supplement for notebook-checking is 20 percent of the base salary. This supplement is too substantial to be neglected by NGOs that have advanced student-centered learning since, by default, student-centered practices result in more formative student assessment and "notebook checking."

The examples provided in this chapter lead us to suggest that NGO-funded projects, as progressive as they might be and as enthusiastically embraced by practitioners as they have been, are not sustainable if they ignore broader policy issues such as, for example, curriculum or teacher salary reform. This applies especially to the Caucasus and Central Asia, where educational practices are regulated in great detail by centralist governments. It is therefore not surprising that NGOs in the region, including the national Soros Foundations, have in recent years attempted to influence educational policy on a larger scale.

A preview on the retrospective

This book examines a unique post-socialist education reform package at the country level by focusing on the role of the OSI and the national Soros Foundations in education reform in the Caucasus, Central Asia, and Mongolia. It reflects on the outcomes of the implementation of the reform package and illustrates a dynamic interaction among various actors—states, donors, and NGOs—in education change. These multiple perspectives are used to introduce an analytical rather than a merely descriptive element into the country-specific case studies. The history of each OSI national foundation will be provided as important background information and supplemented with an overview of, and reflection on, the role of NGOs (including OSI) and civil society building in the corresponding countries. This book highlights the diversity of OSI's responses to education reform and consolidates past experiences, while challenging readers to look at the Caucasus, Central Asia, and Mongolia as unique and dynamic countries.

Following Iveta Silova's overview of the history of educational programming in the OSI and the national Soros Foundations (that is, OSI donor logic) in Chapter 1, the book features nine country-level case studies. Each case study highlights a particular feature of the post-socialist education reform package and reveals the complexity of the sociopolitical, historical, and educational contexts within which international reforms take root. Chapter 2 by Armenuhi Tadevosyan examines the evolution of the *community education schools* concept in Armenia and the role of the World Bank and international NGOs in institutionalizing the initiative in education reform. Chapter 3 by Elmina Kazimzade focuses on international efforts to develop a free textbook-publishing market in Azerbaijan. Kazimzade examines the different perspectives of the government, World Bank, and OSI with regard to textbook reform, uncovering a large rift between vision and reality. In Chapter 4, Anna Matiashvili discusses another feature of the post-socialist education reform package—education decentralization in the Republic of Georgia during the early 2000s. The chapter examines the complex interaction of various actors—the government, World Bank, and the Open Society Georgia Foundation (OSGF). Matiashvili offers a unique analysis of the various factors that account for the selective institutionalization of reforms and discusses the complex conditions under which governments neglect initiatives developed by local NGOs and import ideas from elsewhere.

Chapter 5 by Saule Kalikova and Iveta Silova examines the introduction of OBE in Kazakhstan. Unlike similar curriculum-reform projects funded by international financial institutions across the former socialist region, the OBE reform in Kazakhstan was initiated and implemented locally. This chapter discusses how international NGOs (such as the Soros Foundation–Kazakhstan) had to readjust their strategies to exert influence on Kazakhstan's educational policymaking in an increasingly "donor-free" environment.

In Chapter 6, Alexander Ivanov and Valentin Deichman focus on one of the most ambitious pilot projects of the Soros Foundation–Kyrgyzstan, which aimed at the introduction of the voucher-based teacher training system as a mechanism to improve the quality of in-service teacher training and to offer teachers a choice in selecting professional development courses. The authors reflect on the role of NGOs in generating reform pressure and on opportunities for scaling up the pilot in the future.

Teacher-education reform in Mongolia is discussed by Natsagdorj Enkhtuya in Chapter 7. The chapter deals with a specific type of transfer—cross-institutional borrowing or best practices—and examines the conditions and reasons international donors and NGOs borrow education reform projects from one another and implement them in the same country. The chapter focuses on a project initiated by the Mongolian Foundation for Open Society (MFOS) and its subsequent adoption by other international development agencies in the country.

In Chapter 8 on Tajikistan, Tatiana Abdushukurova reflects on the role of the Open Society Institute Assistance Foundation (OSIAF) in supporting local policy capacity in education reform. She examines the emergence of an independent, locally run organization—Education Reform Support Unit—and its attempts to enter the education policymaking arena in an environment heavily dominated by international donors and subject to strict government control.

The last two case studies provide a unique opportunity to examine reform strategies pursued by international NGOs in some of the most authoritarian countries of the region. Chapter 9 on Turkmenistan by Erika Dailey and Iveta Silova highlights different approaches to education reform—working with the government or implementing education reform initiatives beyond governmental control—and reflects on the complexities and contradictions involved in pursuing both approaches. Chapter 10 on Uzbekistan by Jacqueline Ashrafi examines the legacies of two education programs funded by the OSIAF—the textbook-development program and the in-service teacher-training program—that were miraculously able to survive after the closure of OSIAF in 2004. Following analysis of the education reform context and the role of international NGOs during the transformation period, this chapter reflects on the strategies used by OSIAF to promote open society values through education despite the increasingly authoritarian nature of Uzbek government.

The concluding chapter by Gita Steiner-Khamsi invites readers to step back and reflect on similarities and differences in the post-socialist education reform package across the region. By reviewing a range of strategies used by NGOs to cope with centralist governments, on the one hand, and international donors, on the other, she proposes distinguishing between different strategies of NGOs in dealing with the post-socialist education reforms. She identifies, in particular, three types of NGO-government relations in the post-socialist region. Drawing on case studies presented in the book, she discusses the three types of relationship: the complementary role of NGOs, the cooperative role of NGOs, and the surrogate role of NGOs. The final section of the chapter briefly comments on scaling up strategies of NGOs discussed in the research literature. The Soros Foundation has scaled down the budget for educational projects considerably and at the same time established education policy centers that are expected to scale up the political impact of the Soros Network. Another development highlighted in the chapter is the move from a post-socialist network to a global network in education. These recent developments within the Soros Foundation—scaling up (politically) by scaling down on project expenditures and the intention of going global—are followed with great interest, not only by professionals closely associated with the Soros Network but also by scholars and students in NGO research.

The case studies presented in this book provide detailed contextual information that is necessary to investigate the interplay of various policy actors. This contextualization is indispensable for understanding what a particular reform means in a country and why a reform is supported by some and opposed by others. These country-specific perspectives enable us to engage in a contextual comparison and help to identify similarities and differences in how NGOs, and the national Soros Foundations in particular, have responded to reforms that have been transferred to the Caucasus, Central Asia, and Mongolia.

Notes

[1] For example, the Central Asian republics—Kazakhstan, Kyrgyzstan, Tajikistan, Turkmenistan, and Uzbekistan—were the last ones to declare their independence from the Soviet Union. With the exception of President Askar Akayev in Kyrgyzstan, the leaders of the Central Asian republics supported the coup against Mikhail Gorbachev in August 1991, and an overwhelming majority of the population in these republics voted to remain part of the Soviet Union (Jones Luong 2004; Bremmer and Taras 1996).

[2] For example, armed conflicts broke out in the Caucasus (including the Nagorno-Kharabakh conflict between Armenia and Azerbaijan in 1988–94 and Georgian-Abkhaz conflict in 1990–94) and in Central Asia (including ethnic clashes in the Ferghana Valley in 1989–91, and the civil war in Tajikistan in 1993–95).

[3] It deserves special mention that the most recent Greenbook on U.S. overseas loans and grants (USAID 2004) blurs the line between military and economic assistance. Expenditures previously listed under military assistance are now listed under economic assistance, accounting for a US$1.4 billion shift from military to economic assistance in fiscal year 2003 (USAID 2004, v).

[4] USAID, for example, defines basic education as primary and lower-secondary education. In contrast, the multilateral organizations (U.N. organizations and the development banks) restrict basic education to four-to-six years of primary schooling.

[5] The U.S. government only resumed UNESCO membership in 2003 as part of its global alliance in the war on terrorism.

[6] It is astounding how, without much debate, the EFA FTI has reversed the earlier approach of focusing on soft-type aid, which was conducive to quality enhancement throughout the 1990s. As educational experts in Mongolia remark, the multi-million-dollar project appraisal for EFA FTI Mongolia resembles more a plan of a ministry of construction than a ministry of education.

References

Alesina, Alberto, and David Dollar. 2000. Who gives foreign aid to whom and why? *Journal of Economic Growth* 5(1): 33–63.

Anderson-Levitt, Kathryn. 2003. A world culture of schooling? In *Local meanings, global schooling: Anthropology and world culture theory,* ed. Kathryn Anderson-Levitt, 1–26. New York: Palgrave Macmillan.

ADB (Asian Development Bank). 1998. *A generation at risk: Children in the Central Asian republics of Kazakhstan and Kyrgyzstan.* Report by Armin Bauer, Nina Boschmann, David Jay Green, and Kathleen Kuehnast. Available online.

———. 2004. *Governance: Progress and challenges in Mongolia.* Manila: ADB.

Bassler, Terrice. 2005. *Learning to change: The experience of transforming education in South East Europe.* Budapest, Hungary: Central University Press.

Belkanov, Nikolai. 2000. "Pedagogicheskaya sovetologiya kak nauchny fenomen" [pedagogical sovietology as a scientific phenomenon]. *Pedagogika* 6(5): 81–87.

Bereday, George, and Ina Schlesinger. 1963. Teacher salaries in the Soviet Union. *Comparative Education Review* 6(3): 200–208.

Bremmer, Ian, and Ray Taras, eds. 1996. *New states, new politics: Building the post-Soviet nations.* New York: Cambridge University Press.

Clemens, Michael, Charles Kenny, and Todd Moss. 2007. The trouble with the MDGs: Confronting expectations of aid and development success. *World Development* 35(5): 735–51.

Dollar, David, and Victoria Levin. 2006. The increasing selectivity of foreign aid, 1984–2003. *World Development* 39(12): 2034–46.

Easterly, William. 2002. The cartel of good intentions. *Foreign Policy* 131 (July/August): 40–49.

Gerth, Ilse. 1975. *Zur 18. Generalkonferenz der UNESCO* [the 18th General Assembly Meeting of UNESCO]. Berlin: Akademie der Pädagogischen Wissenschaften der DDR, Arbeitsstelle für Auslandspädagogik.

———. 1976a. *Inhaltliche Analyse und Einschätzung des Entwurfs des UNESCO-Dokuments 19 C/4 (Programm der UNESCO 1977–1982) Bereich Bildung.* [content analysis and evaluation of the UNESCO document draft 19 C/4 (program of UNESCO 1977–1982) Education Sector. Berlin: Bibliothek für bildungsgeschichtliche Forschung, Archiv, APW 15360, AfA, LID/HR—3.339.

———. 1976b. Dreissig Jahre UNESCO [thirty years of UNESCO]. *Vergleichende Pädagogik* 12(3): 353–62.

Gleason, Gregory. 1997. *The Central Asian states: Discovering independence.* Boulder, CO: Westview Press.

Haas, Peter. 1992. Introduction: Epistemic communities and international policy coordination. *International Organization* 46(1): 1–35.

Heyneman, Steven. 2004. One step back, two steps forward: The first stage of the transition for education in Central Asia. In *The challenge of education in Central Asia,* ed. Steven Heyneman and Alan DeYound, 3–8. Greenwich, CT: Information Age Publishing.

Holmes, Brian. 1981. *Comparative education: Some considerations of method.* London, UK: George Allen and Unwin.

Ibrayeva, Aigerim. 2003. Historical roots of third sector development in Kazakhstan. *Central Asian Journal of Management, Economics, and Social Research* 3: 150–57.

International Crisis Group. 2003. *Youth in Central Asia: Losing the new generation.* Available online.

IMF (International Monetary Fund). 2004. *IMF conditionality: A fact sheet.* Washington DC: IMF.

Jansen, Jonathan. 2005. Targeting education: The politics of performance and the prospects of "Education for All." *International Journal of Educational Development* 25: 368–80.

Jones Luong, Pauline. 2004. *The transformation of Central Asia: States and societies from Soviet Rule to independence.* Ithaca, NY: Cornell University Press.

Jones, Phillip. 1998. Globalisation and internationalism: Democratic prospects for world education. *Comparative Education* 34(2), 143–55.

———. 2004. Taking the credit: Financing and policy linkages in the education portfolio of the World Bank. In *The global politics of educational borrowing and lending,* ed. Gita Steiner-Khamsi, 188–200. New York: Teachers College Press.

Kingdon, John. 1984. _Agendas, alternatives, and public policies._ Boston: Little, Brown.

Kuddo, Arvo. 2004. Armenia: The teacher redeployment and severance program. World Bank report. Available online.

Lawn, Martin, and Bob Lingard. 2002. Constructing a European policy space in educational governance: The role of transnational policy actors. _European Educational Research Journal_ 1(2): 290–307.

Mundy, Karen. 1999. Educational multilateralism in a changing world order: UNESCO and the limits of the possible. _International Journal of Educational Development_ 19: 27–52.

Nóvoa, Antonio, and Martin Lawn. 2002. _Fabricating Europe: The formation of an education space._ Dordrecht: Kluwer Academic Publishers.

OSI (Open Society Institute). 2002. _Education development in Kyrgyzstan, Tajikistan, and Uzbekistan: Challenges and ways forward._ Report by Jana Huttova, Iveta Silova, and Hannes Voolma. Available online.

Rose, Richard. 1993. _Lesson-drawing in public policy._ Chatham, NJ: Chatham House.

Rumer, Boris, and Lau Sim Yee, eds. 2002. _Central Asia and South Caucasus Affairs: 2002._ The Sasakawa Peace Foundation. Available online.

Samoff, Joel. 1999. Education sector analysis in Africa: Limited national control and even less national ownership. _International Journal of Educational Development_ 19(4/5): 249–72.

Sandshaasüren, R., and I. Shernossek. 1981. _Das Bildungswesen der Mongolischen Volksrepublik. Beiträge zur Pädagogik, Band 22_ [the educational system in the Mongolian People's Republic. Contributions of education, volume 22]. Berlin, GDR: Volk und Wissen Volkseigener Verlag.

SIDA (Swedish International Development Cooperation Agency). 1998. _Country analysis Mongolia: Transition from the Second to the Third World?_ Report by Ole Bruun, Per Ronnas, and Li Narangoa. Stockholm: SIDA.

Silova, Iveta. 2005. Traveling policies: Hijacked in Central Asia. _European Educational Research Journal_ 4(1): 50–59.

Silova, Iveta, Mark Johnson, and Steven Heyneman. 2007. Education and the crisis of social cohesion in Azerbaijan and Central Asia. _Comparative Education Review_ 51(2): 159–80.

Spreen, Carol Anne. 2004. Appropriating borrowed policies: Outcomes-based education in South Africa. In _The global politics of educational borrowing and lending,_ ed. Gita Steiner-Khamsi. New York: Teachers College Press.

Steiner-Khamsi, Gita. 2006. The development turn in comparative and international education. _European Education: Issues and Studies_ 38(3): 19–47.

———. 2007. _The stavka system in Tajikistan: Background, challenges and recommendations for teacher salary reform._ Dushanbe: Education Modernization Project, Project Management Unit; Washington DC: World Bank, Central Asia Region.

Steiner-Khamsi, Gita, and Ines Stolpe. 2006. _Educational import: Local encounters with global forces in Mongolia._ New York: Palgrave MacMillan.

Steiner-Khamsi, Gita, and William deJong-Lambert. 2006. The international race over the patronage of the South: Comparative and international education in Eastern Europe and the United States. *Current Issues in Comparative Education* 8(2): 84–94.

Steiner-Khamsi, Gita, Iveta Silova, and Eric Johnson. 2006. Neo-liberalism liberally applied: Educational policy borrowing in Central Asia. In *Education Research and Policy: Steering the Knowledge-Based Economy*, ed. Jenny Ozga, Thomas Popkewitz, and Terri Seddon, 217–45. New York: Routledge.

Széchy, E. 1986. Bürgerliche Konzeptionen der permanenten Bildung [bourgeois conceptions of permanent education]. In *Die Bildungspolitik kapitalistischer Staaten*, ed. Zola Malkova, Hans-Georg Hofmann, and Boris Wulfson, 94–106. Berlin: Volk und Wissen Volkseigener Verlag.

UNICEF (United Nations Children's Fund). 1999. *After the fall: The human impact of ten years of transition*. Florence, Italy: UNICEF, Innocenti Research Centre.

———. 2006. *Transmonee database*. Available online.

USAID. 2001. *U.S. overseas loans and grants and assistance from international organization: Obligations and loan authorizations July 1, 1945–September 30, 2001*. Silver Spring, MD: USAID Development Experience Clearinghouse.

———. 2004. *U.S. overseas loans and grants: Obligations and loan authorizations July 1, 1945–September 30, 2004*. Silver Spring, MD: USAID Development Experience Clearinghouse.

Westad, Odd Arne. 2005. *The global Cold War. Third world interventions and the making of our times*. New York: Cambridge University Press.

World Bank. 2003. *Public spending on education in CIS-7 countries: The hidden crisis*. Report by Nicholas Burnett and Rodica Cnobloch. Available online.

1

Championing Open Society

The Education Logic of the Soros Foundation Network

IVETA SILOVA

Since the collapse of the socialist bloc in 1989, the international community has responded "with considerable fanfare and significant resources" to support post-socialist transformation processes in the countries of Southeast and Central Europe and the former Soviet Union (Quigley 1997, 2). Initiatives have ranged from large-scale programs developed by international financial institutions (World Bank, ADB, IMF) and multilateral organizations (UN, EU, OSCE) to smaller projects launched by international NGOs and private foundations. Collectively, these international development agencies aimed to promote a market economy, liberal democracy, and civil society.

In devising their responses, each agency was driven by its own "donor logic," mirroring its mission and objectives. This donor logic was systematically advanced in its target countries (Steiner-Khamsi and Stolpe 2006, 73). For example, the donor logic of international financial institutions was primarily "finance driven," whereas the donor logic of multilateral organizations emphasized "democratic governance" and "rights-based" approaches to international development (Steiner-Khamsi and Stolpe 2006; Quigley 1997). By contrast, many international NGOs were preoccupied with the idea of civil society and the concept of social capital, based on the logic that "funding local advocacy NGOs would help to build independent interest groups in civil society that in turn can provide impetus for democratic reforms" (Adamson 2002, 178; see also Lewis and Wallace, 2000). Documenting the complexity and dynamics of donor logic is extremely important for understanding how international development agencies have interacted with states, NGOs, and other donors, as well as how their initiatives have influenced post-socialist transformation reform processes nationally and internationally.

While considerable attention has been given to educational development assistance of international financial institutions (Heyneman 2003; Jones 2004), multilateral organizations (Mundy 1999; Chabbott 1998), and international NGOs (Burde 2004; Sutton and Arnove 2000; Kamat 2002; Edwards 1998), there has been relatively little discussion devoted to the role of private foundations in post-socialist transformation processes. This chapter attempts to document the donor logic of the OSI and the Soros Foundation Network—one of the major players in education reform efforts in the former socialist bloc. Compared to other international donors, George Soros is often regarded as "the most prominent supporter of democracy assistance projects" with a "considerably higher profile" than many official bilateral assistance programs (Quigley 1997, 87). Not only did Soros make significant investments "to build open, democratic societies"—giving away nearly US$6 billion since the early 1990s and US$417 million in 2006 (OSI 2006, 139)—but he also allowed his national foundations the autonomy to adjust programming to their local contexts. As the OSI moves to other regions of the world and many of the Soros Foundations in the former socialist bloc prepare to become financially independent (or to "spin off") or shut down, a retrospective of OSI education program logic presents a unique opportunity to reflect on the role of the Soros Network in the larger process of post-socialist transformation.

Drawing on document review and in-depth interviews with OSI board members, staff, and consultants, this chapter examines the evolution of OSI education logic since its establishment in the early 1990s. The focus on education logic is purposeful, based on the recognition that there is often a gap between the vision of international development agencies and the actual results they produce. As this book illustrates, OSI educational initiatives have often had mixed and unanticipated outcomes across the post-socialist region. The rest of the chapters in this volume document the complexities involved in translating OSI educational vision into policy and practice in various national contexts. This chapter deals exclusively with the logic of OSI educational programming to provide a historical, philosophical, and organizational background for understanding the broader issues raised: Why and how did the national Soros Foundations develop their strategies in particular countries and in particular points of time? How were these approaches shaped by contextual factors? How did their changing roles, strategies, and partnerships affect national education reform processes?

George Soros, Open Society, and post-socialist transformation processes

George Soros has a controversial reputation as a financier and philanthropist. Globally, he is known simultaneously as "the man who broke the Bank of England" (BBC 1998), "imperial wizard" (Coffin 2003), "Eastern Europe's uncrowned king" (Clark 2003), "the world's most ambitious donor" (Hrab 2003), and "a champion of new democracy" (Abdurakhimov 2004). He is adored by some and hated by others. In most countries of the former socialist bloc he is renowned for his strong commitment to promoting "open societies" by founding a network of NGOs that promote democratic governance, human rights, and legal, economic, social, and education reform. George Soros's vision of an open society is based on "the recognition that nobody has a monopoly on the truth, that different people have different views and interests, and that there is a need for institutions to protect the rights of all people to allow them to live together in peace" (OSI 2007e).[1] It is characterized by the existence of the rule of law, democratically elected government, a vigorous civil society, and respect for minority opinions:

> We need critical thinking; we need institutions and rules that allow people with different opinions and interests to live together in peace; we need a democratic form of government that ensures the orderly transfer of power; we need a market economy that provides feedback and allows mistakes to be corrected; we need to protect minorities and respect minority opinions. Above all, we need the rule of law. Ideologies like fascism or communism give rise to a closed society in which the individual is subjugated to the collective. Society is dominated by the state, and the state is in the service of a dogma

that claims to embody the ultimate truth. In such a society, there is no freedom. (Soros 1995, 113)

In 1979, George Soros established his first foundation, the Open Society Fund (now the Open Society Institute), to "open up closed societies, help make open societies more viable and foster a critical mode of thinking" (Soros 2002, ix). This was followed by the establishment of his first Eastern European foundation in Hungary in 1984 and the Soros Foundation–Soviet Union in 1987. Initially, the main goal of these foundations was to break the monopoly of socialist ideology by creating "small cracks" in the monolithic bloc, hoping that "in a rigid structure even a small crack can have a devastating effect" (Soros 1991, ix). During this time, the foundations' approach to international development assistance was spontaneous. In the words of George Soros "we were practically throwing our money around, like a traditional peasant sowing seeds" (1991, 129). Practically, this meant that the foundation focused on grant-making activities and practically anyone who had a good idea for a project received funding, so long as the proposed project reflected the foundation's mission and fit its criteria. As Soros described it, this approach "was chaotic, appropriate to the confusion of the revolutionary process in Eastern Europe" (1995, 149).

However, as the cracks grew and the former socialist bloc finally collapsed in 1989, the initial approach was no longer effective. The euphoria of the early 1990s was soon replaced by pessimism in the middle of the decade due to the slow pace of political, economic, and social reform. Not only was there a need to devise a new strategy for international development assistance, but it also became necessary to rethink the goals of the foundation. As Soros explained:

Recent experience has taught us a bitter lesson: it is not enough to destroy a closed society in order to bring about an open society. While this is obvious to me now, I cannot claim that I was equally conscious of it at the time when I started the Open Society Fund. I defined the foundation's objectives as helping to open up closed societies and helping to make open societies more viable. What has become my main objective—namely, helping to build the infrastructure and the institutions that are lacking in a closed society but are indispensable to the functioning of an open society—was not part of my original plan. (Soros 1991, xiv)

The revised strategic approach involved a geographic expansion of the network to the newly independent states, an establishment of flexible and participatory management structures in national foundations, development of new operational strategies, and an identification of locally appropriate programmatic priorities. In "the revolutionary atmosphere" of the late 1980s and the early 1990s (Ivacs 2005, 1), national foundations began to emerge everywhere. By 1994, they were active in twenty-four countries of the former socialist bloc. By 2007, the network consisted of national foundations and offices in over thirty countries and included three regional initiatives—the Open Society Initiative for Southern Africa, the Open Society Initiative for West Africa, and Open Society Initiative for East Africa (see Table 3). Combined, the network has reached to over fifty countries worldwide (OSI 2007e).

Unlike other international NGOs, the Soros Foundations have relied on already-existing local initiatives and have generally been managed by nationals of the countries in which they operate. For example, all national foundations are governed by local boards composed of locally prominent individuals (politicians, journalists, human rights activists, education experts, and so on) who determine priorities. Meanwhile, George Soros sets broader policy goals as chairman of the OSI and its network. In addition to locally managed national foundations, with their own operational and grant-making programs, there are also a number of network-wide programs dealing with specific program areas like education, media, health, information, culture, and the justice system. These programs are usually developed by OSI's primary offices (for example, OSI-NY, OSI-Budapest, and OSI-London) and operated through the national foundations. However, the national foundations can decide whether to participate in these network programs. If they do, they are expected to assume responsibility for implementation within their country. Soros describes the interaction between national foundations and network programs as creating "a matrix that combines local needs with professional expertise" (2002, 27). The system is open ended, providing national foundations with flexibility and discretion to operate outside the confines of regional network programs.

Table 3. Open Society Institute/Soros Foundations (2007)

	NATIONAL FOUNDATIONS
Albania	Open Society Foundation for Albania
Armenia	Open Society Institute Assistance Foundation–Armenia
Azerbaijan	Open Society Institute Assistance Foundation–Azerbaijan
Bosnia/Herzegovina	Open Society Fund–Bosnia and Herzegovina
Bulgaria	Open Society Institute–Sofia
Czech Republic	Open Society Fund–Prague
Estonia	Open Estonia Foundation
Georgia	Open Society Georgia Foundation
Guatemala	Fundacion Soros–Guatemala
Haiti	Fondation Connaissance et Liberte
Kazakhstan	Soros Foundation–Kazakhstan
Kosovo	Kosovo Foundation for Open Society
Kyrgyzstan	Soros Foundation–Kyrgyzstan
Latvia	Soros Foundation–Latvia
Macedonia	Foundation Open Society Institute–Macedonia
Moldova	Soros Foundation–Moldova
Mongolia	Open Society Forum
Montenegro	Foundation Open Society Institute–Representative Office Montenegro
Poland	Stefan Batory Foundation
Romania	Soros Foundation Romania
Serbia	Fund for an Open Society–Serbia
Slovakia	Open Society Foundation–Bratislava
South Africa	Open Society Foundation for South Africa
Tajikistan	Open Society Institute Assistance Foundation–Tajikistan
Turkey	Open Society Institute Assistance Foundation–Turkey
Ukraine	International Renaissance Foundation

	REGIONAL INITIATIVES
East Africa	Open Society Initiative for East Africa
West Africa	Open Society Initiative for West Africa
Southern Africa	Open Society Initiative for Southern Africa

	OFFICES
Belgium	Open Society Institute–Brussels
France	Open Society Institute–France
United Kingdom	Open Society Foundation (London)
United States	Open Society Institute–Baltimore
	Open Society Institute–New York
	Open Society Institute–Washington DC

The national foundations function differently depending on specific political, economic, and social context. As the case studies in this book illustrate, national foundations choose to cooperate with the government in some countries (such as the new EU accession countries and more reform-minded governments in other former socialist countries), while in others they use nongovernmental channels (especially in more authoritarian countries of Central Asia and the Caucasus). Soros summarizes:

> They [the national foundations] work with the government when they can and independently of the government when they cannot; sometimes they are in outright opposition. When foundations can cooperate with the government, they can be more effective; when they cannot, their work is more needed and more appreciated because they offer an alternative source of funding for civil society. As a general rule, the worse the government, the better the foundation because it enjoys the commitment and support of civil society. (Soros 2002, 25–26)

OSI education "logic": From demonstration projects to policy impact

Notwithstanding the varied strategic approaches and operational programming across the region, one shared commonality of the Soros Foundation Network has been its high commitment to education reform initiatives. Since the collapse of the socialist bloc at the end of the 1980s, various regional politicians, policymakers, and NGO representatives have persistently approached George Soros to convince him of the importance of education reform to post-socialist transformation processes.[2] Some arguments were so compelling that Soros decided to invest hundreds of millions of dollars in education reform initiatives across the region. For example, Sarah Klaus (2004) describes a meeting of George Soros with Canadian physician Dr. Frasier Mustard in 1993 to discuss strategies for Soros's new regional university (the Central European University in Budapest, Hungary). During the meeting the discussion turned to early childhood development, and Mustard was able to argue "the case for the critical role of early childhood education so convincingly" that Soros decided to invest more than US$100 million to launch the new initiative (Klaus 2004, 3).[3] Since then, education projects have spanned different education levels (from early childhood to higher education), covered different reform areas (from textbook revision to teacher training), and included different target groups (from parents to policymakers).

A strong commitment to education reform is clearly reflected in the annual expenditures of the OSI and its network of national foundations. Of the total, averaging between US$400 million and US$500 million (OSI 2007e), approximately 30 percent is generally committed to education reform initiatives. Since the mid-1990s, education expenditures of the national foundations in the Caucasus, Central Asia, and Mongolia alone have constituted over US$57 million (see Table 4). As Quigley has emphasized in his study on the role of private foundations in democracy assistance efforts in the former socialist bloc, George Soros has instantly recognized "the centrality of education" and made it one of the main priorities of the network, thus going "far beyond the rhetoric of many other funders" and reflecting "an innovative approach in foreign assistance efforts" (1997, 100).

Similar to the experience of other international foundations and NGOs, the OSI's strategic approach to education reform has evolved over time. In the context of frequently changing sociopolitical conditions and the emergence of new foreign development assistance in the region, OSI education logic has undergone major conceptual and organizational shifts. Each of these highlights efforts to ensure long-term sustainability and increase the impact of education reform initiatives. If George Soros "felt quite alone" when he committed his financial resources to helping former socialist countries to make the transition to open societies in the early 1990s (Soros 2002, 154), he soon had to compete with other international NGOs, financial institutions, and multilateral governmental agencies for influence. OSI has faced the need to react to the growing international development "industry" and to adjust its operational and grant-making programming to increase the "comparative advantage" of OSI among other international development agencies in the countries of the former socialist bloc (Soros 1991, 128).

Given the organizational complexity of OSI, the "personality politics" of each national foundation, and the contextual nuances of every country, it is an extremely difficult (if not impossible) task to document the evolution of educational "logic." Any attempt can

Table 4. Education expenditures of the National Soros Foundations

YEAR	ARMENIA	AZERBAIJAN	GEORGIA	KAZAHKSTAN	KYRGYSTAN	MONGOLIA	TAJIKISTAN	UZBEKISTAN	TOTAL
1995			199,520	449,560	1,767,610				2,416,690
1996			459,128	402,323	296,377				1,157,828
1997	12,000	65,000	365,000	757,000	455,000	127,000	1,000	45,000	1,827,000
1998	403,000	377,000	1,575,000	1,721,000	1,157,000	614,000	56,000	356,000	6,259,000
1999	440,000	1,015,000	1,316,000	1,585,000	1,121,000	1,191,000	261,000	516,000	7,445,000
2000	383,000	719,000	2,447,000	1,337,000	740,000	1,119,000	240,000	1,239,000	8,224,000
2001	605,000	946,000	2,689,000	1,089,000	442,000	1,160,000	287,000	1,051,000	8,269,000
2002	504,000	702,000	1,949,000	1,687,000	478,000	571,000	417,000	849,000	7,157,000
2003	243,000	736,000	954,000	1,629,000	532,000	876,000	591,000	756,000	6,328,000
2004	303,000	444,000	471,000	516,000	497,000	550,000	724,000		3,505,000
2005	284,000	306,000	657,000	302,000	373,000	100,000	608,000		2,630,000
2006	303,000	222,000	356,000	61,000	398,000	83,000	551,000		1,974,000
Total	3,491,000	5,532,000	13,437,648	11,535,883	8,256,987	6,391,000	3,736,000	4,812,000	57,192,518

Note: There were no expenditures in Turkmenistan. The above expenditures do not include education expenditures of the network programs.

only scratch the surface of the major conceptual, organizational, and strategic shifts while failing to capture the complexity of the local processes and uniqueness of responses in each national setting. Nevertheless, it is important to map out some of the broader strategic shifts within the education logic of OSI and its national foundations in order to better understand the changing relationships among OSI (as an international NGO), the state, and other transnational actors in the former socialist region.

Generally speaking, it is possible to identify three broad phases of strategic development within the educational programming of OSI and its national foundations. During the first phase national foundations focused their efforts on implementing "demonstration" projects to model best practices at the school level. During the second phase OSI shifted its strategy to ensure greater sustainability of the "demonstration" projects and increase the systemic impact of its education initiatives. During the third phase OSI made concentrated efforts to get involved in national education policymaking to influence reforms on a larger scale through a combination of carefully designed "demonstration" projects, systems-reform activities, and education advocacy initiatives. These three phases have evolved gradually. Yet, they are not necessarily time bound or sequential. For example, some countries (such as the new EU accession countries) advanced through all three phases fairly fast, while others (such as the Central Asian republics), progressed at a slower pace. Furthermore, some countries moved sequentially, while others dealt with all three phases at the same time.

Perhaps the most visible reflection of the strategic shifts in OSI education logic was in the organizational changes of the regional education office in Budapest, Hungary. Established in 1995, the office was initially called the Education Program Support Unit (EPSU). The original goal of the EPSU was to provide "professional support to pilot projects, identify best practices, and disseminate them" on a wider scale (EPSU 1997). Similar to the children and youth programs at OSI-NY (which provided technical assistance to the network of centrally designed programs), EPSU supported the national foundations in implementing locally designed pilot projects in the areas of school improvement, educational leadership, teacher education, textbooks and educational materials, and school success for Roma children. In 1998, the office was reorganized as a result of the strategic shift toward systemic change, which was directly reflected in its new name—Institute for Educational Policy (IEP). Finally, the office was reorganized and renamed again in 2001. The new name—Education Support Program (ESP)—marked a departure from the exclusive focus on policy, and an effort to support national education reforms by "combining best practice and policy to strengthen open society values" (OSI 2007a). The sections below provide a more detailed account of the major strategic shifts and their implications for the network programs and the national foundations.

Phase one: Demonstration projects

The first phase of development of OSI education-related activities was characterized by the piloting of "demonstration" projects at the "base layer of the educational system—the schools and other institutions which are the actual instruments of delivery of the educational process" (IEP, 1999b, 2). The main goal of this process was to model education innovation or best educational practices, which were lacking in countries of the former socialist bloc. During this phase (until the end of the 1990s), OSI-NY developed a number of network programs (also referred to as the children and youth programs) that aimed to "bring innovative approaches to existing social and educational structures that have an impact on the welfare and development of children and adolescents" (OSI 2007e). These programs covered early childhood education (SbS), basic education (RWCT), civic education (Street Law program), and extracurricular activities (Debate program), among others. Combined, these network programs aimed to emphasize "democratic principles" at the school level, and promote "the development of the individual child to his or her full potential" (OSI 2007b) through the introduction of child-centered and interactive teaching/learning, development of critical thinking, and encouragement of participatory education.

During this phase many foundations and most network programs were most successful when they based their programs at the school level. Through supporting teachers, pilot sites, school-based teams, school and community links, and networks of schools, they enabled change to spread "bottom up and across" school communities, national education systems, and even country borders (EPSU 1995, 3). While education ministries and local education authorities were sometimes involved as "gatekeepers of the system," the typical pattern was for foundations and network programs to relate directly to a small number of schools (IEP 1999b, 2). These projects often had a ground-breaking effect by demonstrating quality, innovation, and long-term commitment to education reform efforts. In many countries, these demonstration projects greatly contributed to the legitimacy of OSI in various policy settings, providing a springboard for engaging in wider education reform efforts.

The underlying assumption (and expectation) was that the pilot or demonstration projects would eventually be replicated by the government or other international donors. In fact, in 1997 the OSI published a handbook entitled *Building Donor Partnerships* that emphasized that the "Soros foundations often make an excellent lead partner to provide seed funding or develop a pilot project because of their willingness to innovate, readiness to move human and financial resources quickly, ability to adapt, and their local implementation bases" (Bassler and Wisse Smit 1997). Furthermore, the publication argued that partnerships would be key to the replication and expansion of the pilot projects:

> There may be local demand to expand coverage of the network's Step-by-Step program to more kindergartens and primary schools. The introduction of Internet connectivity through the network's programs may generate the appetite for wider access. Ministries of education may want to distribute textbooks developed by a national foundation of the network to all schools in the country. Other donors with successful programs may approach the Soros foundations for grants to expand. (Bassler and Wisse Smit 1997, 9)

Undoubtedly, the initial approach to educational assistance— developing and piloting demonstration projects—had a number of advantages. These included the possibility of devising fast responses to urgent educational needs and an opportunity to identify "suitable partners with whom to work on issues where they had a comparative advantage and prospects for making a contribution" (Quigley 1997, 107). However, there were also limitations. As the members of the IEP observed: "The cost was sometimes high. The link to systemic change and sustainability was often very weak" (IEP 1999b, 2). Similar to the experience of other international

NGOs in the former socialist region and worldwide, the fear was that "NGO-implemented pilot projects . . . can only ever remain just that—pilot projects" (Klinmhorm and Ireland 1992, 60), or that they may simply become "opulent islands in otherwise empty seas" (Quigley 1997, 101). As summarized by one representative of the national Soros Foundations, "We were strong on mission but weak on strategic thinking" (quoted in IEP 1998a). This realization (along with the increased awareness that OSI education funding is likely to decrease in the future) has led to a major strategic shift toward sustainability and systemic impact of new and existing education reform initiatives.

Phase two: Systemic impact, sustainability, and scalability

By the end of the 1990s, there was a deliberate shift in the OSI education logic from demonstration or grassroots development projects to a "low costs—high impact" pattern of assistance (Rado 2001, 1). This occurred in the context of declining funding for the national Soros Foundations in general, and education reform initiatives in particular. As early as the middle of the 1990s, George Soros had clearly articulated that the national foundations were going to eventually "degenerate" and that they "should not be endowed by the money of a dead man who cannot exercise critical judgment" (1995, 148). As Henry Healey summarized, this meant that OSI and the national foundations had to devise a new strategy to ensure that "there would be something in place to further and sustain the Open Society cause" when the money ran out (1998, 1).

The strategic shift was guided by the IEP, which was established in 1998 and housed at OSI-Budapest. The IEP's main goal was to cooperate with the OSI network, governments, and education institutions in creating "coherent policy frameworks to guide the reforms of general education systems in former communist countries" (IEP, 1998b). As Cameron Harrison, the first director of the IEP, explained, the IEP was established to "take up a newer range of responsibilities" given by George Soros, including (1) developing educational policy for the network, (2) supporting the national foundations and network programs in adjusting their existing programs to reflect the new policy goals, and (3) guiding the development of new large-scale education development programs or "mega projects" in the OSI network (quoted in IEP 1998c). Since its establishment in 1998, the IEP had aggressively embarked on its mission by organizing a series of activities (conferences, workshops, and newsletters) aimed at explaining the meaning of the new strategic shift to the national foundations and building local capacity to ensure implementation.

The IEP's debut (and the turning point in OSI's strategic reorientation) was a regional workshop for the education program directors and education board members of the national Soros Foundations. The workshop, entitled From Mission to Strategy, was held June 3–5, 1998, in Matrahaza, Hungary (and is frequently referred to as the Matrahaza conference). The purpose of the conference was to explore the mission of OSI and its network of national foundations, the relationship between mission and strategy, and systemic approaches to strategy development (IEP 1998a). Although conference participants pointed out that OSI educational programs had many strengths (such as the network's flexibility, lack of bureaucracy, potential for innovation, and autonomy of national foundations), they admitted that weaknesses included not enough strategic planning, monitoring, and evaluation; a growing bureaucracy; poor internal communication; and the absence of a systemic approach. As summarized in the conference proceedings (IEP 1998a), while the national foundations had been "strong at piloting and supporting innovation" at the school level, the next phase of programming should focus more on ensuring sustainability of education initiatives and supporting systemic change in education reform.

The Matrahaza conference signaled a transformation of the Soros Foundation Network. It placed the issues of systemic change, sustainability, and scalability at the top of the OSI education agenda. Within OSI, "systemic change" was defined as "influence on state (or regional) policy or practice in education," which initiated a change within the education system by redirecting "state resources towards the intended goals," and increasing "capacity within the education system to design, initiate, and implement positive change." It was further explained that moving toward "systemic impact" in education meant "engineering a shift" from implementing pilot projects at the school level toward "influencing and supporting change at a higher level," as well as encouraging a system-wide replication of the OSI-initiated pilot projects by the state (Iliff 1999, 1).

In addition to systemic impact, the new strategic approach emphasized the importance of sustainability, defined as "the change initiated by the program," which "continues beyond direct funding from the Foundation" (Iliff 1999, 14). In its initial formulation, the concept of sustainability was closely linked with institutionalization of OSI projects in state educational structures. In particular, Heather Iliff explained that "sustainable programs are those that produce a change that is continued and replicated with regular state resources" to ensure that "the foundations' investment is highly leveraged by significantly larger amounts of state resources" (1999, 16). OSI's definition of sustainability also implied that all projects should have a beginning and an end, or "a clear exit strategy," which was "vital not only to protect investment, but in order to ensure that our activity does not create dependency—the very opposite of our goal" (IEP 1999a, 2).

Finally, the new strategic approach introduced the concept of scalability of pilot projects as "the fundamental problem of reform," by explaining that educational changes (however defined) "cannot break out of the small isolated pockets within which they can be found and become the norm, as opposed to always being the exception to the norm" (Healey 1998, 6). In this context, the IEP encouraged the national foundations to seek partnerships with "middle-layer institutions," which typically connect schools and policymaking institutions within the national educational systems, and are "vital" for pursuing "scalability and breadth of impact," as well as "systemic change and sustainability":

> Some of these intermediate bodies are mainly concerned with administrative and bureaucratic functions; the schools' line managers—regional or municipal authorities. The other bodies in the middle layer have a variety of key functions in the system: one might be a national curriculum agency, for example, another could be a national testing and certification body. One or more of the bodies will certainly be concerned with teacher training; another with adult and community education; and there may also exist a national school Inspectorate. All of these bodies play critical roles in supporting, enabling— or indeed, blocking—the processes of educational development in their countries. (IEP 1999b, 2)

These new strategic concepts—systemic impact, sustainability, and scalability—immediately spread across the OSI global network through newsletters, conferences, and workshops. For example, the 1999 volume of the quarterly newsletter *Open Society Education Update* dedicated each issue to one of the new strategic concepts: sustainability and systemic impact (February 1999), partnerships (April 1999), strategies (July 1999), and large-scale education development programs (October 1999). The main headline of the February issue bluntly asked: "How can we use our experience to influence national systems of education? How shall we design exit strategies for our present programmes?" (IEP 1999c, 1). In the same newsletter (consisting of thirteen pages), the word *sustainability* appeared twenty-two times, *policy* twenty-one times, *systemic* thirteen times, and *impact* ten times, signaling that most of the original reform concepts (such as *pilot projects*, which appeared only three times) had became passe.

Between 1998 and 2001, the IEP organized a number of conferences and workshops to ensure internalization of the new strategic shift within the network of national foundations. Most activities focused on capacity building of staff and policymakers. The conferences featured prominent academics, researchers, and practitioners such as Andy Hargreaves from the Ontario Institute for Studies in Education (addressing reform sustainability), Noel McGinn from Harvard University (speaking on issues of policy, decentralization, and strategic change of educational systems), Tom Alexander from OECD (discussing educational policy processes), James Socknat from the World Bank (focusing on the role of education in national development), Henry Healey from the Research Triangle Institute (focusing on project scalability and systemic change), and numerous other experts from the United States and Europe.

The irreversibility of the new strategic shift had become visible in the massive information campaign and ongoing training opportunities for the representatives of the national foundations and network programs. It was also confirmed by the new criteria for evaluating project proposals and education strategies within OSI and the national foundations. The new standards were prepared by the OSI-NY and OSI-Budapest offices in 1999 and disseminated to all national foundations and network programs later in the year. They prescribed that all education programs should be "time-bound," "replicable," "sustainable," and based on "a partnership with other donors" (see Table 5). All existing and newly initiated education programs and strategies had to meet the above-mentioned criteria in order to secure funding from OSI-NY or OSI-Budapest regional offices. This triggered immediate programmatic responses from the network programs of the national foundations.

Table 5. Criteria for reviewing education strategies and programs (1999)

CRITERIA FOR REVIEWING EDUCATION STRATEGIES

- Vision and mission clear, relevant to open society mission
- Self-sustainability built into the strategy with concrete approaches described
- Evidence of consultation and "ownership" of key stakeholders
- Objectives and outcomes measurable and achievable
- Key points of leverage within the system identified and addressed
- Sustainable, creates long-term effects after funding ends
- Based on adequate and well-grounded needs analysis
- Sound consideration of context, including reform environment, country reality and social demands
- Involves other donors and partners, leverages resources of others
- Realistic in terms of foundation resources and capacity

CRITERIA FOR REVIEWING EDUCATION PROGRAMS

- Promotes a change of attitude/behavior among target groups
- Program is time-bound with sustainability plan built-in
- Goals achievable and measurable
- Directly addresses one or several needs
- Fits with the Foundation's mission, strategy, and priorities
- Is replicable and sustainable
- Feasibility is reflected in clear, measurable, and achievable outcomes
- Integrated with other Foundation programs
- Fits the strengths and capacity of the Foundation
- Program derived from the goals, connected to the mission and strategy
- Includes an evaluation plan with measurable quality indicators

Source: Open Society Institute. 1999. *Category A review process for education programs.* Internal memorandum issued on March 31, 1999.

Implications for the network programs: The "spin-off craze"

Following the strategic shift within OSI's educational programming, the goals of the existing network programs (such as SbS, RWCT, Debate, the English Language program, and others) had to be adjusted (Rado 2001). Although one of the initial recommendations for sustainability, scalability, and systemic impact was to institutionalize these network programs in state education structures (for example, in-service and pre-service teacher education institutions, ministries of education, and other state institutions), the program staff soon realized that this may not be the best option to ensure lasting impact nationally. Reflecting on the history of the SbS early childhood education program, Klaus explained that it began to seem unwise to "turn over a quality-focused initiative to a ministry for safekeeping in a region with strong centralized ministries, economic uncertainty, unstable governments, and a highly politicized education sector" (2004, 6–7). Seeking long-term commitment from election-minded politicians and government-appointed bureaucrats seemed particularly unrealistic, given their often changing priorities and preoccupation with showing quick results. Furthermore, the region was missing "the quality safeguards" in the form of independent professional and parent associations, NGOs, and educational foundations (Klaus 2004, 7).

With an increasingly pressing mandate for sustainability, the only remaining alternative was to transform the network programs into local NGOs, in most cases "spin-offs" of the previous programs (Rado 2001, 1). As Klaus pointed out, the survival of the program no longer depended solely on the quality of the project's implementation and the professional education capacity of the program staff. Sustainability now relied on the ability of country teams to take on "the challenge of establishing and directing new non-governmental organizations in countries that have previously had no history of permitting a strong third sector" (Klaus 2004, 7). Since 1998, OSI-NY has embarked on an intensive initiative to train and support the "panic-stricken" SbS country teams as they went from being members of a project to employees of an NGO (Lorant 2006). In particular, program staff participated in a variety of seminars on topics such as facilitative leadership, strategic planning, financial management, governance, public relations, and proposal writing. Each country team was required to develop a three-year strategic plan for its new NGO, which provided a base for future funding from OSI-NY and fund-raising from other donor agencies.

By 2004, twenty-seven of the thirty SbS programs were operated by independent early childhood organizations, including NGOs and membership associations. Despite the financial fears and programmatic uncertainties associated with the spin-off process during the late 1990s, these newly established NGOs were able to form partnerships and secure independent funding in order to maintain program growth and retain quality. NGOs had initially succeeded in attracting modest funding, but large-scale partnerships with the World Bank, USAID, UNICEF, as well as the EU PHARE and TACIS programs soon followed in many countries (Klaus 2004). As a result, SbS NGOs were able to decrease their financial dependence on OSI-NY. As Klaus highlighted, partner organizations provided over 50 percent of the financial support required by the SbS NGOs in 2002, and almost 70 percent in 2004 (2004, 10). In most countries the SbS NGOs have become important actors in national education reform efforts, filling the void in service provision and advocacy for child-centered early childhood education reform.

While the new organizational status and partnerships had markedly increased the sustainability of the SbS program (as well as other network programs that experienced similar organizational changes during the spin-off processes), the strategic shift also had some unintended consequences. As Klaus pointed out, partnerships inevitably influenced NGO programming. With most international donors in the region showing a strong preference for funding basic education reforms, co-funding for early childhood education programs became more difficult to secure (Klaus 2004). The quest for sustainability and collaborative partnerships had inadvertently led some NGOs to deviate from their original mission in pursuit of external funding. For the SbS program this meant a growing emphasis on basic education instead of the original mission of early childhood education reform. For other network programs (especially the English Language program), the mission drift was more striking, as the newly established spin-offs (English language centers and schools) were forced to become market driven to survive. In some countries, the new market orientation resulted in compromise of some of the original programs goals—such as "fostering social inclusion in order to be in agreement with OSI's mission"

(OSI 2007e). Some spin-offs began to serve more privileged students in order to ensure financial sustainability, charging increasingly high tuition fees that excluded many students.

Implications for the national foundations:
Systemic education reform initiatives, mega projects, and spin-offs

Similar to the network programs, all national foundations had to adjust their programming to the new educational strategy. By 1999, most of the foundations had updated their strategies to reflect the criteria of systemic impact, sustainability, and scalability. One issue of the *Open Society Education Update* summarized enthusiastic responses from the region. For example, Tamara Grdzelidze from Georgia wrote that "one of the main components of the strategy is the building of partnerships with the Ministry of Education, aiming toward synergic efforts in the reform process, and toward ensuring sustainability of OSF [Open Society Foundation] educational programs" (quoted in IEP 1999c, 3). Similarly, Natsagdorj Enkhtuya from Mongolia reported that "the Soros Foundation started the implementation of a large-scale education development program that complements the national education reform," which was "designed to be synergic with the national reform effort, which places greater responsibility on schools for curriculum and management" (quoted in IEP 1999c, 5). Finally, Michael Rezyapkin from Kyrgyzstan reported that the Soros Foundation Kazakhstan's strategy involved "moving from needs-responsive to strategically planned projects. . . . The Foundation thinks about the synergies, of alternative sources of funding, of using the resources created by other programs, of sustainability in developing the 1999 package of educational programs" (quoted in IEP 1999c, 4).

The new strategic plans of the national foundations were soon translated into project proposals and implemented in practice. Not all of these projects led to systemic changes (as documented in Anna Matiashvili's chapter on educational decentralization reform in Georgia), but some resulted in the irreversible transformation of multiple segments of the educational systems. In 2001, for example, the OSI and International Renaissance Foundation in Ukraine formed a partnership with the American Councils for International Education to offer technical support to the Ukrainian government in introducing standardized external testing. This became a mandatory criterion for university admissions to ensure a "fair and transparent" entrance examination process (ESP 2007). The International Renaissance Foundation and OSI's ESP have invested substantial human and financial resources into developing and piloting the project, which was eventually scaled up to become the basis for government reform.[4]

The Central Asian foundations in Kyrgyzstan and Tajikistan began advocating for changes in funding mechanisms, which had far-reaching consequences for the educational systems. As the chapter on Kyrgyzstan by Alexandr Ivanov and Valentin Deichman reveals, these reforms compelled government officials to share power with other education stakeholders, signaling the move from a planned to a demand/supply-driven economy in the education sector. In Tajikistan, the OSIAF was one of the institutional partners in a project funded by the USAID and the World Bank, which piloted student per-capita financing, replacing the policy of incremental budgeting based on instructional hours and number of classes. In Kyrgyzstan, the Soros Foundation supported the voucher-based teacher-training system as part of the USAID-funded project PEAKS (Participation, Education and Knowledge Strengthening). Both of these projects qualify as systemic education reforms and have had major implications for several areas of the education system as they "revamp institutional structures and cultures with an immediate effect" (Ivanov and Deichman in this volume).

Perhaps the most visible reflection of the new strategic shift was the launching of large-scale educational programs—mega projects— by five foundations from the network. As the IEP explained, mega projects were set up to achieve "systemic change through large-scale, single, coherent, powerful" initiatives, focusing on "points of maximum leverage within the system," and "orchestrated in close cooperation with national government" (IEP 1999b, 2). The planning phase of these large-scale education programs lasted one to two years and included needs-assessment strategy development, capacity building for managing the programs, creation of partnerships with the government and other international donors, and consultation with local stakeholders and experts. These large-scale education programs were launched in five countries of the network, including Albania, Georgia, Mongolia, Romania and Russia (IEP 1999c). As documented in Natsagdorj Enkhtuya's chapter on Mongolia, some of the national foundations were able to set a standard for best practices that subsequent donors and implementers adopted in order to gain support from and access to an already established network of innovative schools.

Finally, the national foundations began the process of spinning-off some of their existing education programs into independent NGOs. Similar to the network programs, the establishment of NGOs was intended to achieve two goals. First, the national foundations struggled to decrease their administrative budgets, expecting that the newly established NGOs would be less dependent on OSI funding and eventually would generate their own financial resources. The second goal was to diversify the education market in the region by supporting the emergence of new actors. An overview of Soros National Foundation education strategies (Miljević and Repac 2006) indicates that the number of the national foundations with general education programs dropped from twenty-six in 2000, to nineteen in 2004, and to ten in 2007. However, most education programs are now operated through spin-offs, which collaborate closely with ESP in the broader OSI education network. Some spin-offs have consolidated as one NGO (as in Azerbaijan), while others have remained separate (as in Kyrgyzstan).

By 2007, the national foundations in Central Asia, the Caucasus, and Mongolia (with the exception of Turkmenistan and Uzbekistan) supported the establishment of twenty-five independent education NGOs (Table 6). Some of these NGOs hosted the network programs (such as the SbS and RWCT) while others attempted to combine both policy and practice to increase the impact of their programming on education reform nationally. While some NGOs remained dependent on OSI funding, many were able to generate their resources through grants from the ADB, World Bank, USAID, UNICEF, and other international donors. For example, the Education Initiatives Support Foundation in Bishkek, Kyrgyzstan, was able to raise over US$1,000,000 in 2006 alone, far exceeding the entire education budget of the Soros Foundation–Kyrgyzstan in the same year.

To summarize, the second phase of education development involved a strategic shift from demonstration projects to systemic impact, sustainability, and scalability of existing and newly developed initiatives. As the IEP put it, the goal was to achieve "a systemic impact—impact at a national level, and on a national scale" (1999a, 1). The IEP further argued that the strategic shift would bring several benefits, including (1) increased direct impact, (2)

Table 6. Education NGOs supported by the OSI/Soros Foundations in the Caucasus, Central Asia, and Mongolia

FOUNDATION (year established)	OSI SPIN-OFF (year established)
ARMENIA	
Open Society Institute Assistance Foundation (1997)	Step by Step Benevolent Foundation (2001)
AZERBAIJAN	
Open Society Institute Assistance Foundation (1997)	Baku Education Information Center (1999) Center for Innovations in Education (2004)
GEORGIA	
Open Society Georgia Foundation (1994)	School Family Society Association (2000) Center for Education Initiatives (2001) Center for Social Sciences (2003) Debate Association (2003) International Institute for Education Policy, Planning and Management (2003) The Center for International Education (2005)
KAZAKHSTAN	
Soros Foundation Kazakhstan (1994)	Almaty English Language School (1999) Center for Democratic Education (1999) Educational Center Bilim Central Asia (2004) Educational Center Step by Step (1999) Internet Training Center (1999) National Debate Center (1999) Street Law Kazakhstan (1999)
KYRGYZSTAN	
Soros Foundation–Kyrgyzstan (1993)	Education Initiatives Support Foundation (1997) Center for Information and Support of Economic Education (1998) Child Center "Moltur Koz" (1998) English Language School "Lingua" (1998) Public Foundation "Step by Step" Program (1998) Center of Innovative Education "Peremena" (1999)

CONT.

FOUNDATION (year established)	OSI SPIN-OFF (year established)
TAJIKISTAN	
OSIAF–Tajikistan (1996)	Educational Reforms Support Unit "PULSE" (2002) Public Foundation "International Language School" (2004)
MONGOLIA	
Mongolian Foundation for Open Society (1997)	Open Debate Association of Mongolia (2000) Educational Information and Advising Center (2002) National English Teachers Training Association (2002) Street Law Mongolia (2003) Mongolian Education Alliance (2004)

Note: The above list includes spin-offs (NGOs that were founded by the national Soros Foundations), independent NGOs (organizations that absorbed and continued some of the Soros Foundations Network and/or national programs), as well as newly established independent NGOs (institutions that received substantial financial support from the national Soros Foundations).

increased focus on mission, and (3) increased cost efficiency (1999b, 1). As this book illustrates, this strategic shift had major implications for the network programs and the national foundations, resulting in the establishment of education service-provision NGOs across the region, development of new large-scale mega projects by the national foundations, and the forging of new partnerships with the state, donors, and other NGOs in the former socialist region.

Phase three: Policy-focused development

After the inception of the strategic shift toward systemic impact in the late 1990s, the IEP envisioned that the next phase of OSI education development would be "policy-focused development" (1999b, 3). The rationale was that the national foundations could begin supporting the processes of educational policymaking in their countries when governments were ready for change and the capacity to support such change was established within the national settings. This would create a "knowledge space" around the foundations (IEP 1999b, 4) and improve "information production" in the education sector (Rado 2001, 5), placing the national foundations at the center of educational development efforts in their countries. More specifically, the IEP listed the following advantages of moving to the next phase of strategic development in "appropriate countries":

> Firstly, such activity would, of itself, be a way of supporting directly the democratization of society and the processes of government—both key to our mission. Secondly, it would be an extremely direct and powerful way to influence the process of educational development in the country. Thirdly, such a strategy would incorporate systemic impact and scalability as intrinsic features of the process—they would be inevitable. Fourthly, such an approach may be the only effective way to remove some of the structural and procedural blocks which presently stand in the way of educational development in some countries. Fifthly, Phase Three activities would, by their nature, be an order of magnitude less expensive to fund than Phase Two programs. Finally, and significantly, the leverage obtained on funding by operating in this way would be immense. (IEP 1999b, 3)

Indeed, the strategic shift toward policy-focused development was at least partially motivated by the prospect of decreased funding (especially in the area of education) within the Soros Network. George Soros reiterated this at a board meeting in Budapest on June 24, 2001. He argued that he had been deliberately pushing the foundations toward building open societies through ideas and by influencing policy in the last several years: "This is a necessary progression, since the money will not be there forever" (quoted in OSI 2001, 1). He further explained that although the overall level of expenditure would be maintained until 2010 (approximately US$500 million per year globally), there would be an ongoing reorientation from the original network to other areas of the world. In other words, the national foundations were expected to achieve "a very high measure of impact at low cost" in the years to come (IEP 1999a, 3).

The shift toward policy-focused development required further adjustment of education strategies in the national foundations. In particular, it meant initiating activities to build local capacity in policy analysis and implementation, supporting ministries in the development of policies congruent with Open Society goals, and encouraging the processes of consultation and national debate on educational policy with a range of civil society stakeholders. Furthermore, the new strategic shift triggered the establishment of education policy think tanks, the creation of "an indigenous mechanism for the study and teaching of education policy development and analysis," and the development of intraregional cooperation on relevant topics, including networks for educational policy centers and academic professional associations (IEP 1999a, 3).

Building local capacity in education policy

One of the strategies for national foundations to engage in a policy-focused development was building local capacity in education policy development, analysis, and implementation. As the IEP noted, "the largest single obstacle" to the improvement of the educational practices was the lack of capacity of leading policymakers to understand and analyze existing circumstances, or to plan for educational development (1999b, 5). One possible response was to build local policy capacity. As the IEP explained, training could be provided to key individuals who were involved nationally in leading and supporting the processes of policy development and implementation (1999b). Typically, the national foundations decided to focus on immediate and pressing needs in their countries (given that these needs also reflected the OSI values) and invested in developing local educational policy expertise in a particular area. For example, foundations chose to focus on curriculum reform, textbook revision, student assessment, or education finance.

The chapter by Saule Kalikova and Iveta Silova analyzes the experience of Soros Foundation–Kazakhstan in attempting to influence the policymaking process by building local policy capacity in curriculum reform. In the case of Kazakhstan, this was a fairly successful strategy, which led to a major revision of the existing curriculum. Although local capacity building was a very time-consuming process (lasting over two years), one of the advantages of this approach was local ownership of the new reform. The project succeeded in changing the minds of the "Soviet-bred" specialists—a group of local experts who were highly recognized and well-respected academically, professionally, and politically. The strategic logic was to focus efforts on changing the minds of Soviet-bred specialists by providing opportunities to learn about the latest trends in world educational development, and to form professional partnerships with academics and policymakers abroad. This approach was particularly effective in Kazakhstan's "donor-free environment," where state officials were suspicious of any reform originating from the outside. The government welcomed the initiative, because it allowed local policymakers to engage actively in the reinterpretation and adaptation of the curriculum reform. At the same time, local policy capacity building provided an opportunity for Soros to devise a framework for a qualitatively new process of education policymaking in Kazakhstan.

Establishing education policy think tanks

Another significant opportunity to engage in policy-focused development was through the establishment of education policy think tanks in several countries of the network. As the IEP envisioned, the "real influence and effectiveness" of an education policy unit would be "a product of the quality of its work," and its ability to give "soundly based, well informed, and independent advice on issues of national policy" (1999b, 6). Since the early 2000s, policy think tanks, which were either supported or initiated by the national foundations, have emerged practically everywhere. In many countries, education policy centers became an integral part of larger public-policy think tanks. In some countries policy centers were hosted by education NGOs or universities. By 2007, there were twenty-four education policy centers in twenty-one countries (see Table 7). Notwithstanding the variety of sociopolitical contexts within which these centers are operating, their common feature is that "they are based on strong local knowledge, have developed international contacts, and have built links with key international organizations" (Huttova 2004, 1). The chapter herein by Tatiana Abdushukurova examines the complexities involved in the establishment of a locally run education policy center in Tajikistan. Abdushukurova highlights the challenges and opportunities involved

Table 7. Education policy think tanks supported by the OSI and the National Foundations

THINK TANKS	
Country	**Name of the Center**
Albania	Center for Democratic Education
Azerbaijan	Center for Innovations in Education
Bosnia and Herzegovina	proMENTE Social Research
Bulgaria	Center for Information Society Technologies
Croatia	Center for Educational Research and Development
Estonia	PRAXIS Center for Policy Studies
Georgia	International Institute for Educational Policy, Planning and Management
	Center for International Education
Kazakhstan	Education Policy Analysis Center
Kosovo	Kosova Education Center
Kyrgyzstan	Center for Public Policy
	Foundation "Education Initiatives Support"
Latvia	Center for Public Policy PROVIDUS
Lithuania	Education Policy Center
Mongolia	Mongolian Education Alliance
Romania	Center Education 2000+
Russia	Center for Educational Policy Studies
Serbia	Educational Reform Circles
Slovakia	Center for Education Policy
	Slovak Governance Institute
Slovenia	Center for Educational Policy Studies
Tajikistan	PULSE Educational Reforms Support Unit
Turkey	Education Reform Initiative
Ukraine	Center for Educational Policy

in operating a policy center in a country dominated by international donors and subjected to strong government control.

In many countries, education policy centers played a key role in involving local stakeholders in the policymaking process. They also helped change the terms of public-policy debate by bringing renewed attention to the social costs of post-socialist transformations. As an international review of activities undertaken by the policy units revealed (Rado 2001), the most frequently addressed issues were connected to equity in education. For example, half of all centers engaged in policy analyses of equity-related issues, including dropouts, discrimination in education, gender, and the education of different language groups. Furthermore, the majority of the policy centers addressed key issues in post-socialist education transformation processes (such as textbook revision, curriculum reform, student assessment), thus becoming "major players in designing and promoting the transition process in education" (Rado 2001, 13).

Regional policy networking and professional partnerships

As the education policy think tanks matured nationally, they increasingly recognized "the value of a regional focus in education development" (Kovarovic 2001, 4). This was especially important in order "to broaden the support base for sustainable reforms in general education and to promote, within these alliances, a specific agenda to further OSI goals" (ESP 2004, 6). In 2003, they joined together to become the Network of Education Policy Centers to promote "flexible, participatory, evidence-based, transparent education policies embedding open society values" (Network of Education Policy Centers 2007, 1). The idea was that acting as a network they would each have a stronger voice in advocating open society values internationally. Since 2003, the Network of Education Policy Centers has conducted two cross-national education monitoring studies, including *Education in a Hidden Marketplace: Monitoring of Private Tutoring* (OSI 2006) and *Monitoring of School Dropouts* (OSI 2007d). The network was formalized in 2006 with core funding from OSI.

In addition to the policy network, OSI supported two regional networks and a number of professional (or issue-focused) education networks. The regional networks included the South East European Education Cooperation Network, which was co-financed by OSI and the Austrian government as part of the Stability Pact, and the Central Asian Education Cooperation Network, which was jointly funded by OSI and the ADB. Both of these networks are virtual networks, which aim to facilitate information exchange and to "democratize the debate" about education reforms by establishing "links among grassroots initiatives, NGOs, regional education policy makers, and international institutions" in their respective regions (OSI 2007c, 1).[5] Furthermore, OSI supported several professional networks, including ISSA, the International Debate Education Association (IDEA), and the RWCT International Consortium. With varying success, some OSI-supported educational networks have been attempting to position themselves as advocates for open society values globally by engaging in policy debates with national governments, international financial institutions, bilateral and multilateral agencies, and other NGOs (Jurko 2007, 1).

Developing graduate programs in education policy

Although the initial strategy of the IEP envisioned the establishment of graduate degree programs in the area of education policy across the region (including Central European University), this has only happened in Russia (1999b). In 2002, the Moscow School of Social and Economic Sciences launched the Centre for Educational Policy Studies "for training a new generation of Educational Policy professionals" (Yablonskene 2005, 1). With the initial assistance of the OSI's Higher Education Support Program the center developed a two-year M.A. level program in educational policy and management for Russian-speaking education professionals. Given the lack of education policy study programs in other countries, the center attracted a large number of education professionals and policymakers from other countries of the former Soviet Union, especially Central Asia and the Caucasus. In addition, the ESP organized a series of online courses for education professionals from the region in cooperation with Teachers College, Columbia University. These courses covered a range of key topics in international and comparative education, including program evaluation and education policy studies. Efforts to introduce graduate training in education policy aimed at developing local capacity in education policymaking, thus lessening "dependency on Western resources and experts" in the region (IEP 1999a, 2).

Unfortunately, the IEP itself failed to achieve one of its initial goals of becoming "a center for professional development for educational staff" in the area of education policy (IEP 1998b). It appeared to be a policy institute in name but not necessarily in practice.[6] In 2001, the IEP was formally reorganized into the ESP, which involved a return to its original mission of providing technical support to the national foundations in education program development and implementation. As Eliason noted, the goal was to rebalance policy and practice because of the vital information that feedback and monitoring provided—"keeping one's finger on the pulse of rapidly changing circumstances and contexts" (2003, 13).

For most of the national foundations in the countries of Southeast/Central Europe and the former Soviet Union, the third phase— policy-focused development—has been primarily associated with developing exit strategies to ensure that education initiatives under way would be institutionalized within state structures, existing NGOs, or newly established entities. In the beginning of the 2000s, the ESP itself was involved in the spin-off process. The initial intention was that the ESP would close down its operation by the mid-2000s, after accomplishing the complex tasks of capturing the best practices developed by OSI over the last two decades, assisting the national foundations in developing exit strategies for their education programs, and helping to increase sustainability of the newly created spin-offs. Several national foundations were closed, and most of the education initiatives continued through an increasingly larger network of local spin-offs, newly established NGOs, and other OSI partner institutions (ESP 2004, 4). The underlying logic was that these independent organizations would continue to contribute, in one way or the other, to ongoing educational reform processes in the region by promoting open society values.

The programmatic "crisis" and re-balancing policy and practice

While a strong emphasis on education policy had many advantages (such as increasing systemic impact and sustainability of education initiatives), it also led to "a dispersed engagement on a very wide spectrum of educational issues" in each national setting (ESP 2006, 1). Increasingly, an exclusive emphasis on policy made OSI engagement in education "too technical" and far removed from the open society agenda, leading less often to deeper expertise in any particular area.[7] Instead of directly addressing educational issues related to promoting the open society values—equity, justice, and critical thinking—education programming became dominated by technical aspects of policy reform such as per capita funding, vouchers, and assessment. As some program staff noted, the open society mission began to get lost in the technicalities of policy jargon, making it increasingly more difficult for OSI to make the link between education and the fundamental mission of building open societies.

This programmatic "crisis," which was also accompanied by personality politics within the OSI regional offices, has recently led to rethinking the OSI education logic. In particular, OSI education logic was reformulated within the social justice framework to ensure a more coordinated effort across OSI and the national foundations in directly linking education initiatives to the open society agenda. OSI's education mission now persuasively focuses on justice in education, advocating for equal opportunity for every child and adult in three priority areas. First is the focus on combating social exclusion. Education is perceived as a fundamental human right, entailing equal access to quality education for low-income families, minority groups, and inclusion of children with special needs. Second, the new strategy advocates for openness and accountability in education systems and education reforms, including reconciling the power symmetries between governments and polities through the promotion of equitable and efficient state expenditures on education, anti-corruption and transparency, accountable governance and management, and citizen participation. Third, the new strategy promotes open society values in education, advocating for social justice and social action, diversity and pluralism, critical and creative thinking, as well as relevant curricula and learner-centered methodologies (ESP 2007, 1). As the ESP emphasized: "The current mission emphasis on education justice is the national and logical culmination of a maturing realization within OSI education network over a number of years. It is a mission that has grown from the bottom up" (2007a, 3).

Furthermore, the new strategic vision recognizes the importance of combining policy, practice, and advocacy to increase the impact of OSI education initiatives on education reforms nationally and internationally. Moving away from an exclusive emphasis on policy-focused development, which dominated OSI education logic at the turn of the century, the current education initiatives aim to promote innovation (through demonstration projects), advocacy (through targeted policy initiatives), and activism (through encouraging civic participation in education development). In Central Asia, for example, an initiative co-funded by OSI and the OECD focuses on at-risk children, including those with physical disabilities, learning difficulties, and other disadvantages (ESP 2007). The initiative combines both demonstration projects and advocacy. The rationale for demonstration projects is to identify the best practices of service delivery for at-risk children inside and outside of traditional systems in order to replicate and share them across the region. The demonstration projects are supplemented by building government and civil society capacity in order to initiate advocacy for the educational rights of at-risk children. Combined, the focus on policy and practice could substantially increase the impact of OSI initiatives on education reform in the region.

From post-socialist transformations toward the global open society

In the past few years OSI education programming has been undergoing yet another, perhaps conceptually greater, strategic shift. In an interview with Gints Grube (2002), George Soros explained that his interests and philanthropic activities "shifted from the problems of transition to the problems of globalization." With eight countries of the former socialist bloc becoming members of the EU in 2004, and two more joining in 2007, the problems of post-socialist transformation have become less urgent. The OSI has become increasingly engaged in advancing the idea of a global open society. In fact, Soros went so far as to say that "the transition paradigm is now being exhausted." He continued:

> There was, in fact, a moment of transition, a historic moment, an evolutionary moment when the old system collapsed—it was a total collapse, the most far-reaching collapse that you could imagine, because it involved politics, the economic system, and it was a moral collapse as well, because the communist system had been so comprehensive. So you had that moment, and that was a moment of great opportunity, and also chaos, but now

things have settled down and you now have the beginnings of a new system that has emerged. (in Grube 2002)

Soros has become increasingly engaged in advancing the idea of a "global open society" that would mobilize efforts "to correct and contain the system's deficiencies" of global capitalism (Soros 2002). Programmatically, the emphasis on the "global open society" has involved a reconceptualization of existing education initiatives and led to the proposal to develop "a coherent global education program" that would promote "justice in education through upholding this right" (ESP 2006, 1). In particular, the ESP aims to position itself as a global player in order "to draw international attention to local needs and informal international advocacy around a central mission with local insights and understanding" (ESP 2007, 2). For example, the 2007 strategy states that "ESP seeks to build on the momentum of mainstream education reform processes" (including EFA, FTI, and MDGs) while also raising issues that are of importance to OSI national foundations, yet may not be "fashionable" in the global arena (ESP 2007, 4).

Undoubtedly, this new phase of OSI strategic development opens up unique opportunities for OSI and the network of national foundations to engage in "global advocacy" by building on the momentum of mainstream education reform processes internationally (ESP 2007; 2004). However, a new emphasis on global education initiatives is also marking a historic shift from the original network of Soros Foundations in the countries of the former socialist bloc to different geographical areas, including Africa, Central and Latin America, West and Southeast Asia. For the national foundations in the original network, this shift has had major implications. Whereas the national foundations received financial and technical assistance from OSI in their initial phases, they are now required to generate their own income or seek funding from other donors as they continue to champion the open society values in increasingly complex post-socialist environments.

Notes

[1] Soros bases his philanthropic activity on the concept of an open society, which was popularized by Karl Popper in *Open Society and Its Enemies* (Princeton, NJ: Princeton University Press, 1945).

[2] Based on an interview with Liz Lorant.

[3] This early childhood education initiative has become known as the Step by Step program and is currently administered independently of OSI by the International Step by Step Association (ISSA).

[4] According to the ESP (2007), a 2005 presidential decree declared that transition to the external examination system for university entrance should be carried out in 2005–2006. A subsequent Cabinet of Ministers' decree stated that 2006 should be an experimental year, and 2007 and 2008 should be transition years for external examination reform to be implemented nationwide. In 2006, the Ukrainian government introduced a national examination reform, which linked secondary-school exit exams with higher-education entrance exams. All universities were obliged to accept external testing certificates in lieu of entrance exams. The government allocated substantial resources for these changes and established the Center for Educational Quality Assessment to head the reform.

[5] For more information on these regional networks, see http://www.see-educoop.net/ (for the South East European Education Cooperation Network) and http://www.educasia.net/ (for the Central Asian Education Cooperation Network).

[6] Based on personal communication with Hugh McLean, director of the ESP of the OSI in London (2007).

[7] Ibid.

References

Adamson, Fiona. 2002. International democracy assistance in Uzbekistan and Kyrgyzstan: Building civil society from the outside? In *The power and limits of NGOs: A critical look at building democracy in Eastern Europe and Eurasia,* ed. Sarah E. Mendelson and John K. Glenn, 177–206. New York: Columbia University Press.

Abdurakhimov, Sadriddin. 2004. George Soros in Central Asia. *Central Asia and the Caucasus* 4(28). Available online.

Bassler, Terrice, and Mabel Wisse Smit. 1997. *Building donor partnerships.* New York: OSI.

BBC News. 1998. *The man who broke the Bank of England.* Available online.

Burde, Dana. 2004. NGOs and best practices: The art of educational lending. In *The global politics of educational borrowing and lending,* ed. Gita Steiner-Khamsi, 73–187. New York: Teachers College Press.

Chabbott, Colette. 1998. Constructing educational consensus: International development professionals and the World Conference on Education for All. *International Journal of Educational Development* 18(3): 207–18.

Clark, Neil. 2003. *The uncrowned king of East Europe.* Available online.

Coffin, Heather. 2003. *George Soros: Imperial wizard/double agent.* Available online.

Edwards, Michael. 1998. Are NGOs overrated?: Why and how to say "no" (editorial). *Current Issues in Comparative Education* 1(1). Available online.

Eliason, Leslie. 2003. *Developing expertise to shape policy change in education.* Presented to EPS program leaders in Bratislava, Slovak Republic. November 28.

ESP (Education Support Program). 2004. *Education Support Program (ESP) strategy: Update and outlook, 2004–2007.* Strategy paper. Hungary, Budapest: ESP.

———. 2006. *Education Support Program: Strategy overview.* London: ESP.

———. 2007. *Education Support Program: 2008–2010 strategy.* London: ESP.

EPSU (Education Program Support Unit). 1995. Conference on education for an open society. Budapest, Hungary. September 18–22. Available at the osi.hu website.

———. 1997. Priority areas for 1997. Available at the osi.hu website.

Grube, Gints. 2002. *The critical philanthropist.* Available at the policy.lv website.

Healey, Henry. 1998. *Towards Open Society education systems: Strategic considerations for the Soros Foundation Networks and the Institute for Educational Policy.* Paper presentated at the OSI education strategy meeting (From Mission to Strategy), Matrahaza, Hungary. June 3–5.

Heyneman, Steven. 2003. The history and problems in the making of education policy at the World Bank, 1960–2000. *International Journal of Educational Development* 23: 31–37.

Hrab, Neil. 2003. *George Soros: A bridge to radicalism.* Available online.

Huttova, Jana. 2004. Why the network of education policy centers? Why the newsletter? *Education Policy: Newsletter of Education Policy Centers* 1: 1. Available at the soros.org website.

Iliff, Heather. 1999. *Strategic planning.* Presented at Education Strategy Conference. Budapest, Hungary. February 22–24.

IEP (Institute for Educational Policy). 1998a. *Proceedings from the workshop for the education program directors and education board members of the Soros Foundations "Mission and Strategy."* Organized by the IEP, Matrahaza, Hungary. June 3–5.

———. 1998b. *About us.* Available at the osi.hu website.

———. 1998c. *Open Society Education Update* 2(1). Available at the osi.hu website.

———. 1999a. *Education sub-board network strategy paper.* Available at the osi.hu website.

———. 1999b. *Network education development strategy—next steps.* Budapest, Hungary: IEP/OSI.

———. 1999c. *Open Society Education Update* 2(5). Available at the osi.hu website.

Ivacs, Gabriella. 2005. *An appendage to the history of democracies in transition: A preliminary appraisal of the records of Soros Foundation Hungary.* Available at the osa.ceu.hu website.

Jones, Phillip. 2004. Taking the credit: Financing and policy linkages in the education portfolio of the World Bank. In *The global politics of educational borrowing and lending,* ed. Gita Steiner-Khamsi, 188–200. New York: Teachers College Press.

Jurko, Lana. 2007. Editorial: The 1st General Assembly and future of the Network of Education Policy Centers. *Education Policy: Newsletter of Education Policy Centers* 1: 1.

Kamat, Sangeeta. 2002. *Development hegemony: Non-governmental organizations and the state in India.* New York: Oxford University Press.

Klaus, Sarah. 2004. Stepping into the future: A history of the Step by Step program. *Educating Children for Democracy* 8: 3–13.

Klinmhorm, Somthavil, and Kevin Ireland. 1992. NGO-government collaboration in Bangkok. In *Making a difference: NGOs and development in a changing world*, ed. Michael Edwards and David Hulme, 60–69. London: Earthscan Publications.

Kovarovic, Jan. 2001. *IEP policy workshop report.* Budapest, Hungary. November 22–24. Available at the osi.hu website.

Lewis, David, and Tina Wallace. 2000. *New roles and relevance: Development NGOs and the challenge of change.* Bloomfield, CT: Kumarian Press.

Lorant, Liz. 2006. Personal communication.

Miljević, Gordana, and Igor Repac. 2006. *OSI education strategies overview.* Budapest, Hungary: ESP.

Mundy, Karen. 1999. Educational multilateralism in a changing world order: UNESCO and the limits of the possible. *International Journal of Educational Development* 19: 27–52.

NEPC (Network of Education Policy Centers). 2007. *About us.* Available at the edupolicy.net website.

OSI (Open Society Institute). 2001. *Meeting of the foundation boards.* Budapest, Hungary. June 24. Minutes of the meeting by Katie Jamieson.

———. 2006. *Education in a hidden marketplace: Monitoring of private tutoring.* Edited by Iveta Silova, Virginija Budiene, and Mark Bray. Available online.

———. 2007a. *Education Support Program: About this initiative.* Available at the soros.org website.

———. 2007b. *Children and youth programs: About this initiative.* Available at the soros.org website.

———. 2007c. *SEE ECN: South East European Educational Cooperation Network.* Available at the soros.org website.

———. 2007d. *Monitoring of school dropouts.* Edited by Virginija Budiene, Indra Dedze, and Mercedes del Rosario. Available online.

———. 2007e. *Frequently asked questions.* Available at the soros.org website.

Quigley, Kevin. 1997. *For democracy's sake: Foundations and democracy assistance in Central Europe.* Washington DC: The Woodrow Wilson Center Press.

Rado, Peter. 2001. *An emerging network of the new century: Comparative overview of the education policy centers in Eastern Europe and Central Asia.* Keynote address, Conference for Institutional Development of Teacher Education Institutions. Tbilisi, Georgia. Education Development Project of the Open Society Georgia Foundation.

Soros, George. 1991. *Underwriting democracy: Encouraging free enterprise and democratic reform among the Soviets and in Eastern Europe.* New York: PublicAffairs/Perseus Books Group.

―――. 1995. *Soros on Soros: Staying ahead of the curve.* New York: John Wiley and Sons.

―――. 2002. *On globalization.* New York: PublicAffairs/Perseus Books Group.

Steiner-Khamsi, Gita, and Ines Stolpe. 2006. *Educational import: Local encounters with global forces in Mongolia.* New York: Palgrave Macmillan.

Sutton, Margaret, and Robert Arnove. 2000. *Civil society or shadow state? State/NGO relations in education.* Greenwich, CT: Information Age Publishing.

Yablonskene, Nataliya. 2005. A success story for educational policy: Centre for Educational Policy Studies (CEPS). *Education Policy: Newsletter of Education Policy Centers* 7 (February). Available at the epc.objects.net website.

2

The Parallel Worlds of NGOs, Multilateral Aid, and Development Banks

The Case of Community Schools in Armenia

ARMENUHI TADEVOSYAN

Promoting community participation in education development has become both a "new orthodoxy" (Burde 2004, 73; see also McGee 2002; Swift-Morgan 2006) and a "new tyranny" (Cooke and Kothari 2001). These differing perceptions are reflected in the multiple and at times competing meanings that governments, donors, NGOs, and international financial institutions attach to the concept of participation. Proponents as varied as the World Bank and the OSI have increasingly advocated for community participation in education development across the former socialist countries of Eastern Europe, Central Asia, and the Caucasus. From the perspective of development banks (World Bank, ADB, and others) community participation can channel badly needed resources into the underfunded education sector. For activists and NGO workers (such as the OSI/Soros Foundations), it has the potential to empower communities to become involved in the educational decision-making processes that directly affect their lives. For post-socialist governments, it serves as a mechanism to create new educational spaces,

I would like to thank Iveta Silova and Gita Steiner-Khamsi for their help in formulating the interpretation of this case study and substantially editing an earlier version of the chapter.

signaling a move toward Western education practices. The concept of community schools has resonated with education stakeholders across the former socialist bloc because of "the intense hunger for collective action" that has been lost since the collapse of the Soviet Union:

> People really do want to work collectively. They understand that they cannot manage their problems alone. I don't want to create too rosy of a picture because there is corruption and mismanagement and there are abuses of power in schools, but community schools are needed. . . . The community school is an idea whose time has come, especially because it wasn't something that was implanted here. . . . The ideas from the outside just helped unleash our natural trends. (Kortunov 2006, 1)

Apart from a general sense that community participation is something positive, and worth promoting, there is no shared understanding between donors and governments in post-socialist countries of what it should entail. Furthermore, community members themselves—students, teachers, parents, residents, and education authorities in school districts—are rarely consulted on their understanding of community participation or their roles and responsibilities in education development. Few international projects promoting community participation pursue objectives commonly associated with participation in donor countries. Community participation does not necessarily mean more decision-making authority granted to the community or more active involvement of the community in the school. Rather, the term refers to services *for* the community offered by the school, such as transforming the school library into a district public library, the school computer room into a public Internet center, or the classroom for instructional media into a village movie theater. In many countries the post-Soviet variant of community participation also encourages schools to charge fees for services, turning community participation projects into income-generating activities.

Notwithstanding these different conceptual orientations, much of the policy framework surrounding the move toward community participation in education has been associated with shifts toward education decentralization (Bray 2003). At the level of policy talk, especially at the stage when a loan or grant needs to be approved by a donor organization, the language of the donor countries is spoken and community participation is presented in the context of shared governance and finance. In the countries of the former socialist bloc, the move toward decentralization has been closely coupled with education democratization. Increasingly, community participation in education has been referred to as "an outright democratic value" (Uemura 1999, 7) and "a fundamental element of democratic civil society development" (Fomina 2005, 1). In the context of political transition from authoritarianism to democracy, the concept of community participation in education has become one of the key components of the post-socialist education reform package, strongly promoted by governments, NGOs, and international financial institutions across the region.

Armenia's experience in promoting community participation in school reform is unique. The country contains various models of community schools supported from the outside by institutions such as the World Bank, and initiated from within by local and international NGOs, such as the OSI, Project Harmony, and others. Many NGOs, in particular the OSIAF in Armenia, have seen themselves as incubators of innovative practices, expecting that these practices will eventually become mainstream and funded by other sources. In the case of Armenia, OSIAF has initiated the development of community schools and attempted to disseminate the model across the educational system. While the concept of community schools has been widely acknowledged by education stakeholders, its institutionalization has been selective, with some components eagerly embraced and others overlooked by national policymakers.

This chapter traces the emergence of the concept of community schools in Armenia within the larger context of education reform. It documents the dynamic interplay among various actors pursuing community participation projects. From 2000 to 2004, several community schools projects were initiated in Armenia at two-year intervals by various organizations. OSIAF started its community schools projects in 2000. In 2002, the U.S. State Department's Bureau of Educational and Cultural Affairs funded Project Harmony, which drew on the network, experiences, and resources developed in the OSIAF project. In 2004, the World Bank launched the Education Quality and Relevance Project, with a strong focus on the development of community schools. This concentration of activity raises the question of what governments and donors should do when implementing a project similar to one that already exists in the recipient country. Should they work to enhance what already exists, selectively borrow components from current projects, or disregard what is in place to create a parallel network by funding separate districts, schools, and, possibly, different beneficiaries?

The hope of every donor is that its projects will have a lasting impact on a system or, at least, be funded by other sources once the original financing dries up. The issue of sustainability is important for all donors. As this chapter and other chapters in this book illustrate, the OSI, in the first phase of its activities in the Caucasus, Central Asia, and Mongolia, often conceived its educational initiatives as pilot projects that were to be subsequently either institutionalized by the government or picked up by other donors (World Bank, USAID, EU, among others) and continued on a larger scale. For the OSI, the expectation was that every project would eventually be integrated into the educational system. In some cases, projects required tremendous support before being acknowledged by the government. In others, the initiative was absorbed without much delay. This chapter examines the notion of community schools promoted within a short period of time by three different donors in Armenia, including the OSIAF, the U.S. State Department's Bureau of Educational and Cultural Affairs, and the World Bank. Following an examination of the context in which the concept of community schools emerged, I discuss different rationales for the development of community schools in Armenia.

Community-driven development amid educational crisis in Armenia

From the earthquake in 1988 to the dissolution of the Soviet Union in 1991 and the Nagorno-Kharabakh War[1] in 1988–94, Armenia's education system has faced natural, economic, and social disasters. Reflecting on the state of education since the collapse of the Soviet Union, Armenia's Minister of Education Sergo Eritsian stated simply that "the education system was destroyed" (Radio Free Europe/ Radio Liberty 2006). Armenian public funding for education has been drastically reduced since independence. Throughout the 1990s and since the turn of the century, public spending on education as a percentage of GDP has fluctuated around 2.5 percent. This is well below the Organisation for Economic Co-operation and Development (OECD) average in other transition economies of 4.7 percent (World Bank 1997; 2003). Private spending was also low (less than 0.5 percent) as was education as a proportion of public spending (11 percent) (World Bank 2003).

A crisis in funding combined with high emigration has resulted in declining enrollment. In addition, the education system has experienced a significant drop in quality, reflected in the deterioration of school infrastructure, inadequate investment in teacher training, reduction of teachers' salaries, and lack of textbooks and materials. According to the World Bank the deterioration of education quality was "undocumented but undoubted" (2003, 48). While data on academic achievement of Armenian students compared with those in other countries is lacking, there is widespread agreement that general education has fallen to such a low level that employers do not trust degrees and diplomas awarded by Armenian schools or universities (World Bank 2003). At the start of this decade, extreme poverty was highest among young people (up to age twenty-five), as was unemployment. These are indicative of a decline in educational quality and relevance, due to a dramatic drop in public expenditure since the early 1990s (World Bank 2003).

As the World Bank report put it, "The fact that the Armenian education system had not collapsed under the pressures of low spending and external shocks since independence was remarkable" (2003, 16). According to the *Social Assessment Report on the Education and Health Sectors in Armenia* (Gomart 1995), the general population was keenly aware of the crisis in education. Fifty percent of respondents named education as the number-one problem facing the country, and over eighty percent ranked it as one of the top three problems (Gomart 1995). According to focus group and survey data, the main concerns of parents are the high cost of education, lack of availability of textbooks, deteriorating quality (especially in rural areas because of the lack of specialists and lower access to textbooks), and lack of motivation among teachers due to low salaries.

It is in this context of educational crisis that the government of Armenia has begun educational reforms with the assistance of international partners, including the World Bank. Reforms in general education can be provisionally divided into two stages. The first stage (1998–2002) involved fundamental structural changes and the creation of a basis for content reforms in education. The second stage (2003–present) has involved initiating those reforms as well as continued structural reforms. Structural reforms were directed toward decentralization, increasing school autonomy, introducing a new system of school finance and management, improvement of the management capacity of school administration, and increasing school efficiency. While the rationale behind these structural reforms lay in shedding financial responsibilities linked to the provision of educational services to lower levels of the educational system, the Ministry of Education and Science (1997, 2) framed it within the policy discourse of greater community responsibility for education:

> The state is not the only performer responsible for education. Citizens also have their own responsibility for education and its expenses. . . . Development of private financing will improve the situation, remove some of the burden from government shoulders, [and] create competitiveness in the sphere. . . . The process of school autonomy will be complemented by a gradual increase of parental and community involvement in the school governance.

This position was readily supported by the World Bank, which confirmed that "achieving adequate funding to improve quality will also depend on mobilizing additional non-budgetary resources," including mechanisms "to encourage, formalize and target community and parental contributions to schooling" (1997, 4). The World Bank's Education Financing and Management Reform Project (approved in 1997 for a loan of US$15 million) promoted community and parental participation in school funding and management. It also supported the policy of school autonomy by channeling resources for school improvement directly to the schools. The objective was to mobilize additional resources and formalize community contributions for their funding and management.

Under the Education Finance and Management Reform Project, the government has begun providing autonomy to schools and communities. By 2004, all schools in Armenia had transferred to the new per capita financing system and were managed by school boards (World Bank 2004). Schools thereafter should have the ability to manage their own budgets (including retaining any savings), based on per student funding, and have the right to hire and fire teaching and non-teaching staff. Furthermore, communities were supposed to assume responsibility for school governance through participation on school boards by mobilizing resources for school improvement and managing resources (Ministry of Education and Science 1997). Whether these reforms have actually taken place is another question.

Surprisingly, parents and communities have become major players in education reform efforts. Their new responsibilities were reinforced by the concept of community-driven development introduced by the World Bank at the end of the 1990s. According to the World Bank, community-driven development is "the process by which communities assume control and authority over decisions and resources in development projects." It implies a devolution of control and accountability from central authorities to communities, which can then take "a greater role in initiating, planning, implementing, operating, maintaining and evaluating development projects, with agencies playing a supportive role." Furthermore, the World Bank argues, community-driven development "should be seen as complementing decentralization, improving the effectiveness and responsiveness of local governments, and strengthening partnerships between local governments, community organizations, and citizens" (World Bank 2000, 1).

> A strong community-driven development emphasis has been shown to lead to greater development effectiveness, sustainable institutional change, greater citizen involvement, and greater accountability and transparency of local governments. There is general consensus among Bank staff working in Armenia that greater involvement of communities in development could enhance development outcomes. (World Bank 2000, 1)

As the World Bank itself admitted, however, community participation in education reform efforts has not produced the desired outcomes, because of "the lack of a comprehensive and consistent decentralization policy; blurring and confusion of roles and responsibilities among local, municipal, regional and national level government; limited local government capacity and resources; and lack of viable and legitimate community organizations and institutions" (World Bank 2000, 7). In particular, partial decentralization of schools in the education sector has left questions of ownership unresolved; local governments operate and maintain schools, but the state owns them. This means that local authorities cannot take full control over their schools. There has also been significant conflict between local governments and school administration, in part because officials have not respected school autonomy, but rather have attempted to use schools in local patronage systems by placing political appointees in administrative positions (World Bank 2000; 2003).

Furthermore, the World Bank notes that traditional hierarchical relations may have dampened the reform initiative. In school communities, for example, parents were willing to articulate ideas, but felt that they had neither the right—nor the responsibility—to propose practical solutions. Similarly, teachers took responsibility within their own classrooms, but agreed with parents that school directors were the key decision-makers (World Bank 2000, 8). The combination of these complications suggests that Armenia's parents and communities were simply not prepared to take on new responsibilities. They were neither fully aware of their new roles nor equipped with the necessary skills to become involved in school life in a meaningful way.

Filling the vacuum: OSIAF strategy in supporting community schools

By the end of the 1990s, decentralization reform had made it clear that schools must formulate their own educational programs, teaching methods, and development plans. The decentralization reform was legalistic and did not pay attention to the professional development of practitioners. Schools were not only expected to function flawlessly by providing quality education to all students, but they were also required to assume new roles and responsibilities in communities where other important public infrastructure (such as libraries and cultural centers) could no longer survive due to poor economic conditions. In many areas, particularly small rural communities, schools became the only functioning public institutions and the only sources of information. It seemed they might not be able to fulfill their new roles and responsibilities.

It is in this context that OSIAF-Armenia initiated a pilot project aimed at developing community schools. Similar to many other NGOs and international organizations, OSIAF-Armenia saw itself as an incubator of innovative practices. OSIAF-Armenia supported the creation of a progressive education environment that would serve the needs of the educational community. OSIAF-Armenia believed that the development of a community school model would fill the vacuum in educational reform by building the capacity of schools and communities to address their needs and solve their problems.

In 2000, OSIAF piloted a community school model (Community TeleCenters) at twelve secondary schools in various regions of the country. Community TeleCenters set up partnerships between schools and other local institutions to offer a wide range of support and educational opportunities for children, youth, families, and communities. Schools became community centers, open to everyone. The expectation was that schools would take the lead in answering community needs and improving the quality of life by organizing training sessions and workshops, acting as cultural and recreational centers, and focusing on the concept of lifelong learning. The project also aimed at improving student learning through the introduction of a participatory approach to education. The Community TeleCenter worked to incorporate information technologies into the teaching process and to create school-based training capacities. The idea was that schools would become intellectual centers, initiators of innovative ideas, and agents of change in their communities.

Community TeleCenters were established at public schools during the first phase of the project. They were furnished with computers, telecommunication facilities, and Internet access. The program started with twelve schools in urban areas and was later expanded to twenty-eight schools in both urban and rural areas of the country. In order to prepare for their new role, participating schools first had to improve their infrastructure. OSIAF organized training for school directors, teachers, and school-board members in areas such as school leadership, managing the process of change and conflict resolution, new teaching and learning methodologies, school and community relationships, and partnership building, as well as needs assessment and proposal writing. Internet access facilitated communication among schools in Armenia and abroad. In addition, a group of teachers from each school was given computer training. Participants were provided with textbooks and other educational materials. Later, training was extended to other teachers, students, and community members.

To reinforce its comprehensive approach to strengthening community schools, OSIAF undertook additional initiatives such as Armenian language e-content development, teachers' ICT training, and interschool web-portal creation. OSIAF assumed that having computers and teachers trained to use them would not be sufficient to result in the integration of ICT into the educational process or the creation of lifelong learning opportunities for the community. Schools also needed appropriate teaching and learning content. OSIAF prioritized development of the necessary e-curricula in Armenian by creating eleven CDs covering different academic subjects.[2] These were distributed to schools, along with relevant training for subject teachers. This initiative served as a tool to provide endorsement of up-to-date curricula and teaching methodology, as well as to ensure access to high-quality education by reaching out to students. The pilot project also aimed to strengthen community schools by providing ongoing networking opportunities through the creation of the interschool web portal (www.schoolnet.am). The portal became an important source of educational curricula and other information, as well as a space for the exchange of ideas for educators and students.

In 2004, OSIAF commissioned an outside evaluation (Gyuzalyan et al. 2005). The findings revealed that the Community TeleCenters addressed the main challenges of education decentralization by opening schools to the community and engaging the community in the education process. The evaluation confirmed that community schools have developed into community resource centers providing a wide range of educational opportunities (Gyuzalyan et al. 2005). Many community schools have started publishing newspapers and developed specialized training for adults. The evaluation also revealed that TeleCenters have become entry points for the active use of ICT tools and methods in educating students and members of the community. The development of electronic curricula in the

Armenian language, in particular, was perceived as a necessary component for the meaningful use of technology.

Finally, the evaluation confirmed that the Community TeleCenters have the potential to become a sustainable and important resource for even the most deprived regions of Armenia (Gyuzalyan et al. 2005). The report also suggested that successful implementation would require substantial investments in human and physical resources, investments most international financial institutions and NGOs could not afford because of limitations in time and funding. As the World Bank itself admitted, "real capacity building is resource intensive and often beyond the scope of a single project" (2000, 8).

Institutionalizing the concept of community schools in Armenia's education reform

A unique feature of the OSIAF pilot was that its commitment to local capacity building and the subsequent positive outcome of school and community empowerment have become visible in Armenia's education reform environment. OSIAF pilot-project components are reflected in other education initiatives implemented by governmental organizations and NGOs in Armenia. The community schools concept, in particular, has become an important component of the Armenia School Connectivity Program grant. This grant was awarded in 2002 to Project Harmony by the U.S. Department of State's Bureau of Educational and Cultural Affairs. It is significant that some components of the OSIAF community schools project are reflected in the second World Bank loan to the education sector through the Education Quality and Relevance Project.

Community schools in Project Harmony's Armenia School Connectivity Program

The cooperation between OSIAF-Armenia and Project Harmony began when both organizations were piloting their education reform projects.[3] OSIAF's community schools model (including teacher training in ICT and development of e-curricula) was acknowledged by Project Harmony as having great potential to contribute to the Armenia School Connectivity Program. The program's main focus areas—technology, education, and community—closely overlapped with the OSIAF project components, thus providing a unique opportunity for both organizations to build on each other's experiences and utilize existing networks and human resources for wider program dissemination (see Table 8). In 2002, Project Harmony received a large grant from the U.S. Department of State to establish 330 Internet computer centers in Armenian schools. In addition, the grant provided for seminars, conferences, and training for school representatives and community members on the integration of technology into education, sustainability, and the creation of Armenian-language Internet resources. The Armenia School Connectivity Program provides opportunities for students, educators, and community members to access and share information, to engage in online collaborative projects, and to develop marketable technical skills. The program increased school-community interaction and civic engagement on the local, national, and international levels.

OSIAF-Armenia's community schools entered the Armenia School Connectivity Program in 2002 and immediately became involved in all project activities. Close cooperation with the Armenia School Connectivity Program allowed OSIAF to disseminate the concept of community schools to over three hundred schools. The close partnership between these two NGOs allowed both organizations to scale up their initiatives nationwide in order to have a profound impact on education reform in Armenia.

Community schools in the World Bank's Education Quality and Relevance Project

The concept of community schools has also been reflected in the Education Quality and Relevance Project (2004–8), funded by a World Bank loan of US$19 million. The World Bank recognized that there had been insufficient support of community involvement in sector-wide reforms during the first education project (1998–2002). The World Bank was also aware of the experience of NGOs in encouraging community participation. The World Bank acknowledged that if communities are to take on more responsibility for their own social and economic development through partnerships with local government and the private and nongovernmental sectors, then "enhanced capacity must become an important development goal for the Bank." The World Bank has officially called for a shift "from the current focus on facilitating participation to support Bank instruments . . . to more of a capacity-building approach to participation" (2000, 8).

This transformation is reflected in the Education Quality and Relevance Project, which echoed many of the OSIAF community schools components (see Table 8). The World Bank project consisted of four areas: (1) development of a more relevant and inclusive general education national curriculum, state educational standards, and assessment system; (2) incorporation of ICT in the learning and teaching processes; (3) professional development of teachers; and (4) improvement of the management capacity and efficiency of the education system by supporting decentralized schools, increasing community and parent involvement in school management and financing aspects, training school management and administrative staff, and further developing the Education Management Information System (EMIS)[4] to support effective decision-making at all levels of the education system (central, regional, and school).

Several components of the World Bank project stood out due to their close resemblance to the OSIAF's community schools project: (1) the development of infrastructure for community schools (school learning centers); (2) professional development opportunities (school centers); (3) community partnerships; and (4) e-content development. The World Bank project aimed to introduce school learning centers in six hundred schools across the country. According to the World Bank (2003), these centers—computerized classrooms containing a wide range of media and information materials—could be used by students and communities for various educational purposes. Second, the World Bank's project introduced the concept of school centers (to be implemented in fifty locations) that would disseminate new models of school improvement and school-based educational development to surrounding schools (referred to as school clusters). The World Bank project also aimed to support the education decentralization process by increasing community and parental involvement in school management and financing (World Bank 2003).

While similarities between the OSIAF and World Bank education reform initiatives are undeniable, there were also some differences, the most obvious in project budget coverage and procurement policy. The World Bank project undertook a fundamental reform

Table 8. OSIAF, Project Harmony, and World Bank community schools models

OSIAF-ARMENIA'S COMMUNITY SCHOOLS (2000–present)	PROJECT HARMONY'S ARMENIA SCHOOL CONNECTIVITY PROGRAM (2002–2007)	WORLD BANK'S EDUCATION QUALITY AND RELEVANCE PROJECT (2004–2008)
CREATING THE NECESSARY INFRASTRUCTURE		
Community Schools (TeleCenters)	**Armenia School Connectivity Program**	**Educational Technologies in Schools (component 2)**
• Established TeleCenters in forty secondary schools. • Equipped schools with computers with Internet access. • Organized three types of ICT training for teachers, including basic training for school teachers, advanced training for school network administrators, and web and e-curriculum development. • Developed e-curriculum for eleven subjects and organized teacher training to ensure effective use of the software. • Developed inter-school web portal (www.schoolnet.am).	• Established 330 Internet computer centers in secondary schools. • Selected site monitors, all trained in basic computing, network administration, web design, and other ICT-related themes, to administer centers. • Established a mobile Internet computer lab (www.hf.am), which serves remote communities in Armenia.	• Built necessary infrastructure for integration of ICT into general education. • Established and equipped school learning centers (computer labs) in approximately six hundred schools in Armenia. • Funded an Internet-connected school network for approximately 150 schools. • Funded technical assistance to develop educational software, manuals, and teacher-training modules. • Funded development and maintenance of the educational portal.

CONT.

Table 8. OSIAF, Project Harmony, and World Bank community schools models, con't

OSIAF-ARMENIA'S COMMUNITY SCHOOLS (2000–present)	PROJECT HARMONY'S ARMENIA SCHOOL CONNECTIVITY PROGRAM (2002–2007)	WORLD BANK'S EDUCATION QUALITY AND RELEVANCE PROJECT (2004–2008)
PROFESSIONAL DEVELOPMENT		
School-based Teacher Professional Development	**School-based Teacher Training**	**Teacher Professional Development (component 3)**
Teacher training in ICT and e-content usage was provided by teachers who had attended the training sessions described above (one-year grant).	In addition to staff development activities, the program provided seminars, conferences, and training for school representatives and community members on the integration of technology into education, the sustainability of centers, and the creation of Armenian-language Internet resources.	Teacher training in the use of ICTs. The pilot of the school-based professional development was implemented through grants to approximately sixty school centers.

CONT.

Table 8. OSIAF, Project Harmony, and World Bank community schools models, con't

OSIAF-ARMENIA'S COMMUNITY SCHOOLS (2000–present)	PROJECT HARMONY'S ARMENIA SCHOOL CONNECTIVITY PROGRAM (2002–2007)	WORLD BANK'S EDUCATION QUALITY AND RELEVANCE PROJECT (2004–2008)
SCHOOL AND COMMUNITY PARTNERSHIPS		
Management Training and Community Involvement	**Community-based Activities**	**System Management and Efficiency (component 4)**
School directors, teachers, and school-board members participated in training in school leadership; managing the process of change and conflict resolution; teaching and learning new methodologies; school and community relationships and partnership building; needs assessment and proposal writing. It is now possible to conduct computer training for school staff and local community members, and to deliver educational, cultural, and various informational services both to the community and to other secondary schools and institutions in their regions.	Community is one of the integral parts of the program. Targeting community needs and integrating the Internet computer centers into the daily life of local communities will make the centers self-sustaining. For this reason sustainability training was organized for all the network schools. By conducting "open door" days and organizing community-engaging events, the centers' monitors tried to create an environment in which visitors' professional and technical needs could be accommodated. A series of community support and service projects were implemented throughout Armenia.	The goal was to improve the management and efficiency of the education system by supporting decentralized schools, and by increasing community and parent involvement in school management and financing aspects.

of the national general education curriculum and the educational standards and assessment system; established the National Center for Educational Technologies; and enlarged EMIS. While the World Bank project initiatives were wider in their conceptual scope and geographic coverage, they nevertheless closely followed the principles of the OSIAF pilot project, especially its commitment to the previously overlooked problem of supporting community participating in education reforms (see Table 8).

Conclusions:
Dealing with community participation
of the other .

It is important to bear in mind that OSIAF, the U.S. government, and the World Bank were not alone in promoting community participation in Armenia. In one way or another, all international organizations, including Save the Children U.K. and UNICEF, have advanced the idea of community schools. As mentioned at the beginning of this chapter, community participation is both the "new orthodoxy" (Burde 2004, 73) and the "new tyranny" (Cooke and Kothari 2001) in aid-recipient countries and has been coopted by all major donors in development. Given that all actors pursue various types of community participation, the question becomes how to define it, and what to do with community participation projects previously funded by other donors. This chapter examined the notion of community schools, promoted within a short period of time by three different donors:

- OSIAF: The Community Schools project, launched in 2000.
- U.S. government: The Armenia School Connectivity Program, implemented by the NGO Project Harmony and launched in 2002.
- World Bank: The Education Quality and Relevance Project, in particular components 2 (educational technologies in schools) and 3 (professional development).

All three projects included features of ICT and professional development of school staff, and all three projects drew on the rhetoric of community participation in schools. How did donors deal with the fact that similar projects already existed? In the U.S.-funded Armenia School Connectivity Program, there was a close connection between what already was in place, funded by OSIAF, and what the new U.S.-funded project initiated. In retrospect, one can consider the OSIAF project as a successful pilot for the larger Armenia School Connectivity Program. OSIAF and other national OSI Foundations tend to see themselves as incubators of innovative practices. The take-over by Project Harmony and the continuation of OSIAF-initiated activities by other means were seen as an indication that the OSIAF project was effective. The World Bank–funded project, in contrast, drew minimally on networks, resources, and expertise already existing in the two other programs. For example, the World Bank adopted only three of the forty OSIAF-funded community schools as partner schools.

An international comparative perspective helps us to reflect on why subsequent donors, such as the World Bank, disregard similar existing projects. In the case of Armenia, three reasons explain why the "latecomer" did not draw from the existing experiences, staff and networks generated in the two previous projects: (1) stakeholder replacement, (2) distributive practices, and (3) competition.

Every project tends to draw on or train its own experts and personnel. Similarly, each project tends to create new alliances with stakeholders that are supportive of the organization. By signaling the novelty of a project that, on closer scrutiny, is not much different from what other donors have already implemented, the organization is able to use its own experts and establish its own alliances (see Luschei 2004). Stakeholder replacement is an important motive for organizations and often the main reason why organizations choose not to borrow existing project ideas or models from other organizations. By not borrowing what already exists and instead insisting that the project is unique, an organization can create its own network of loyal individuals and institutions.

Second, one legacy of the socialist past is the tendency for governments in the Caucasus, Central Asia, and Mongolia to engage in distributive practices. They view donor involvement as a form of resource transfer, secured from external sources by politicians and channeled to the local level. Often ministries of education feel compelled to include new schools that did not previously benefit from international projects. This distributive practice is, to the dismay of international organizations, very common. The discomfort with distributive practices that international donors frequently feel has to do with the pressure to demonstrate to their own organization that the project has been successfully implemented. Donors typically want to have a greater say in which participants or institutions are selected. In contrast, governments must deal with complaints from schools that have not benefited from the resources, both human and financial, that come with involvement in an international project.

Finally, donors compete to influence governments. Even though there is a limited number of reforms circulating, every donor insists on having its own variant or best practice of community participation. Different donors continuously redefine community participation in terms of the particular mission of their organization. It is not surprising that the meaning of community participation has become quite broad, with different connotations depending on which organization is using it. Advancing a concept, a best practice, or a project always implies advancing the mission of an organization as well.

Notes

[1] Nagorno-Karabakh is a de facto independent republic located in the South Caucasus, officially part of the Republic of Azerbaijan, about 270 kilometers (170 miles) west of the Azerbaijani capital of Baku and very close to the border with Armenia. The region is predominantly Armenian, and it became a source of dispute between the republics of Armenia and Azerbaijan when both countries gained independence from the Russian Empire in 1918. After the Soviet Union expanded into the South Caucasus, it established the Nagorno-Karabakh Autonomous Oblast (NKAO) within the Azerbaijan SSR in 1923. In the final years before the dissolution of the Soviet Union, the region was again a source of dispute between Armenia and Azerbaijan, culminating in the Nagorno-Karabakh War. Since the end of the war in 1994, most of Nagorno-Karabakh and several regions of Azerbaijan around it have remained under joint Armenian and Nagorno-Kharabakh Defense Forces control, and Armenia and Azerbaijan have been holding peace talks mediated by the OSCE Minsk Group.

[2] Since 2001, e-curricula have been developed in chemistry and biology (for the ninth and tenth grades), chemistry (for the seventh and ninth grades), biology virtual laboratories (for the ninth grade), ecology and informatics (for the ninth and tenth grades), history of Armenia (for the fifth and sixth grades) and physics (for the ninth grade).

[3] An American NGO implemented two pilot projects in Armenia— Internet Community Development and Armenia School Connectivity Program.

[4] EMIS was first introduced in 1999 as part of the World Bank's Education Management and Finance Reform project.

References

Bray, Mark. 2003. Community initiatives in education: Goals, dimensions, and linkages with governments. *Compare* 33(1): 31–46.

Burde, Dana. 2004. Weak state, strong community? Promoting community participation in post-conflict countries. *Current Issues in Comparative Education* 6(2): 73–87.

Cooke, Bill, and Uma Kothari, eds. 2001. *Participation: The new tyranny?* New York: Zed Books.

Fomina, Elena. 2005. *Community schools movement reaches from Flint to Siberia.* Available online.

Gomart, Elizabeth. 1995. *Social assessment report on the education and health sectors in Armenia.* Consultant report. Washington DC: World Bank.

Gyuzalyan, Gayk, Adrine Babloyan, Arusyak Sevoyan, and Anna Arutunyan. 2005. *Evaluation report of the secondary education program of OSIAF-Armenia and its future strategic development* (in Russian). Yerevan, Armenia: OSIAF.

Kortunov, Andrei. 2006. Russian NGO leader discusses philanthropy and community schools. Available online.

Luschei, Thomas S. 2004. Timing is everything: The intersection of borrowing and lending in Brazil's adoption of "Escuela Nueva." In *The global politics of policy borrowing and lending,* ed. Gita Steiner-Khamsi, 154–67. New York: Teachers College Press.

McGee, Rosemary. 2002. Participating in development. In *Development theory and practice: Critical perspectives,* ed. Uma Kothari and Martin Minogue, 92–116. Basingstoke, UK: Palgrave.

Ministry of Education and Science. 1997. *Strategy for reform of the general education system of the Republic of Armenia.* Yerevan, Armenia: Ministry of Education and Science.

Radio Free Europe/Radio Liberty. 2006. Armenia: Education minister challenged by post-Soviet transition. Available online.

Swift-Morgan, Jennifer. 2006. What community participation in schooling means: Insights from Southern Ethiopia. *Harvard Educational Review* 76(3): 339–68.

Uemura, Mitsue. 1999. *Community participation in education: What do we know?* Washington DC: World Bank.

World Bank. 1997. *Staff appraisal report: Education financing and management reform project in the Republic of Armenia.* Report no. 16474–AM. Washington DC: Human Development Sector Unit, Europe and Central Asia Region of the World Bank.

————. 2000. *Scaling up community driven development in Armenia: A strategy note.* Washington DC: World Bank.

————. 2003. *Project appraisal document on a proposed credit to the Republic of Armenia for an education quality and relevance project in support of the first phase of the education sector reform program.* Report no. 26266–AM. Washington DC: Human Development Sector Unit, Europe and Central Asia Region of the World Bank.

————. 2004. *Education in Armenia.* Annual booklet. Yerevan, Armenia: World Bank.

3

The Free Market
in Textbook Publishing

Visions and Realities in Azerbaijan

Elmina Kazimzade

In the mid-1990s, Annabel Jones was conducting training sessions for prospective textbook authors in Azerbaijan. The training sessions were part of a publishing project organized by OSIAF in Azerbaijan. The goal was to establish teams of authors who could create a new generation of innovative textbooks in cooperation with publishers. Teachers and academics interested in more creative approaches to developing textbook content were invited to learn how to write the types of books they would prefer to use in their classrooms. Annabel, who had devoted her life to improving British textbooks after being promoted from schoolteacher to editor at a well-known publishing company, asked her audience, "In your opinion, what are the benefits of a textbook?" There were many replies, emphasizing the importance of textbooks for national development and increasing the quality of education. But none of the participants gave the response she was waiting for. When they ran out of ideas, Annabel offered an answer that surprised the participants by its simplicity and clarity: "The textbook is a teacher's assistant—it helps make teacher's work easier and more creative." This was a real novelty to those who had been brought up on the Soviet notion of the textbook as something complex and authoritative, exhausting everyone from the authors themselves to the teachers who routinely used them in their classrooms to the students who ultimately learned to hate them.

This story exemplifies one aspect of textbook reform in Azerbaijan and other former Soviet socialist countries. The question is how to alter previous notions of what a textbook is supposed to be among teachers, writers, and publishers. Textbook quality, adequate and efficient financing, and liberalization of the textbook market are just three factors that may determine whether the outcome is positive or a source of disillusionment for various actors—donors, school communities, and government officials. These three strands of reform—quality, finance, and liberalization of textbook publishing—reflect the "Age of the Market" (Sneath 2002) and have been emphasized by international financial institutions as manifestations of the new free market in education. Following the collapse of the socialist bloc in the early 1990s, market-oriented textbook reform has become universal across the region (Pinter and Slantcheva 2000), instituted as a regular component of the post-socialist education reform package.

This chapter examines Azerbaijan's experience in developing a free textbook publishing market and the complex partnerships among various actors—the Ministry of Education, the World Bank, and OSIAF—in the process of reform. Following discussion of the major issues affecting textbook-publishing reform during the post-socialist transformation process, and the specifics of education reform in Azerbaijan, this chapter examines different perspectives of the government, World Bank, and OSIAF with regard to textbook reform, uncovering a large rift between vision and reality.

Issues affecting textbook provision in the period of post-Soviet transformation

In the post-Soviet era newly independent states view education as an important means for transmitting normative expectations of appropriate values, attitudes, and behaviors of the ideal citizen (Tse 2003; Asanova 2007). This is a question of political and cultural change, directly reflected in curricula, textbooks, and educational materials promoting new national values. Across the former Soviet Union, textbook reform has become among the highest priorities of education transformation for governments, international donors, and local NGOs. This has resulted in major changes in content, curricular strategies, and ideological goals.

Issues surrounding post-Soviet textbook reform generally concern breaking away from the old, centralized system of provision to a more open, fair, and competitive publishing market. Up until 1991, all textbooks in the Soviet Union were developed, produced, and manufactured by Prosveshcheniyie, the state-owned textbook publisher based in Moscow, then shipped to various republics and translated by the local state publisher. Though uniform and rarely revised, they were at least durable, affordable, plentiful, and reliably supplied (Hunt and Read 2000).[1] Schools maintained textbook libraries and loaned books to students free of charge. Replacement copies were provided every four years. The system was hierarchical but successful, and every child had access to a complete set of inexpensive books in acceptable condition.

Since the collapse of the Soviet Union in 1991, the situation has changed. The economic crisis accompanying the transition to a market-based economy severely affected most countries in Central Asia and the Caucasus. This led to serious cutbacks in education finance and demonstrated many of the weaknesses of a centrally planned educational system. Because of budgetary constraints, funds for recurrent costs have not been adequate. There has also been little investment in the educational sector, and almost no maintenance of educational facilities. Additional barriers to the adequate provision of textbooks have been the lack of experience of newly independent governmental bodies, the inertia demonstrated by the persistence of antiquated approaches to decision-making, and the abrupt interruption of economic and cultural contact with other former Soviet republics. As Pinter and Slantcheva summarize, other factors influencing textbook provision throughout the region have been the strong dependence upon books published and printed in Russia, state monopoly in educational publishing and printing, outdated and unreliable printing equipment, and the necessity of importing most of the materials—including paper—required for manufacture. Textbook reform was further hampered by the legacy of an ideology that stressed the existence of only one truth. Traditional educators across the region are still searching for definitive textbooks to replace the old ones (Pinter and Slantcheva 2000). It is in this context that post-Soviet education reformers, with limited funds, have been attempting to change textbook publishing markets.

In Azerbaijan, similar to other former Soviet republics in Central Asia and the Caucasus, textbook shortages have become increasingly severe since independence. Parents also are now required to buy books for their children in grades five to eleven. Existing textbooks are often inappropriate—they correspond to outdated curricula, contain excessive text, have insufficient illustrations, and are generally hard to understand. The language of instruction has changed from Russian to Azeri as historical and cultural orientations have shifted from Soviet concerns to local values and interests. Even the script has been changed from Cyrillic to Roman, in part a reflection of the increased interest in studying foreign languages such as English, German, French, and Turkish.

The shock of change has been considerable for all concerned—from government officials down to districts, schools, students, and parents. It has also affected publishers, distributors, booksellers, and printers who are, or were, principally involved in the process of textbook provision. A lack of local expertise in textbook development, information about modern educational methodology, and exposure to clear evaluation parameters and criteria have been among the main reasons for the slow pace of textbook reform in Azerbaijan. In this context it has become necessary not simply to replace the old textbooks (using the "old" textbook development methodologies), but to create the preconditions for transition to a new quality standard of textbook provision.

This new quality standard of textbook provision emphasizes market principles, with a particular focus on quality, finance, and liberalization of the textbook publishing market in Azerbaijan. Undoubtedly, it has been strongly influenced by international financial institutions (for example, a World Bank education loan of US$73 million for the period 2003–13),[2] as well as international NGOs, such as OSIAF-Azerbaijan and its textbook publishing program. The World Bank emphasized textbook-reform principles such as "quality within the constraints of affordability and sustainability" (World Bank 2002, 7) and "the development of a sustainable private publishing industry to support the ongoing reforms and dissemination of knowledge to the whole country" (World Bank 2003, 22). Similarly, the goals of OSIAF's publishing program included developing "a new model of textbook provision" in order to help "de-monopolize" authorship, improve pedagogical and technical quality by stimulating competition among publishers, and open up the market to provide a wide range of free textbooks and teaching/learning materials (Crighton 2001, 19). Finally, the government's Ten-Year Education Reform Strategy, developed within the framework of the World Bank loan, included matching strategic priorities, such as increasing the availability and quality of textbooks and ensuring adequate provision of new learning materials to schools (quoted in World Bank 2003, 15).

The main players of school textbook reform in Azerbaijan—the government, World Bank, and OSIAF—share a fundamental vision of creating a new market. They also agree (at least rhetorically) about the main principles of textbook reform, including emphasis on quality, market liberalization, and finance. While this is a unique example of complex collaboration among various partners, it also reveals a gap between the visions and realities inherent in implementation. The following sections identify the different—and often conflicting—agenda of each partner, with a focus on three main components—textbook quality, market liberalization, and finance.

Textbook quality

The traditional approach to textbook authorship in Azerbaijan, as in other former Soviet republics, has focused almost exclusively on the content of information delivered to students, without consideration of issues such as age, appropriateness, design appeal, and ease of use. Authors were also often involved in curriculum development or came from academic backgrounds. The textbooks they wrote were seen as logical extensions of the curriculum. In fact, the subject/level curriculum guide, produced by one of the two curriculum-development institutions, made direct reference to the textbook and how to teach it. Traditionally, teachers were viewed only as textbook users and barred from the realm of academics solely responsible for writing them. It is not surprising, therefore, that many teachers perceived textbooks as irrelevant to classroom needs, and inappropriate to the age of their students. As one teacher explained in a personal communication at a meeting of history teachers at the In-Service Teachers' Institute in Baku in March 1999:

> I dreamt of meeting textbook authors and asking them why they use such sophisticated language—difficult to understand

and implement in everyday classroom work. But this was impossible because textbook authors were unreachable. For us— the teachers—they were like the Olympian Gods of Ancient Greece. I had a simple solution to this problem—teachers themselves must be textbook writers, and their voice must be heard before textbooks are delivered to schools.

During the period of post-Soviet transformation, textbook revision has become one of the highest priorities of education reform in Azerbaijan. The goal was to develop a new generation of textbooks that would reflect national values, correspond to the new curriculum, and meet the quality standards of age appropriateness, design appeal, and ease of use for students and teachers. Despite general awareness of the urgency of textbook revision, various partners have had different perspectives on how the quality of the new generation of textbooks should be improved. For the government of Azerbaijan, the most important goal was to ensure that the new textbooks instilled nationalism. In the context of budgetary constraints, however, the government also expected that the new books would be developed by the "old" authors, using traditional methods of development.

For the World Bank, the notion of textbook quality has encompassed wider concerns and is connected to the overall improvement of general education in Azerbaijan. According to the World Bank, the aim was "to assist the government to prevent further deterioration of the quality of general education through a set of specific interventions," including "the development and provision of new textbooks based on the new curriculum" (World Bank 2003, 17). The World Bank's Azerbaijan Education Sector Development Project envisioned that new textbooks would improve the learning outcome of the students and consequently contribute to their empowerment (2003, 22). Furthermore, the World Bank report explained that curriculum and textbook reform must place "much greater emphasis on developing skills in problem solving, critical thinking, and effective communication" (2003, 7). Compared to the government's priorities, the World Bank approach is comprehensive, emphasizing the importance of revision of ideological content and skills development.

For OSIAF-Azerbaijan, one of the key areas was capacity building and design through the training of new teams of authors. At the end of the 1990s, OSIAF initiated the World History Textbook Project to establish authors' groups and form teams of publishers, designers, academics, and teachers who would collaborate. Unlike the traditional Soviet approach to textbook development, designers worked together with authors from the very beginning to ensure that illustrations matched content and pedagogical objectives. Furthermore, new textbook authors learned to work with feedback from textbook users—teachers and students. This was an important stage in the textbook development cycle, missing during the Soviet period, and for which no procedures existed after independence. The textbook development process now included piloting in schools and content revision. Compared to the traditional approach (that is, relying exclusively on input from academics in content development), a collaborative textbook development process piloted by OSIAF was more time consuming. But though it took more than two years for the team of authors to develop the history textbook, it was in the end an exciting and rewarding opportunity for teachers, academics, designers, and publishers.

While some publishers enthusiastically adopted ideas from the OSIAF pilot (for example, making qualitative improvements in textbook design), the government was reluctant to embrace new ideas for improving quality through the introduction of mechanisms of collaborative development and piloting in schools. The involvement of teachers, in particular, was generally perceived as too time consuming and costly, potentially slowing the pace of education reform. Moreover, the government decided not to grant ministry approval to the history textbook developed in the OSIAF pilot, recommending it only as an alternative. The OSIAF book was not able to compete with a single, state-funded history textbook. So, although OSIAF was successful in demonstrating new, innovative approaches to quality improvement, it has not necessarily changed the culture of textbook development in Azerbaijan.

Liberalization of the textbook market

One of the fundamental problems of the Soviet system of textbook publishing—the state monopoly on development and production—has stifled the quality of school textbooks in the post-Soviet era. The process whereby curriculum and syllabus development merged with authorship and the editorial process was particularly problematic (Hunt and Read 2000). Textbook writers were commissioned (usually informally, but sometimes through some type of "open competition") by the Institute of Education Problems, and most authors tended to be members of the institute's staff or the Methodological Board for the subject curriculum.[3] Authors who were not part of the established group of curriculum and textbook writers could apply for their manuscripts to be approved, but there were very few cases where alternative textbooks were actually approved by the Ministry of Education. Furthermore, textbook evaluation and approval lacked a fixed and publicly available set of criteria or established methodology. Evaluation results were never published, and the reasons for choosing one manuscript and one set of authors rather than another were never made available (Hunt and Read 2000). This may not have been a major problem in the closed, Soviet system, because there was only one textbook for every subject and grade level (except for experimental editions), and one or two publishers supplied all the books.[4] However, this practice has come under increased scrutiny in the emerging context of competition and choice in Azerbaijan.

Since independence, liberalization of the previously state-controlled textbook publishing market has become a priority, symbolizing Azerbaijan's progress toward Western ideals. International experts (including World Bank consultants advising the government on textbook reform) made strong arguments about the urgency of de-monopolizing textbook publishing, with stark comparisons between the Soviet-style, state-controlled educational-publishing system, and the Western system of private, commercial competition. For example, Hunt and Read explained:

> In the Western private sector tradition it is the job of the state to provide the curriculum; it is the task of private sector authors and publishers to provide competitive interpretations of the curriculum, from which individual schools may select the course materials that suit their needs the best. Thus, curriculum and textbook development activities are clearly separated in most western countries, whereas they are combined under state supervision and control in the previous Soviet system. This is a critical developmental issue that needs very careful consideration by policy makers in Azerbaijan. (Hunt and Read 2000, 9)

After increased international pressure to adopt market principles and make the textbook publishing market more vibrant, the Ministry of Education officially declared its interest in doing so at the end of the 1990s. The goal was to provide opportunities for the development of "competing, alternative textbooks for each subject and grade and thus in the provision of a choice of textbooks for the teacher" (quoted in Hunt and Read 2000, 4). The main problem, however, was the lack of practical experience within Azerbaijan with systems of choice and competition for textbooks. Inevitably, the government looked for outside technical assistance in textbook reform, identifying the World Bank and OSIAF-Azerbaijan as main partners in moving toward the goals of textbook-market liberalization.

While assisting the Azerbaijani government in liberalizing the textbook publishing market, the World Bank's main priority was to contribute to "the development of a sustainable private publishing industry" (World Bank 2003, 22). Furthermore, the World Bank's *Operational Guidelines for Textbooks and Reading Materials* emphasized the importance of "transparent and competitive processes in the selection or purchase of books for educational use or for contracting publishing or printing services" (2002, 2). In particular, the guidelines stated that "the selection process must be transparent to maintain credibility before producers (publishers) and consumers (schools and communities)." The World Bank's logic was that "book choice can lead to the adoption of more and better quality books" (World Bank 2002, 5). In 2003, the "transparent and competitive processes"—if not yet "book choice"—were put to the test when the textbooks required for the Learning and Innovation Reform Project were tendered according to World Bank–approved procedures.

Similarly, OSIAF aimed to influence textbook policy in Azerbaijan by providing technical assistance to introduce a more open, effective evaluation and approval system, which would "demonopolize" authorship and "stimulate competition among publishers" (Crighton 2001, 19). In 2002, OSIAF's strategy was to pilot the alternative textbook evaluation and approval system through the establishment of a Textbook Approval Board as an external and independent body that would set specifications for competition and criteria for textbook evaluation. The Textbook Approval Board was duly appointed by the minister of education, and its first task was to set standards and evaluate entries submitted in a pilot textbook competition organized by OSIAF together with the textbook department of the ministry. The competition was deemed a success; it resulted in the publication of seven textbooks at the primary and secondary levels that met quality standards and proved popular with teachers and students. The outcome, it was hoped, was for the Textbook Approval Board to be adopted by the Ministry of Education for all textbook activity, assisting in the formulation and implementation of policy, stimulating and overseeing an open system of national competitive bidding from state and private publishers on an equal footing, ensuring that proposed textbooks are evaluated by subject panels on the basis of specific criteria, awarding and managing contracts with successful publishers, carrying out periodic quantitative and qualitative impact studies of textbook reform in primary and secondary schools, and providing feedback to the ministry with recommendations for textbook policy or regulatory changes. The strategy was to encourage different publishers to take risks in the textbook market.

Undoubtedly, both the World Bank and OSIAF have had a major impact on textbook market liberalization. The pilot textbook competitions have proved that tendering with objective standards can work successfully. The Ministry of Education, however, was at this stage reluctant wholly to embrace principles underlying the success of these pilots. Nevertheless, some changes had already taken place. Following the liberalization of the market, school textbooks could be printed by state-owned bodies, private companies, and privatized (formerly state-owned) printers. Since 1999, for example, Maarif and Tahsil have had to compete as the market opened to private publishers. New publishers did not have big printing houses, but they were more flexible and ambitious. Some named their companies after their places of birth, others chose philosophical symbols. They were ready to take risks, but they perceived textbook publishing as a commercial game with high stakes. New publishers were also primarily interested in printing rather than development, since the former is more profitable. Ironically, the opening of the textbook market in Azerbaijan has created opportunities for new publishers, but it has not necessarily contributed to the improvement of the quality of the textbooks as originally envisaged by the World Bank and OSIAF.

Textbook finance

Azerbaijan's Law of Education (1992) states that all primary (grades one through four) and lower secondary (grades five through nine) students should receive textbooks free of charge. In practice, however, this policy has faced serious problems. Throughout the 1990s, budgetary constraints have allowed only primary-level books to be supplied. Many parents continued to buy textbooks for their children either out of necessity (textbooks are poor quality or unavailable) or by choice (they don't want their child to have to share a book). According to one survey, 61.3 percent of students were supplied with books, 32.2 percent were partially supplied, and 6.6 percent were not supplied at all (Dundar et al. 2000). The situation was better in elementary grades, where 76.7 percent of students received books, 22.1 percent received some, and only 1.3 percent received none. This was as compared with respective indices of 53.2 percent, 37.6 percent, and 9.2 percent in secondary grades (Dundar et al. 2000, 40).

At the start of the decade, however, the government made a commitment to supplying all students with free textbooks. This decision was a reciprocal obligation within the Education Sector Reform Project. A five-year period was established for using textbooks, during which they would pass from one student to another through the school library. Since 2003, textbooks for all school subjects have been distributed gratis to all students. Minister of Education Misir Mardanov, speaking at the National Education Conference, September 5, 2006, said:

> Textbook provision was one of the main achievements. All students from grades 1 through 11 were supplied with textbooks free of charge. Azerbaijan was the first country among the former-Soviet republics to implement free textbook provision for all general school students. In 2006, this work has continued with the publication of 108 new titles—and a total of 5 million books. However, polygraph quality [technical quality] and textbook content require further improvement. ... Development of a new generation of textbooks requires setting up new mechanisms and models of textbook development as reflected in the government's textbook policy.

In 2006, the Ministry of Education spent over US$5.5 million in printing and distribution of free textbooks. While the new finance scheme has equipped all students with books, it has undermined some of the most important elements of the overall reform—choice for schools and competition for publishers. First, the government has funded only one textbook for each subject. Theoretically, schools may choose alternatives and require parents to buy them, but this has proven unrealistic given the budgetary constraints of many families in Azerbaijan. Second, the new finance policy has severely restrained competition among publishers. While open tenders have been made to promote liberalization of the market, the same company was often awarded state funding for the production of free textbooks, leading to a new monopoly by one (usually government-sponsored) firm. The production of alternatives was simply not attractive to new publishers, because there was no demand among schools, parents, and students. Ironically, the new textbook finance policy has once again left parents, teachers, and schools out of the decision-making process, thus strengthening state control over which textbooks should be used in Azerbaijani schools.

Visions and realities of textbook-publishing reform

Undoubtedly, international financial institutions (for example, the World Bank) and NGOs (for example, OSIAF) have had a tremendous impact on textbook-publishing reform in Azerbaijan. In addition to direct impact (for example, setting up the Textbook Approval Board, training textbook authors, and funding textbook publishing), a partnership among the government, World Bank, and OSIAF has yielded important indirect benefits by raising awareness about textbook issues in the Ministry of Education and among teachers and teacher trainers. This partnership has also had the effect of defining and disseminating the notion of "quality" in textbooks, raising interest in new methods of evaluation, tendering/bidding, and financing. It has also promoted a greater acceptance of teamwork and input from classroom teachers in textbook writing.

This chapter has highlighted an emerging difference between intentions and outcomes of textbook reform in Azerbaijan. This could be explained by several factors. First is the government's fear of losing control over ideological aspects of education as it attempts to redefine its role in a new, free-market environment. Although the government has accepted principles of market liberalization (for example, through the tendering of textbooks) and allowed (at least theoretically) competition among publishers, it has not necessarily provided textbook choice for schools. As during the Soviet era, most schools in Azerbaijan continue to rely on one state-approved textbook for each subject, provided to schools free of charge. In the context of budgetary constraints faced by many families in Azerbaijan, the purchase of alternative textbooks by families is simply not feasible.

Second, the creation of a free market for textbooks in Azerbaijan has undoubtedly opened opportunities for publishers, but it has not necessarily contributed to the improvement of the quality as originally envisaged by the World Bank and OSIAF. While government officials generally regard quality as a priority, there are no proper mechanisms to ensure it. The government is more interested in replacing "old" ideological values with "new" ones than in reforming the process of quality control in textbook publishing. Following recommendations of the World Bank and OSIAF, the government in 2006 established one quality-control mechanism—an independent Textbook Approval Board—with its own set of procedures for evaluation, selection, approval, and procurement of textbooks. However, as of May 2007, no books have been put through the board's mechanism; nor have quality standards for pedagogy and design been properly specified in government tender documents. Furthermore, the tendering process used by the government only covers the cost of printing and binding, not authorship and development. As a result, publishers are primarily interested in production.

A final weakness is the lack of consumer influence in product quality and the publishing process. Not only are grassroots stakeholders (teachers, schools, communities, and parents) not experienced or confident enough to engage actively in the developing textbook market, but there are no mechanisms in place to provide decision-making capacity to schools and parents. According to the government's education reform plan, textbook choice and finance will be further decentralized by 2010 to provide direct access to publishers for communities, school, and parents. However, it is not clear how and to what extent a new policy would support textbook choice.

Experience throughout the former Soviet Union has shown that education reform is a slow and uncertain process. As the case of textbook-publishing reform in Azerbaijan has illustrated, envisaged reforms do not necessarily reach goals and objectives, and policy intentions may be seriously obscured by the various interests of key partners. While Azerbaijan represents a unique case of mutual agreement among key partners—the government, World Bank, and OSIAF—in the overall direction of reform it highlights a rift between visions and realities in implementation. As this chapter discussed, the goal was to break away from the old centralized system to a more open, fair, and competitive market. In practice, however, the varying and often conflicting interests of different partners have led to selective implementation of reform. This has sacrificed the principles of choice and quality—promoted by OSIAF and the World Bank—for the control of textbook publishing—desired by the government.

Notes

[1] The low cover price of textbooks in the Soviet Union was a result of the application of input subsidies (e.g., paper, printing, etc.) and a single, dominant language of instruction (Russian). These factors, along with the absence of competition (and thus waste) and fixed (and thus artificial) pricing policies allowed for very time-consuming print runs.

[2] The World Bank's Azerbaijan Education Sector Development Project (2000) involves a loan in the amount of US$73 million, and consists of three phases over a period of ten years (2003–13). The first phase (US$18 million for 2003–7) aims to establish the capacity to implement, monitor, and evaluate the program and address the improvement of the quality and relevance of general education, including (1) beginning curriculum reform for general education; (2) development and provision of textbook and reading materials based on the revised curricula; (3) piloting the provision of information and communication technologies in selected districts; (4) training of teachers and principals; and (5) assessing the results of student learning outcomes in selected core subjects. The second phase (US$25 million for 2007–10) will support the government's reform program to expand coverage and extend scope of interventions and develop further management skills, particularly at local levels, based on evolving needs. The third phase (US$30 million for 2010–13) will aim to achieve full national coverage, consolidate interventions, and review the achievements of the reform program.

[3] Cole (1999) demonstrated that textbook authors also often wrote the curriculum. For example, the authors of the current textbooks for primary

mathematics were also the authors of the new mathematics curriculum for grades three and four.

[4] Until the end of the 1990s, virtually all schoolbooks in Azerbaijan were printed at the state Ministry of Press and Information. Maarif was the sole provider of all approved books for grades one through four, and Tahsil was the official publisher for grades five and above.

References

Asanova, Jazira. 2007. Teaching the canon? Nation-building and post-Soviet Kazakhstan's literature textbooks. *Compare: A Journal of Comparative Education* 37(3): 325–43.

Cole, Peter. 1999. *Development of the curriculum in the Republic of Azerbaijan.* Report submitted to the World Bank.

Crighton, Johanna. 2001. *OSI-Azerbaijan World History Textbook Project.* Evaluation report submitted to OSIAF-Azerbaijan. Cambridge, UK: Cambridge Assessment and Development in Education.

Dundar, Halil, Geoff Howse, Ayfer Bartu, Rasim Ramazanov, Larissa Lemberanskaya, and Rajab Sattarov. 2000. *Social assessment of Azerbaijan education reform.* Baku, Azerbaijan: Sigma.

Hunt, Tim, and Tony Read. 2000. *School textbook provision in Azerbaijan: A study comprising an analysis of current problems with options and recommendations for future strategies.* Report submitted to the World Bank. London: International Book Development Ltd.

Pinter, Frances, and Snejana Slantcheva. 2000. *Education for all 2000: Textbook provision at the end of the century.* Available online.

Sneath, David. 2002. Mongolia in the "Age of the Market?": Pastoral land-use and the development discourse. In *Markets and moralities: Ethnographies of postsocialism,* ed. R. Mandel and C. Humphrey, 191–210. Oxford: Berg.

Tse, Kwan Choi. 2003. Civics and citizenship. In *International handbook of educational research in the Asia-Pacific region,* ed. John Keeves and Ryo Watanabe, 555–68. Dordrecht, Netherlands: Kluwer Publishers.

World Bank. 2002. *Operational guidelines for textbooks and reading materials.* Washington DC: The World Bank Education Sector.

———. 2003. *Azerbaijan Education Sector Development Project.* Project Appraisal Document. Washington DC: World Bank.

4

On Being First

The Meaning of Education Decentralization Reform in Georgia

ANNA MATIASHVILI

Decentralization has been called "a fashion of our time" (Manor 1999, 1), with a wide variety of countries pursuing it for numerous reasons. Many are decentralizing because they believe it can help stimulate economic growth and reduce poverty. Others see it as a way to move financial responsibilities onto lower level governments. Yet others perceive it as a way to strengthen civil society and promote democracy. As Kamat observes, decentralization has become "a common rallying point," bringing together diverse actors such as NGOs, state bureaucracy, and international aid agencies. This is because, historically, it has been equated with democracy, in terms of greater local sovereignty and increased responsiveness to the needs of communities (2002, 111). The connection between democratization and decentralization explains increased efforts in pursuing the latter in former socialist-bloc states since the early 1990s. In fact, over 80 percent of countries in Eastern and Central Europe, with widely differing political orientations and economic bases, have been decentralizing since the collapse of the Soviet Union (Manor

I would like to express my appreciation for the consultations and invaluable information provided by the leadership of OSGF, especially Nino Chinchaladze. I would also like to acknowledge the contribution of the International Institute for Education Policy, Planning and Management team in the creation of this document and to express my special thanks to Nino Kutateladze for her expertise and valuable recommendations on earlier drafts of this chapter.

1999). In education, decentralization has been secured as an inseparable component of the post-socialist education reform package, reflecting strong aspirations of post-socialist governments to democratize educational systems across the region.

Comparative analysis of education decentralization has shown that there are various models of decentralization (Bray 1996). The most common typologies attempt to distinguish between the various functions and resources being decentralized, and presume four broad categories—administrative, fiscal, political, and market (Rondinelli 1986). Not surprisingly, donors attach different meanings to decentralization reform. The UNDP lays emphasis on political decentralization to promote the stability of public institutions and national capacity for organizing and evaluating varying responsibilities, while the OSI and other NGOs define decentralization in terms of civil society involvement (UNESCO 2005, 15). Alternatively, international financial institutions such as the World Bank have framed decentralization as a cost-sharing measure between the center (national government) and periphery (local government).[1] Only after 2002, when the World Bank added good governance as a condition for providing loans and grants, was decentralization promoted as a means to emphasize, to use World Bank terminology, the "demand side." It is indicative that the World Bank created its own terminology *(social accountability)* for civic involvement in public policy, even though the meaning is closely associated with what NGOs have been saying all along.[2] The question becomes which models of education decentralization become institutionalized where, how, and why.

During the post-socialist transformations of the 1990s, donors competed to determine which definition(s) of decentralization would prevail. In an era when decentralization was presented in a multitude of ways and regarded as a cure-all for every educational crisis, donors hastened to leave their imprint on the reform. This chapter discusses education decentralization reform in the Republic of Georgia during the early 2000s and examines the complex interaction of various actors—the government, the World Bank, and the OSGF. The chapter traces how the original concept of administrative decentralization and civil society involvement, developed by the government and piloted by OSGF, was eventually replaced by the World Bank's model of finance decentralization. The chapter also discusses why the Georgian government did not draw on the existing pilot project, local experience, and professional capacity (promoted by local NGOs and OSGF) and instead imported a completely new education reform package funded by the World Bank. Following examination of the education reform context, the chapter offers a review and analysis of the various factors that account for the selective institutionalization of education decentralization reform in the Republic of Georgia. This case study demonstrates the complex factors and conditions under which governments neglect initiatives developed by local NGOs and import ideas from elsewhere.

The reform context: Declining education finance, deteriorating quality, and ineffective management

The educational system in Georgia has experienced a sharp decline in funding since independence. According to the World Bank, this drop was among the most severe in the region and unique in the history of education systems worldwide. In real terms, the state budget for the education sector in 1996 was only 5 percent of what it had been in 1989. This was a consequence of an overall 75 percent reduction in GDP between 1991 and 1994, and a drop in the share of education within it, from more than 7 percent in 1991 to less than 1 percent in 1994. Public-education expenditure quadrupled between 1995 and 1998, and its percentage of the total amount of public expenditure has gone from 6.7 to 11.3. Meanwhile, the GDP increased to an estimated 2.4 percent in 1998 (World Bank 2001). In 2004, education expenditure as a percentage of GDP constituted 2.9 percent (UNESCO 2006). Notwithstanding this modest recovery, education's share of GDP remained low by international standards (for example, education expenditure as a percentage of GDP constitutes 4–6 percent in OECD countries).

Limited funding had serious implications for education quality, teacher salaries, access to learning materials, and maintenance of school facilities. The Georgian educational system encountered other serious challenges, such as insufficient and inadequate learning materials and infrastructure, lack of information and transparency in resource allocation, inefficient use of resources, growing inequities, and weak governance and management capacity. The existing legal and regulatory education framework was inadequate—

too rigid, often contradictory—to support the implementation of education-sector reforms. At the same time, the system demonstrated failures in organization and implementation, as the majority of school administrators, directors, and other personnel lacked the management experience necessary for succeeding in the post-Soviet environment. The system seemed overburdened by bureaucratic layers with overlapping responsibilities and accountabilities. In some cases tasks were duplicated between the Ministry of Education and regional education departments. In other instances newly created district-level offices found themselves without clearly defined functions. There was a lack of effective coordination and administrative and financial management capacity at nearly every level.

It is in this context that education decentralization reform was formulated as a strategic priority by various stakeholders, including the government, international donors, and NGOs. The case for education decentralization reform was largely based on the assumption that the government should be more knowledgeable about, and responsive to, people's demands, and should be locating decisions on services closer to the people they serve (World Bank 2003). In post-Soviet Georgia the state bureaucracy appeared heavy, slow, and unable to tackle the emerging education crises of the 1990s. Decentralization appeared to be the solution for increasing efficiency in management and governance of schools and for allowing faster identification of needs and development of possible solutions for existing problems. In this context, education decentralization was commonly equated with the democratization of the education system.

Georgia's education decentralization reform: Changing visions, shifting priorities

In 1999, the government of Georgia developed the *Draft Decree on the Status of a State Institution for General Education* (Decentralization Decree) to initiate reform. The draft decree reiterated that the initiative was a direct response to a lack of democratic governance and management, insufficient civil society involvement, and inefficiency and effectiveness within education management. The decree focused primarily on administrative decentralization of secondary-education institutions and discussed such issues as institutional autonomy, appointment and responsibilities of school principals, and the role of boards of trustees. While the document included some education-finance provisions, it referred mainly to the management of existing financial resources by the newly established boards of trustees and their responsibility for overseeing the available budget and attracting additional financial resources to schools.[3]

In 2000, the government of Georgia signed a cooperation agreement with the OSGF to pilot test several models of administrative decentralization in the education sector. The agreement stipulated that the OSGF would play a leading role in pilot testing education decentralization reform models, which would then be used in schools nationwide. The cooperation agreement confirmed that the Ministry of Education would "support piloting of the programs in education institutions of Georgia," guarantee the participation of professors from higher-education institutions, along with school staff, in training seminars, courses, and workshops organized by the OSGF, while fully mobilizing and involving teachers and students "according to the project needs." The original strategy was to develop local capacity in education decentralization processes at the school level.

With the arrival of the World Bank, however, the reform model abruptly shifted from administrative to finance decentralization, and the OSGF project remained at the pilot stage. The Ministry of Education was closely involved in every phase of the pilot, from the initial stage of development, to signing the memorandum of collaboration, to attending training sessions, conferences, and round-table discussions. Though the evaluation of the outcome was positive, the ministry chose to disregard it and instead introduced an entirely new decentralization package as a part of the World Bank Education Realignment and Democratization Project. Moreover, the World Bank did not use any locally existing expertise developed from the OSGF pilot project. Before discussing the factors leading to the "failed institutionalization" of the OSGF project, this section provides a brief description of the two models implemented by OSGF and the World Bank, tracing a conceptual shift in decentralization reform and distinguishing more clearly between "administrative" and "finance" decentralization in the education sector.

Decentralization of education governance: OSGF's Education Decentralization and Management Development Project

By the time the World Bank entered the donor scene, OSGF was already well established in Georgia. In 1998, George Soros pledged substantial support for initiation of educational reform, though actual program development had already begun by the end of 1996 with the formation of a working group. The first program proposal was completed in July 1997. Two months later Soros doubled education program funding from US$3 million to US$6 million dollars to support implementation of the multi-component education reform project. The original project strategy was called Partners in Education and contained three components: (1) developing Parent-Teacher Associations (PTAs), (2) reforming early childhood education (SbS program), and (3) revising textbooks. The original strategy, however, was revised in 1998–99, when the entire Soros Foundation Network in Central/Southeastern Europe and the former Soviet Union was mandated to rethink its approach to ensure systemic impact and long-term sustainability in education reform in the countries where it functioned. In May 1998, the IEP (currently the ESP), began to work closely with the foundation to develop a new strategy for education reform—a mega project that would reflect both the needs of the system and the OSI agenda. With increased involvement of international donors in Georgia, the goal was to target those areas where they would not be working, or alternatively, to lay the groundwork for good practice that would later leverage World Bank money when loans were disbursed.

While the revised OSGF strategy contained the original program components, it also introduced new initiatives based on a needs assessment, constituting an important part of the development process. Needs assessment was undertaken with technical reinforcement from the ESP of OSI Budapest, and resulted in the development of three new program areas: (1) local education policy capacity development (for example, the creation of the local education think tank), (2) pre-service teacher-education reform (for example, professional development for staff of pre-service teacher education institutions), and (3) education decentralization. During the needs-assessment mission, the Georgian government and OSGF staff agreed that education decentralization was one of the main priorities and proposed that the process should encourage wider participation of stakeholders while simultaneously providing management training for local-level administrators.

The main aim of the Education Decentralization and Management Development (EDMD) project was to create and test several models of more decentralized and democratic educational arrangements and to build capacity within the system to manage them. The project was also intended to design and pilot the "Mini Decree" for general secondary schools in thirty-two locations throughout the country. The "Mini Decree" was a shortened version of the *Draft Decree on the Status of a State Institution for General Education* developed by the Ministry of Education in 1999. It dealt with basic issues of decentralized governance, such as the election of boards of trustees and boards of teachers, and enabled the EDMD project to pilot democratic mechanisms in the thirty-two schools. An important component was providing training for education stakeholders at all levels, including authorities at local education departments, school principals, administrators, teachers, and parents. The purpose was to develop various competencies in management and governance among school staff. Implementation began in 2000 and covered four geographic regions: Tbilisi, Imereti, Kvemo Kartli, and Adjara.

The findings of the evaluation[4] indicate that the project was successful and well received in participating schools (Kochoradze et al. 2002). A major theme emerging from interviews was the importance of the new skills participants acquired—teamwork, democratic management, independent thinking, new information on decentralization issues, and rights and responsibilities within the process. One of the strengths of the EDMD project was increased community involvement within schools. As the evaluation highlighted, increased responsibility among teachers and parents brought a sense of ownership over the quality of education offered by schools (Kochoradze et al. 2002). More important, most pilot schools welcomed democratic processes resulting from decentralization reform, and all respondents confirmed the importance of established boards of trustees in ensuring fair governance. The pilot project played an important democratizing role and empowered school staff, teachers, parents, and local communities to take an active part in decision-making.

Decentralization of education finance: The World Bank Education System Realignment and Strengthening Program

The development and planning process of the World Bank's Education System Realignment and Strengthening Program (adaptable program credit) began in 1999 and was approved in March 2001. It was designed to have three four-year phases, starting in the summer of 2001. The Adaptable Program Credit was a US$60 million, twelve-year program, supporting primary and general secondary education in Georgia. Project components aimed at (1) developing and implementing an outcome-based national curriculum for primary and general secondary education; (2) strengthening the management capacity at central and local levels through development; and (3) implementing policies to improve financial, human, and physical resource management. As stated in the program document, development of management and policy capacity focused on strengthening the central level in its redefined role within a decentralized system, and improving internal efficiency and quality in the system. However, the project document stated that "as the pace of decentralization evolves, subsequent phases will support capacity development at local and school levels and will move on to address equity and external efficiency policy issues as well" (World Bank 2001, 1).

The program aimed to strengthen management capacity at central and local levels. It was also meant to develop required tools like new financing formulas and funding mechanisms, school mapping and consolidation plans; to improve decision-making; to increase transparency; and to ensure accountability. In terms of resource allocation, the World Bank focused on developing new financial formulas, introducing professional-development incentives for teachers, maximizing student-teacher ratios, and promoting cost-effective use of school infrastructure. While the program included various components (teacher training, curriculum development, and so forth), the primary focus was decentralization of finance in general secondary schools.

Although the World Bank recognized the government's decentralization efforts as "a positive step towards autonomy" (2006, 22), it reframed the original concept in terms of education finance. The World Bank justified the need for reform based on the lack of resources in the education sector. One World Bank document in particular stated:

Less than 20 percent of all schools in Georgia have received any type of maintenance (and often a superficial one) in the past 20 years and resource allocation for capital expenditures has been minimal. Lack of maintenance minimizes substantially the returns of the investment since it reduces the lifespan of a building by roughly 30 years. . . . To address these issues, Georgia is trying to decentralize school ownership (without selling-rights) to autonomous School Boards. . . . In theory, School Boards will assume responsibility for capital development and maintenance of school buildings, reducing (but still having) legal dependence on local governments for this purpose. (World Bank 2006, 76)

The World Bank initiatives in the decentralization of finance have resulted in a number of legislative changes in Georgia. One of the most important was the Law on General Education (2005), which placed greater financial autonomy and accountability at the school level. The new law recognized decentralized management of schools through the operation of the existing boards of trustees and gave them new governance and financial management authority. The new law stated that school-board responsibilities included election of school directors from a list of three candidates provided by the Ministry of Education and Science; approval and management of the school budget and school curriculum; and approval of the staff manual and internal regulations.

The World Bank supported Georgia's education decentralization process through the establishment of a network of seventy-two educational resource centers with two main areas of responsibility. First, the resource centers, each of which serves clusters of twenty-five to forty schools, performed managerial and administrative functions, including monitoring school accounting, bureaucratic requirements, data management, and professional practices and standards. Second, they provide instructional and professional services for the Ministry of Education and Science, training, supplementary materials in curriculum and assessment, and support for school management and councils. This reform model corresponds, as mentioned earlier, to the minimum definition of decentralization commonly held by educators and public servants: offering provisions outside the capital or center. According to the World Bank (2006), each

Resource Center helped schools with financial planning, statutory and legal requirements, professional development, data and communications and—where needed—language specialists.

The results of the Rapid Social Assessment[5] (quoted in World Bank 2006) revealed that education stakeholders viewed decentralization of financing as "a very positive concept, causing more freedom in school level expenditure and decision-making" (World Bank 2006, 79). However, respondents also noted that decentralization reform had not been fully implemented due to the scarcity of funds transferred to schools. School directors explained that budgets were insufficient to pay teachers optimum salaries, let alone to improve the physical condition of schools or provide resources like technical labs and teaching materials. In the view of most education providers, the scarcity of funds transferred to schools did not enable them to be more competitive or attract more students. As the World Bank explained, securing extra funding for schools remained a function of the school director and, depending on the individual efforts and personalities of the schools directors, "poorer schools that historically were lagging behind struggling may weaken further" (World Bank 2006, 79).

Furthermore, the Rapid Social Assessment revealed that the creation of school boards—another important aspect of the decentralization reform—was not fully understood by most users and some providers. The majority of respondents who knew about the boards were skeptical, fearing nepotism would determine membership (World Bank 2006, 79). Ironically, the World Bank recommended more active involvement of local NGOs, who had been entirely left out of the education decentralization process initiated by the World Bank, to ensure that school boards and local communities were more aware of their new responsibilities and had access to relevant information and training:

> Although the reform is viewed as positive, there seems to be a need for better information of the public as well as providers of education. More importantly, all schools should be trained on the formation of School Boards and the community involved need to be informed and trained as well. Using local NGOs or any local institutions in this regard will be very positive to involve communities, parents, and other stakeholders. Information dissemination through public media and involvement

of local NGOs are very important in this regard. (World Bank 2006, 79)

Failed institutionalization
of a locally developed decentralization reform

Why did the Georgian government disregard a locally developed model of administrative decentralization, piloted by OSGF, and instead import an entirely new package through the World Bank? What factors accounted for the failure to institutionalize the locally developed model? At the end of the 1990s attempts were made to coordinate donor assistance in education reform. At least rhetorically, the World Bank intended to mobilize and coordinate donor support and considered the possibility of forming a working relationship with OSGF. Since OSGF was recognized as among the most active donors in Georgia, the World Bank believed both groups could operate better by coordinating their initiatives and building upon one another's experiences. One World Bank document emphasized the need for a "participatory approach" to education reform, and noted a "special partnership" with the OSGF in the reform process:

> The preparation of the project had a participatory approach all along. The opportunity to do sector work prior to preparing an investment operation gave time to develop trust and a constructive dialogue between WB staff and MoES officials. ... Efforts to promote donor coordination and partnership have also been undertaken from the start: meetings with potential donors have been scheduled regularly to inform about activities and a special partnership has been developed with the Georgia Open Society Foundation. (World Bank 1999, 34)

While some initial meetings did take place between the World Bank and OSGF, the education initiatives funded by the former disregarded local capacity developed by the latter. The result was that the OSGF project was not institutionalized. A detailed analysis of local policy context is paramount for understanding the complexity of factors that led to this neglect. It is clear that the political nature of the decision-making process and the financial incentives provided by international financial institutions played a crucial role in the government's decision to abandon the existing model of education reform.

The politics of dissociating from the "old" regime

One of the contextual factors explaining the failed institutionalization of the locally developed education decentralization reform in the Republic of Georgia is recent political instability. Changes in the country's leadership while the project was being implemented had negative consequences in terms of effectiveness and sustainability. Components and activities were significantly delayed several times, as OSGF obtained re-approval for some of its activities and renegotiated certain project components with new officials.

An abrupt change of government in 2003 complicated things even further. In November the political unrest—or Rose revolution—resulted in the displacement of President Eduard Shevardnadze, who had led the country from the collapse of the Soviet Union to the transformation of government in 2003. The new administration, headed by newly elected President Mikheil Saakashvili, enjoyed great popular support and benefited from a broad public consensus. The government launched reforms demonstrating its resolve to build a stable, modern democracy and to prove its legitimacy. Many believed that a completely new era began after the revolution. Reaching an agreement with new authorities on issues endorsed by the "old" leadership was not an easy task. Possibly, they wanted to dissociate themselves from reform initiatives undertaken before the Rose revolution. In their view, any connection with the "old" regime could provoke mistrust. Unsurprisingly, prior policies were often dismissed or replaced with new ones, as was the case with the education decentralization reform piloted by OSGF at the end of the 1990s.

Stakeholder replacement

The change in government resulted in a replacement of stakeholders in the education sphere, including staff of the Ministry of Education and Science. As discussed earlier, human capacity developed through OSGF activities represented a valuable resource, which could have been used to supplement initiatives funded by the World

Bank. However, the new government decided to develop capacity among its own support group to maintain greater control over the reform process and to ensure its own interests. Stakeholder replacement resulting from changes in political administration has been well documented in education policy literature (for example, Luschei 2004). New administrations tend to demand new beginnings to exert their authority, generate hope, and disempower past experts funded from other sources. One way of displacing existing local capacities is to import something new from the outside. Georgian experts and practitioners working within the OSGF decentralization project became superfluous. Their knowledge and skills were of little use to a project no longer defined by civil society involvement and narrowly focused on financial decentralization.

Financial incentives and interests

Another reason for the failed institutionalization of the OSGF education decentralization project has to do with the desire of the new government to obtain substantial funding from the World Bank. International financial institutions worldwide have often made decentralization of education systems a precondition for financial assistance (Bjork 2003). A loan of US$60 million was a significant contribution to Georgia's deteriorating education sector, but in receiving it the government also had to accept the World Bank's agenda and political conditionalities. Not surprisingly, decentralization of governance and finance was top of the list. What had begun in 1999 as a presentation of possible solutions to educational problems was soon prescribed (in a considerably altered form) as a condition for international loans and grants.

In addition to political conditionalities, much of the attractiveness of financial decentralization lies in the extent to which it is able to relieve governments of the burden of education financing by providing an alternative source for channeling resources to the education sector (Bray 1996). According to Bray, "Where governments are prosperous, community financing seems to attract relatively little official attention, but where governments are hard pressed, it is given more recognition" (1996, 44). Similarly, UNESCO observes that governments with serious financial problems may be particularly attracted to the potential that decentralization holds for "shedding financial responsibilities linked to the provision of educational services" in schools (2005, 13). The financial crisis that beset the Georgian government during the 1990s greatly increased official interest in the phenomenon of financial decentralization in education and prospects for community financing.

Legitimizing a contested education reform

Justifications were necessary for economic reasons. The government legitimized a substantial loan by belittling already-existing projects funded by NGOs, OSGF in particular. The government was in a bind—in need of approval from an external authority to pass an unpopular reform. Thus, consideration of political factors may help explain why it chose to import the World Bank package. Similar to any other reform, education decentralization is often resisted by a wide group of interest groups and stakeholders—political authorities reluctant to give up power, in particular (Dethier 2000). A detailed analysis of the education policy context in Georgia revealed that some powerful central- or regional-level actors were opposed due to interest in managing financial activities or fear of losing authority. Some also resisted taking on new responsibilities for fiscal and political reasons, fearing increased administrative burdens with the transfer of authority.

Decentralization of education finance was unpopular with schools and local communities reluctant to assume greater responsibility for school financing. Many perceived it as simply a transfer of financial burden from the central level to the local level, raising concerns about exacerbating social inequalities among different geographic regions. Similar to other former Soviet republics, many communities hoped to revive the legacy of "free and uniform" education, funded entirely by the government, and did not seek contributions from already impoverished communities. Presenting the contested initiative as an internationally imposed, rather than locally formulated, solution enabled the transfer of blame to an outsider: the World Bank.

The politics and economics of selective institutionalization of education reforms

Undoubtedly, shifting meanings of education decentralization in Georgia highlight the political and economic context of reform processes in the post-socialist period. Originally, reform was initiated locally to democratize educational governance, marking the country's move to a more open, democratic environment. The original concept—emphasizing decentralization of governance—was developed by policymakers and piloted by OSGF to build local capacity for implementation. However, it soon became a condition for international loans and grants. With acceptance of funding from the World Bank, the concept of the reform abruptly shifted from decentralization of governance to decentralization of finance, resulting in the failed institutionalization of the OSGF initiative.

Factors accounting for the selective institutionalization of decentralization reform in Georgia are multiple and complex, highlighting the politics and economics of importing educational ideas from elsewhere. Not only was the government interested in receiving a substantial loan from the World Bank for education reform, but it also used the newly imported package to pursue multiple political interests locally. World Bank funding also distanced the government from reform initiatives undertaken by the previous regime, including the decentralization of education governance begun at the end of the 1990s. Since the new government inherited serious financial problems, it was particularly attracted to the potential for shedding responsibilities from the central to local levels. Finally, importing the new reform package from the World Bank provided an opportunity for the Georgian government to present an unpopular and contested education reform as an imposition from the outside, transferring blame to the World Bank.

Notes

[1] There is yet a third definition of decentralization that should not be neglected. The Ministry of Education and Science also occasionally refers to means provision (for example, in-service teacher training or resource centers) as decentralization.

[2] The various meanings of decentralization might also be a result of the failure to decentralize finance in the post-socialist region. In fact, many laws and regulations of the 1990s were reversed and educational finance was "recentralized" (see Steiner-Khamsi and Stolpe 2004).

[3] The decree did not provide for decentralization of the education-finance system as such (for example, transferring responsibility to local education authorities or to the schools themselves).

[4] A formative objectives-oriented evaluation was conducted to compare real project outcomes within stated objectives to expected ones.

[5] The overall objective of the Rapid Social Assessment was to ensure that reforms intended to increase access to quality education, particularly for low-income families, did not cause unintended consequences. The Rapid Social Assessment used a combination of quantitative and qualitative methods, including a survey among parents and focus groups and in-depth interviews with education providers and students (World Bank 2006).

References

Bjork, Christopher. 2003. Local responses to decentralization policy in Indonesia. *Comparative Education Review* 47(2): 184–216.

Bray, Mark. 1996. *Decentralization of education: Community financing.* Washington DC: World Bank.

Dethier, Jean-Jacques. 2000. *Some remarks on fiscal decentralization and governance.* Paper presented at the Conference on Decentralization Sequencing, Jakarta, Indonesia, March 20. Available online.

Kamat, Sangeeta. 2002. Deconstructing the rhetoric of decentralization: The state in education reform. *Current Issues in Comparative Education* 2(2): 110–19.

Kochoradze, Badri, Ji Sun Lee, Rocio Rivas, and Natalya Shablya. 2002. *Education Decentralization and Management Development Project.* Evaluation report. Tbilisi, Georgia: Educational Policy, Planning, and Management.

Luschei, Thomas. 2004. Timing is everything: The intersection of borrowing and lending in Brazil's adoption of *Escuela Nueva.* In *The global politics of educational borrowing and lending,* ed. Gita Steiner-Khamsi, 154–67. New York: Teachers College Press.

Manor, James. 1999. *The political economy of democratic decentralization.* Washington DC: World Bank.

Rondinelli, Dennis. 1986. Assessing decentralization policies in developing countries: The case for cautious optimism. *Development Policy Review* 4: 3–23.

Steiner-Khamsi, Gita, and Ines Stolpe. 2004. Decentralization and recentralization reform in Mongolia: Tracing the swing of the pendulum. *Comparative Education* 40(1): 29–53.

UNESCO. 2005. *Decentralization in education: National policies and practices.* Education Policies and Strategies series 7. Paris: UNESCO.

———. 2006. *Global education digest 2006: Comparing education statistics across the world.* Montreal, Canada: UNESCO Institute of Statistics.

World Bank. 1999. Georgia: Education System Realignment and Strengthening Program. Report no. PID7940. Washington DC: World Bank.

———. 2001. Project appraisal document: Georgia Education System Realignment and Strengthening Program. Report no. 20952–GE. Washington DC: World Bank.

————. 2003. *2004 world development report: Making services work for poor people.* Washington DC: World Bank.

————. 2006. Education System Realignment and Strengthening Project in support of the second phase of the Education System Realignment and Strengthening Program in the Republic of Georgia. Report no. 36513–GE. Washington DC: World Bank.

5

From Educational Brokers to Local Capacity Builders

Redefining International NGOs in Kazakhstan

SAULE KALIKOVA AND IVETA SILOVA

Foreign aid is frequently associated with generating dependency and implies an imposition of reforms by international donors (Moss et al. 2006; Dichter 2003; Brautigam 2000; Maren 1997). However, what if a country, such as Kazakhstan, does not depend on foreign aid, and yet engages in international cooperation? There are numerous countries such as Saudi Arabia, United Arab Emirates, and Iran that are not aid dependent. Yet they seek international technical assistance to ensure that their reforms are in line with international

As we were finishing this chapter, we received tragic news about the unexpected death of Hannes Voolma, an Estonian education consultant and colleague who played an important role in curriculum reform processes in Kazakhstan. During 2002–3, Hannes made important contributions to the development of the overall framework for curriculum reform by preparing a series of training conferences, seminars, and discussions for education policymakers, and inviting international experts. The project benefited tremendously from his deep knowledge of the post-Soviet education realities, his understanding of education reform processes in Kazakhstan, as well as his professional outlook on a variety of educational issues. His personal qualities—honesty and kindness toward his colleagues, commitment to the values of education equity, and ability to initiate a constructive dialogue with the representatives of opposing points of view—were important lessons for anyone involved in curriculum reform in Kazakhstan.

developments and standards in education. Kazakhstan is an interesting case because it has moved from being aid-dependent to donor free within the past decade. How has this decreasing dependency on foreign aid influenced the work of international NGOs in Kazakhstan?

In December 1999, the president of Kazakhstan, Nursultan Nazarbayev, announced that his country would substantially reduce the number of loans it accepted from international donors; it would instead finance education and health-sector reforms with internal resources (ADB 2002a). This has resulted in a substantial reduction in foreign aid and debt, making Kazakhstan one of the most donor-independent countries in Central Asia and the Caucasus. An important corollary is that the influence of international financial institutions on the government has also declined. In fact, the government of Kazakhstan canceled some ongoing education-sector reform projects before the original loan-closing date, leaving several incomplete (ADB 2002b). Instead, the government has used its own resources for education reform, emphasizing the need for closer collaboration with local experts. In his state-of-the-nation speech on February 28, 2007, President Nazarbayev summarized Kazakhstan's continuous effort to develop local "human capital" and an "economy of the mind" rather than relying on foreign expertise to shape Kazakhstan's future:

> We are no longer a country of the Third World. This is the main result of our work in the past 10 years. . . . Today, having secured a firm foundation for our economy and sovereignty, we are confidently moving on to a new stage. . . . Almost all successful modern states which are actively integrated into the international economic system have created an "economy of the mind." To do this we must focus on developing our own human capital. (Nazarbayev 2007)

This chapter examines the changing relationships among the government, international donors, and NGOs in light of Kazakhstan's decision to curb foreign aid to the education sector drastically. How did the role of international organizations change in a donor-free policy environment? What strategies did international organizations use to exert influence on Kazakhstan's educational policymaking, given that foreign aid was no longer a source of political leverage? Following a brief discussion of Kazakhstan's changing policy context, this chapter examines how one international NGO—Soros Foundation–Kazakhstan (SFK)—has redefined its operational strategy by prioritizing the development of local capacity in education policy. We focus on a national curriculum reform (often referred to as outcomes-based education or OBE), which has been initiated and implemented locally, unlike similar curriculum reform projects funded by international financial institutions across the former socialist region.

Reform context: Declining foreign aid and a rising demand for local policy capacity

Following the collapse of the Soviet Union in 1991, international financial institutions (such as the IMF, the World Bank, and the ADB) have used foreign aid as a way to promote neoliberal education reforms in Central Asia and the Caucasus. During the 1990s, Kazakhstan's education system adopted a number of structural adjustment reforms under international pressure to "improve efficiency in the use of available educational resources," "reduce excessive reliance on state funding," and "create conditions for the development of the private sector" (World Bank 2000, 162–63). These reforms led to decentralization of education finance, rationalization of school staff, and optimization of schools. These are just a few examples of the reforms typically found in the post-socialist education reform package in Kazakhstan, as well as other former socialist countries.

With few exceptions, these structural adjustment reforms were conceived by international consultants with little or no knowledge of Kazkahstan's education reform context. As is typically the case, reforms were primarily "driven by the agendas and procedures of the funding and technical assistance agencies, with constrained national participation, limited national control, and very little sense of national ownership" (Samoff 1999, 249). Not surprisingly, some reforms have become examples of institutional reform failure. School rationalization, for example (1995–98), "rationalized" education expenses by enlarging classes and liquidating "cost-ineffective" educational institutions (ADB 2002b, 46). Introduced during the economic crisis of the 1990s, the reform led to the closure of preschools and small rural schools throughout the country, leaving thousands of children without access to education.[1] In 2000, the school rationalization reform was reversed by a government resolution, "Guaranteed State Minimum for Educational Institutions' Network," which aimed at restoring the network of small rural schools in Kazakhstan.

While struggling to reverse some of the most damaging outcomes of structural adjustment reforms in the education sector and to gain tighter control over national education reforms, Kazakhstan decided to reformulate policies regarding foreign aid. This led to the decision to finance education and health reforms through internal resources (ADB 2002a). The windfall from higher world oil prices at the end of the 1990s increased government resources significantly, thus reducing Kazakhstan's external borrowing needs for financing domestic reforms (ADB 2006). As the result of a more cautious borrowing policy, official development assistance (ODA) received by Kazakhstan has fallen from 1.1 percent of Gross National Income (GNI) in 2000 to 0.5 percent in 2005 (OECD 2007). At the same time, Kazakhstan's ratio of sovereign debt to GNI has fallen from 26.5 percent in 2000, to an estimated 8.8 percent in 2005 (*Kazakhstan News Bulletin* 2005). Having redefined its relationship with international donors, Kazakhstan has substantially decreased its dependency on foreign aid.

Following the displacement of foreign donors, the government of Kazakhstan adopted the Law on Social Contracts (2005) to "outbid" local NGOs and end "reliance on foreign funding" (Ovcharenko 2006, 2). The new law provided an opportunity for local NGOs to apply for state grants or "state social contracts" to address a growing demand for social services among the population. In 2005, the government distributed the equivalent of US$3.5 million and promised that by 2010 this figure would reach US$8 million (quoted in Ovcharenko 2006). Driven by the belief that donors determine the agenda of the NGOs they finance, Kazakh officials attempted to set the policy of local NGOs by promising them state financing instead of international funding. Ironically, the new law triggered the establishment of governmental NGOs (GONGOs—see Fisher 1997), thus undermining the government's original intent of "luring [authentically independent] NGOs away from foreign financing" (Ovcharenko 2006, 5).

It is in this context of decreasing dependence on international donors and increasing reliance on local policy capacity that SFK and its spin-off NGOs have reasserted themselves as institutions capable of developing local capacity in education reform. This move has coincided with a larger programmatic shift within the international network of OSI/Soros Foundations, whereby national foundations are encouraged to move from "demonstration projects" to "systemic education reforms," to produce "impact at a national level, and on a national scale" (OSI 1999, 1). Similar to the intention of Kazakh government officials, the OSI's strategy across the region is to "lessen dependency on Western resources and experts" (OSI 1999,1–2). This has made SFK a legitimate partner in implementing a large-scale curriculum reform at the start of the millennium.

From demonstration projects to systemic education reform

SFK was established in 1994 and registered as a local NGO in July 1995. The first educational program, Transformation of Humanities Education (1995–97), supported a competitive approach to school textbook revision and provided small grants to schools for the introduction of innovative approaches to school governance. In 1996, the SFK's educational portfolio expanded with the introduction of network programs, initiated by the OSI-NY office and introduced across the former socialist region. These included SbS (1996–99), Debate (1997–99), RWCT (1998–99), Street Law (1998–99), Visual Thinking Strategies (1998–2000), I*EARN (1998–99), Summer University (1997–2003), and Scholarship Programs (1996–2003). These pilot or demonstration projects encompassed the whole educational system from the preschool to university level. They were intended to introduce new educational approaches, ideas, and concepts to Kazakhstan's educational system. The assumption was that these demonstration projects would eventually be institutionalized in state education structures, with the government of Kazakhstan assuming financial responsibility for their ongoing implementation.

At the end of the 1990s, SFK's educational strategy began to shift from demonstration projects to a more systemic impact on national education reform. This strategic shift occurred in the context of three interrelated developments. First, it was driven by SFK's motivation to scale up its activities in order to ensure sustainability of its pilot projects. Second, it coincided with a larger programmatic shift within the international network of the OSI/Soros Foundations. Soros had become increasingly aware of the limited impact of its education development activities and had begun to consider a range of strategies to influence policy. Third was the Kazakh government's rejection of foreign aid, combined with an increased emphasis on the importance of local expertise in social-sector reforms. It is in this context that SFK began to redefine its role as an important player in national education development by attempting to connect educational initiatives to wider education-sector reforms.

The shift was initially reflected in SFK's effort to institutionalize its operational programs (that is, network programs) as independent NGOs in order to increase their competitiveness in education-service provision. In 1999, for example, SFK spun off some of the most popular programs (SbS, RWCT, Debate, and Street Law) by registering them as independent NGOs (Educational Center Step by Step, Center for Democratic Education, National Debate Center, and Street Law Kazakhstan, respectively). A year later SFK made a more active attempt to influence national education policy by introducing the National Education Program (2000–2003), which consisted of three components: (1) education policy, (2) support of education NGOs, and (3) schools as community centers. The first component repositioned SFK as a major player in national education reform. The goals were to initiate a constructive dialogue of key policy issues among state institutions and society and to create a precedent for developing an independent analysis of issues to be used in the national education policymaking process.

This approach was tested by SFK's involvement in the National Curriculum Reform (2001–3). This reform forged new alliances among representatives of the SFK, state institutions (the Ministry of Education of the Republic of Kazakhstan, Republican In-Service Teacher Training Institute, Kazakhstan Academy of Education, and local education authorities), and local NGOs. SFK facilitated a qualitatively new education policy process by mobilizing different education stakeholders in the policy formulation process and building local capacity in curricula development. Ultimately, SFK's emphasis on local capacity building in education policymaking resulted in a major policy shift. The proposed curriculum extension reform—a simple lengthening of the state curriculum to twelve years—became broad revision of curriculum content. This led to the introduction of OBE in Kazakhstan.

Entering the education policy scene: SFK and the changing focus of national curriculum reform

SFK entered the education policy scene when the Ministry of Education and Science was considering extending secondary education to twelve years. The impetus for the reform stemmed from both domestic and international considerations. The challenge for Kazakhstan and other Central Asian governments had been to avoid further disintegration of their education systems. They needed to recapture previous levels of quality, while striving to build systems that would reflect an elusive "international standard." This would prepare graduates who could be competitive for positions in more globally oriented economies (Chapman et al. 2005).

Domestic pressure for reform came from higher-education administrators and academics, who had complained about the decreasing quality of graduates entering universities. Fears of declining education quality, initially driven by widespread concern among academics, were validated by the results of the National Unified Testing in 1999. The scores revealed that many students were poorly prepared for undergraduate studies. Almost one-third (28–30 percent) of those who took the test failed. Equipped with firm evidence of inadequate schools, higher-education administrators and academics put increased pressure on policymakers to initiate secondary education reform, including revision of the existing curriculum.

Kazakhstan's domestic "quest for quality" (Chapman et al. 2005) was accompanied by a process of international higher-education reform, after Kazakhstan signed the Lisbon and Bologna conventions in 1997 and 2004.[2] Ratification of these conventions emphasized the importance of reforming secondary education to ensure that students are better prepared for undergraduate studies. In particular, ratification of the Lisbon convention required the extension of secondary education to realign both primary and higher education systems with European standards. The driving force behind the reform in Kazakhstan was the creation of a new "education space" (Steiner-Khamsi, Silova, and Johnson 2006). As explained by the former minister of education, Nuraly-Sultanovich Bektourganov, the reform was necessary to ensure that Kazakhstan would "gradually occupy its place in the international educational space," and produce "competitive school graduates able to continue their studies in the higher educational establishments in Europe" (Bektourganov 2002).

In other former socialist countries the extension of schooling was part of the post-socialist education reform package promoted by international donors. In Kazakhstan, reform was initiated locally in the context of decreasing influence of international donors in education-sector reforms. The fact that Kazakhstan's policymakers were adopting some features of the post-socialist education reform package on their own, without direct international pressure, meant that they were trying to control the content and pace of reform. In fact, the initial attempt to formulate the curriculum extension policy did not involve any major revision of existing curriculum content. Many education officials were unwilling to admit weaknesses in the current curriculum inherited from the Soviet Union (usually described as centralized, rigid, inflexible, and overloaded). As Yulya Semikina noted, many experts questioned the need to extend education to twelve years, given that the Soviet model was so successful—"fundamental, substantive, and strong in tradition" (Semikina 2001). Similarly, parents were not supportive of the reform, anticipating that it would cost more to have their children enrolled in schools for an additional year. Referring to Soviet educational achievements in math and science, one parent explained: "Why should we emulate Western models when they [the West] actively cultivate our educational models and schemes?" (quoted in Semikina 2001).

Given the unfavorable policy environment and increased pressure to meet world standards, the initial discussion revolved around the idea of leaving the existing curriculum intact and simply adding one additional year of schooling at each end. Some experts argued that the first year could better prepare children to enter elementary school, while the final year could be used either for more intensive college preparation or to develop professional vocational skills. The result was that though the broad concept of the policy was accepted, its implementation did not mean major changes in the old Soviet system (Steiner-Khamsi, Silova, and Johnson 2006). The first draft of the "Concept of Twelve-Year General Education in the Republic of Kazakhstan" (2001), prepared by Ministry of Education and Science experts, did not emphasize the need for a qualitative revision of the existing curriculum and did not mention OBE even once. Instead, stretching the curriculum (without content revision) was proposed as a solution to the lack of public consensus on how to reform it systematically. This would have required the consolidation of an overloaded curriculum where each subject was allocated only a few instructional hours, and a grouping of subject matter into different areas.

Redefining the national curriculum reform

The draft concept came under heavy criticism from many teachers, academics, and representatives of NGOs. In 2001, the SFK commissioned an opinion survey to document public attitudes toward the proposed curriculum extension reform. According to the survey (Komkon-2 Eurasia 2002), the majority of government officials (62 percent) supported the reform, while only 46 percent of school directors, 29 percent of teachers, 20 percent of high-school students, 19 percent of parents, and 15 percent of education experts were in favor of it. Although most education stakeholders were convinced of the need for a major education reform, the overwhelming opinion was that "stretching" would not alone solve problems existing in Kazakhstan's education system.

The lack of public support for the curriculum reform created a convenient entry point for SFK into the education policy scene. At the end of 2001, SFK brought together a group of approximately seventy policymakers, academics, teachers, and NGO representatives to assess the weaknesses of the existing curriculum and to discuss whether and how the proposed curriculum extension reform would address them. Following several meetings organized by SFK, participants highlighted some of the weaknesses of the current secondary-education system. First, the system did not adequately reflect the new education paradigm, which emphasized individualization and diversification and allowed upper-secondary students to choose between academic and vocational studies. This represented a significant change from the centralized curriculum model during the Soviet period. Second, current education curriculum was outdated and overloaded, raising major concerns for the quality of education and the health of children. Third, many secondary-school graduates who did not enter higher education institutions faced difficulties finding employment after graduation due to lack of basic vocational skills. Finally, there was growing concern for the quality of general secondary education, including a lack of child-centered teaching/learning methodologies and assessment systems.

Having identified specific problems facing the educational system of Kazakhstan, SFK saw the proposed curriculum extension reform (also called the twelve-year education reform) as an opportunity to revise the entire curriculum. This would redefine the concept of education quality in Kazakhstan. The goal was to initiate a more democratic policy-deliberation process by undertaking a thorough analysis of the existing curriculum structure and content. This meant studying the experience of other countries in curriculum reform and considering a variety of policy options appropriate for Kazakhstan. The strategy was to involve Kazakhstan's key education stakeholders—ministry officials, education experts from the Academy of Science and the Republican In-Service Teacher Training Institute, representatives of schools, and representatives from the NGO sector—in a qualitatively new policymaking process in order to ensure national ownership and support for the reform. SFK's role as an international NGO changed from "broker" of education innovations imported from abroad to local facilitator of the education reform process. The former had meant implementing and institutionalizing demonstration projects. Now SFK would be mobilizing local education stakeholders and building their capacity in education policy.

The comparative advantages of SFK were its deep understanding of the local policy context, strong connections to a wide network of local education stakeholders, and relatively easy access to international policy elites and organizations. Having mobilized a group of stakeholders and identified weaknesses in the existing curriculum, SFK's next step was to invite international experts to facilitate a discussion of possible alternatives for curriculum reform. From 2001 to 2003, a "global network of education agencies and academics was mobilized" (Seddon 2005), including experts from former Soviet republics (Russia, Latvia, and Estonia), East and Central Europe (Hungary, Romania, Slovenia, and Slovakia), as well as Finland, South Africa, Australia, and the United States. The idea was to invite education experts from countries that had previously undertaken major curriculum reform.

The focus of the first meeting was developing a vision for education in Kazakhstan. A key feature of the meeting was a presentation by the former director of education and social policy at the OECD, Tom Alexander, who was then a member of the Education Sub-Board of the OSI. His presentation highlighted features of the changing global context and argued for a specific approach to education reform. He established a framework for policymaking based on the synergies among policy areas such as education, the labor market, and social issues. He also argued that education should not be an isolated domain, concerned with inducting young people into established knowledge traditions, but should focus on developing the kinds of capacities that enable young people to learn how to learn and to demonstrate the kinds of literacies that will help them get a job and become socially aware. According to Seddon, this framework challenged the established Kazakh view that education was just about the acquisition of knowledge. Education in Kazakhstan should emphasize skills (2005).

Developing local capacity in curriculum reform

Although highly contested initially by many conference participants, these ideas laid the foundation for more focused work by a smaller group of Kazakh educators, later referred to as the Analytical Group. The Analytical Group was endorsed by the Ministry of Education and Science and received ongoing support from SFK through regular training, workshops, and meetings with different international experts. The group consisted of ten people, including representatives of key educational institutions such as Kazakhstan's Academy of Education, Republican In-Service Teacher Training Institute, National Center of Corrective Pedagogy (targeting children with special needs), Kazakh National University, and Almaty Pedagogical University. In addition, the group included a representative from an NGO and an expert from the Ministry of Economics and Budget Planning (Department of Social Projects).

The core of the Analytical Group consisted of nationally recognized educational experts who had previously contributed to development of the *State Standard of Secondary Education* (1996–2000), used as an educational foundation by every school in Kazakhstan. The involvement of these experts was necessary to demonstrate that the reform was initiated by local experts who commanded high regard and respect among academics, professionals, and politicians nationally. The strategy was to focus on changing the thinking of "Soviet-bred" specialists by providing opportunities to learn about the latest trends in global educational development and to form professional partnerships with academics and policymakers abroad. In other words, the goal was not educational borrowing per se (that is, adopting best practices from abroad), but rather the development of basic frameworks and the creation of favorable conditions that would help policymakers to assess, understand, and address national education issues in a broader comparative context.

For two years (from November 2001 until November 2003) the Analytical Group participated in all SFK project activities, including a total of eighteen conferences, workshops, and seminars (see Table 9). Most of these were intended to develop local capacity and knowledge, necessary for initiating, formulating, and implementing curriculum reform. They included different philosophical approaches to curriculum organization, international review of curriculum policies, and the relationship between curriculum and teaching/learning, as well as techniques and approaches to reform. Furthermore, some seminars provided a broader foundation for effectively engaging in education policy processes, including skills in assessing specific policy contexts, generating policy options, evaluating policy options, making policy decisions, planning policy implementation, and assessing policy impact. In addition, members of the Analytical Group participated in workshops designed to develop their coalition-building, public speaking, and media development skills. These regular, bi-monthly training sessions were supplemented by informal working meetings (skillfully facilitated by an international consultant, Hannes Voolma) in which the group had the opportunity to translate theory into practice by developing a draft of the policy paper on curriculum reform in Kazakhstan. Members volunteered to organize presentation workshops and round tables in their own institutions to share new knowledge and skills with their colleagues in the Kazakh Academy of Education, Republican Institute of In-Service Teacher Training, and other institutions.

Table 9. An overview of project activities organized and funded by the Soros Foundation–Kazakhstan to develop local policy capacity in curriculum reform (2001–2003)

CONFERENCES	
• National Curriculum as an Instrument of Education Policy	November 2–3, 2001
• Development and Implementation of a National Curriculum in the Context of the Transition to Twelve Years of Education	February 6–10, 2002
• Outcomes-based Education: International Experience of Curriculum Reform in Basic and Secondary Education	December 5–6, 2003

A SERIES OF SEMINARS FOR EXPERTS IN CURRICULUM DEVELOPMENT THEORY AND METHODOLOGY	
• Development of National Standards in Secondary Education in the Context of a Changing World (Module 1)	March 28–31, 2002
• Development of National Standards in Secondary Education in the Context of a Changing World (Module 2)	August 15–17, 2002
• Development of National Standards in Secondary Education in the Context of a Changing World (Module 3)	June 9–11, 2003

A SERIES OF SEMINARS FOR EDUCATION EXPERTS IN DEVELOPING A LEGAL BASIS FOR THE NATIONAL CURRICULUM REFORM (LEGISLATIVE ACTS AND REGULATIONS)	
• Methods/Techniques of Developing Normative Acts to Regulate Curriculum Content in Outcomes-based Education Reform	November 20–22, 2002
• Methods/Techniques of Setting Expected Learning Outcomes in Specific Education Areas	March 5–7, 2003

CONT.

A SERIES OF SEMINARS FOR EXPERTS IN EDUCATIONAL ASSESSMENT

• Education Process as a Basis for Constructing Educational Content and Assessment System	October 18–20, 2002
• A National Assessment of Learning Achievement at the Pre-university Education Level: An Experience of Scotland	April 2–3, 2003

SEMINAR FOR TEACHERS AND SCHOOL ADMINISTRATORS

• Outcomes-based Education: Issues of Professional Development of Teachers and Schools	September 23–25, 2002

A SERIES OF SEMINARS FOR PROJECT WORKING GROUPS IN SPECIFIC EDUCATIONAL AREAS

• Perspectives of Psychological Directions in the Educational System: In Search of Cohesion	January 28, 2003
• Relationship between Education and Individual Psychological Development of a Child	February 13, 2003

WORKING SEMINARS FOR THE ANALYTICAL GROUP

• A working seminar	May 15–17, 2002
• A working seminar	June 29–30, 2002
• A working seminar	January 31–February 1, 2003

MEETINGS OF THE WORKING GROUP ESTABLISHED BY THE MINISTRY OF EDUCATION AND SCIENCE TO DEVELOP A POLICY PAPER ON SECONDARY EDUCATION STANDARDS

• A working seminar	September 2003
• A working seminar	October 2003

As a result of this intensive series of conferences, workshops, and seminars, the Analytical Group built its capacity as a new policy actor in Kazakhstan's education reform. In 2002, the group prepared a policy paper that outlined the dimensions of change and proposed a new, previously unarticulated solution for school reform—introduction of OBE in the context of the twelve-year secondary-education reform. The policy paper presented OBE as "an approach to system-wide improvement in education" that would define clear statements of expected outcomes to guide the organization of the learning process, introduce learner-centered models, professionalize the role of teachers, and increase community participation in the learning process. The group continued to work together on a regular basis, organizing public discussions, conferences, and workshops across Kazakhstan in order to disseminate and discuss the idea of OBE with a larger group of education stakeholders.

In 2003, some members of the group were included in a working group organized by the Ministry of Education and Science and made key contributions to the development of the "State Program of Education Development in the Republic of Kazakhstan for 2005–2010" and a new policy paper, "General Secondary Education Standards in the Republic of Kazakhstan: Current Situation, Exploration, Alternatives." In fact, the draft of the latter acknowledged the importance of financial and intellectual support of the SFK in the development of the draft policy document as well as the individual contributions of some members of the SFK Analytical Group. These two documents became the first policy instruments to institutionalize the idea of OBE in education legislation. The "State Program of Education Development in the Republic of Kazakhstan for 2005–2010," in particular, outlined the main principles of OBE, which included a shift from "facts-based" to "skills-based" learning, a move from "teacher-centered" to "learner-centered" education models, as well as a transition from "knowledge-acquisition" to a "systematic understanding of the world, society, and people . . . ability and desire to independently and creatively use, broaden, and deepen this understanding" (p. 28). In addition, the document underscored the importance of critical thinking, reasoning, and reflection as some of the main goals of the teaching/learning process. Finally, it introduced the idea of national education standards "oriented at student outcomes in a form of basic learner competencies" (p. 29). The draft "National Standards Concept" further elaborated these ideas and defined a concrete plan for development and implementation of OBE in Kazakhstan, including concrete activities and budget for the period from 2005 to 2010. Combined, the adoption of these policy documents signified a major reorientation of international NGOs (such as the SFK) in Kazakhstan's donor-free environment, confirming that international NGOs could continue to be active players in education reform by devising new ways of influencing local education policies.

New ways of influencing local education policies in a donor-free environment

Curriculum reform in Kazakhstan provides an interesting case study to examine how the relationship between a state and the community of international NGOs is altered once the former decides to become less dependent on foreign aid and more reliant on its own local policymaking capacity. Government officials in Kazakhstan felt pressure to adapt to international standards in education, yet were reluctant (and sometimes openly hostile) to readily accepting structural adjustment reforms imposed by international financial institutions and NGOs. Kazakhstan's government successfully curbed foreign aid in education in the wake of economic growth and attempted to gain tighter control of international and local NGOs. The underlying assumption was that reforms imposed from the outside could be harmful to Kazakhstan's education system without appropriate adaptation by local education experts.

Emerging mistrust of government officials toward internationally initiated reforms and increased state control over education reform processes forced international NGOs to devise new ways of influencing education policies and practices to carry out their missions and maintain leverage. For SFK, this meant a strategic shift from a traditional NGO role of implementing demonstration projects to a more systemic support of education reform. More precisely, SFK attempted to influence education policy in a subtler, yet equally effective way—through building local capacity in education policy assessment, analysis, formulation, and implementation.

SFK prioritized capacity building of local policymakers over the excessive use of Western education experts—a strategy that coincided with the government's aspirations. This made SFK a legitimate partner in implementing a large-scale curriculum reform at the start of the millennium.

This strategic shift—from demonstration projects to systemic reform support—provided opportunities for piloting new approaches as old development orthodoxies came under strain in Kazakhstan's donor-free environment. While many international NGOs appeared reluctant "to shed their traditional roles" and insisted on remaining "deliverers of development designed or imported from outside" (Edwards, Hulme, and Wallace 2000, 11), the strategic reorientation of SFK presented a unique case. It allowed SFK to enter the education policy arena of Kazakhstan without being accused of imposing international reforms. In particular, Kazakhstan's government welcomed the initiative, because it allowed local policymakers to engage actively in the reinterpretation, indigenization, and adaptation of international reforms. At the same time, however, local policy capacity building provided an opportunity for SFK to devise a framework for a qualitatively new process of education policymaking. This helped policymakers to assess, understand, and address national education issues in a broader international and comparative context. Against this background, government officials, policymakers, and NGOs in Kazakhstan saw the rise of the local policy capacity as an important tool for effectively repositioning their country within the international education space, while at the same time maintaining local control and ownership over national reform processes.

Notes

[1] The number of preschools was reduced by 3,667 institutions (from 5,226 to 1,558), and the number of secondary general schools fell by 590 (from 8,694 to 8,104) during the four years of the reform (ADB 2002a).

[2] In 1997, Kazakhstan was one of the first Commonwealth of Independent States countries to sign the Convention on the Recognition of Qualifications concerning Higher Education in the European Region. Ratification of this document requires general education extension with the further recognition of higher education quality. In 2004, Kazakhstan signed the Bologna

Convention, which aims "to establish a European Higher Education Area by 2010 in which students and staff can move with ease and have fair recognition of their qualifications. This overall goal is reflected in the main action lines defined in the Bologna Declaration: adoption of a system of degrees essentially based on two cycles; co-operation in quality assurance and recognition; [and] promotion of mobility" (Nyborg 2004).

References

ADB (Asian Development Bank). 2002a. *Analysis of the education reform process in the Republic of Kazakhstan: Sub-regional cooperation in managing education reforms.* Regional technical assistance report no. 5946–REG. Almaty, Kazakhstan: ADB.

————. 2002b. *Kazakhstan country strategy and program update 2003–2004.* Available online.

————. 2006. *Asian Development Bank and Kazakhstan: A 2007 factsheet.* Available online.

Bektourganov, Nuraly-Sultanovich. 2002. *Education in Kazakhstan: Stepping into the twenty-first century.* Available online.

Brautigam, Deborah. 2000. *Aid dependence and governance.* Stockholm, Sweden: Almqvist and Wiksell.

Chapman, David, John Weidman, Mark Cohen, and Malcolm Mercer. 2005. The search for quality: A five country study of national strategies to improve educational quality in Central Asia. *International Journal of Educational Development* 25(5): 514–30.

Dichter, Thomas. 2003. *Despite good intentions: Why development assistance to the Third World has failed.* Boston: University of Massachusetts Press.

Edwards, Michael, David Hulme, and Tina Wallace. 2000. Increasing leverage for development: Challenges for NGOs in a global future. In *New roles and relevance: Development NGOs and the challenge of change,* ed. David Lewis and Tina Wallace, 1–14. Bloomfield, CT: Kumarian Press.

Fisher, William. 1997. Doing good? The politics and antipolitics of NGO practices. *Annual Review of Anthropology* 26: 439–64.

Kazakhstan News Bulletin. 2005. Kazakhstan will repay $849,000,000 in loans ahead of schedule. November 29. Aavailable online.

Komkon-2 Eurasia. 2002. *Opinions of education stakeholder about the transition to twelve year education.* Almaty, Kazakhstan: SFK.

Maren, Michael. 1997. *The road to hell: The ravaging effects of foreign aid and international charity.* New York: The Free Press.

Moss, Todd, Gunilla Pettersson, and Nicolas van de Walle. 2006. *An aid-institutions paradox? A review essay on aid dependency and state building in Sub-Saharan Africa.* Working Paper no. 74. Available online.

Nazarbayev, Nursultan. 2007. Address by the president of the Republic of Kazakhstan Nursultan Nazarbayev to the people of Kazakhstan. February 28. Available online.

Nyborg, Per. 2004. The influence of the Bologna Process on reform processes in higher education in the Caucasus and Central Asia. *Twelfth OSCE Economic Forum.* Prague, Czech Republic. Available online.

OECD. 2007. *International development statistics.* Available online.

OSI (Open Society Institute). 1999. *Education sub-board network education strategy paper.* Budapest, Hungary: IEP/OSI.

Ovcharenko, Vsevolod. 2006. Government financing of NGOs in Kazakhstan: Overview of a controversial experience. *The International Journal of Not-for-Profit Law* 8(4). Available online.

Samoff, Joel. 1999. Education sector analysis in Africa: Limited national control and even less national ownership. *International Journal of Educational Development* 19(4/5): 249–72.

Seddon, Terri. 2005. The global encounter: Kazakhstan. Course materials. Available online.

Semikina, Yulya. 2001. The twelfth floor. *Kontingent* 15(53): 1–4.

Steiner-Khamsi, Gita, Iveta Silova, and Eric Johnson. 2006. Neo-liberalism liberally applied: Educational policy borrowing in Central Asia. In *Education research and policy: Steering the knowledge-based economy*, ed. Jenny Ozga, Thomas Popkewitz, and Terri Seddon, 217–45. New York: Routledge.

UNDP. 2006. *United Nations human development report.* Available online.

World Bank. 2000. *Kazakhstan: Public expenditure review.* Vol. 2. Washington DC: World Bank.

6

A Voucher System
for Teacher Training
in Kyrgyzstan

ALEXANDER IVANOV AND VALENTIN DEICHMAN

At the turn of the millennium, OSI and the national foundations began moving from an emphasis on demonstration projects toward influencing actual education policy. The national Soros Foundations have subsequently initiated an increasing number of fundamental reforms in different parts of the former socialist region. Besides advocating for changes in the funding mechanisms in the education systems of Tajikistan and Kyrgyzstan, the Soros Foundation Network also advanced the introduction of standardized university entrance examinations in Ukraine as a means to curb corruption in higher education. These projects qualify as fundamental reforms because they have important repercussions in several areas of the education system; they have an immediate impact on student assessment, trigger curriculum reform in general education, and revamp institutional structures and cultures with immediate effect.

Changes in funding mechanisms involve some of the most far-reaching consequences for the educational system of any reform. They signal the transformation from a planned to a demand/supply-driven economy in the education sector and force government officials to share power with other stakeholders. The Soros Foundation has supported two such reforms in the Central Asia region. In Tajikistan, it was among the institutional partners, including USAID and the World Bank, that piloted student per capita financing. This replaced incremental budgeting based on instructional hours and number of classes. In Kyrgyzstan, the Soros Foundation supported the voucher-based teacher training system as part of the USAID-funded PEAKS project. Both reforms of funding mechanisms lead to less concentration of power at the central level. In the student per capita system, final decision-making authority is granted to schools. In the voucher-based teacher-training system, teachers ultimately determine which courses are offered in the following year, based on the demand for those they took the previous year.

This chapter examines one of the more ambitious pilot projects in the Issyk-Kul region *(oblast)* of Kyrgyzstan, which aimed at the introduction of a voucher-based teacher-training system. We investigate whether the quality of in-service teacher training was improved by giving participants the option to select courses. The project was supported by the Soros Foundation–Kyrgyzstan and PEAKS. It acted as one of the consortium partners along with the Academy of Educational Development, Save the Children UK, Save the Children US, and Abt Associates. The Foundation for Support of Educational Initiatives, a Kyrgyz NGO based in Bishkek, was selected as the project implementation agency. Vouchers were distributed to teachers, and for the first time they were able to choose not only courses but also training providers. As simple as this may sound, the introduction of vouchers triggered a landslide of reforms that could be called revolutionary. As a result, government-sponsored teacher-training institutes lost their monopoly and had to compete with other training providers. They were also forced to share their budget with NGOs. Enrollment in in-service teacher training soared the first year the voucher system was introduced (in 2005). As this chapter demonstrates, when teachers are given a choice, they enroll in courses that are relevant for their work.

Antecedents of the pilot project

The pilot was designed as a two-year project, starting in 2005 and ending in 2007. Preparations began in 2003, and in the following two years voucher-based teacher-training systems in other countries were studied, conferences were organized, and working groups were set up to explore possibilities for implementing a pilot in Kyrgyzstan. As part of the preparatory phase a study tour to Samara, Russian Federation, was organized to evaluate the voucher-based teacher-training system that had been in place since 1997. In 2003, the Foundation for Support of Educational Initiatives organized—jointly with the Soros Foundation–Kyrgyzstan—the international New School–New Teacher conference (Deichman 2006; Foundation for Support of Educational Initiatives and Soros Foundation–Kyrgyzstan 2003). The conference presentations examined the demands placed on teachers in light of ongoing educational reforms. A few presenters reported on their qualitative research on the professional development of teachers or, more accurately, the lack thereof. They ultimately generated a consensus on the need to reform in-service teacher training (Foundation for Support of Educational Initiatives and Soros Foundation–Kyrgyzstan, 2003). Another outcome of the conference was a commitment to lifelong learning for teachers. Rather than allowing teachers to participate in extensive in-service courses for five years, an agreement was reached that teachers should be eligible to attend shorter professional-development courses annually throughout their careers.

During the preparatory phase in 2004, the Issyk-Kul *oblast* was selected as a pilot site, because it satisfied the following three conditions: First, the request for reform originated locally; second, political actors offered support; and third, the resources existed for implementation (PEAKS 2006a). Schools themselves had pressured the educational authorities to increase the supply of in-service training in the Issyk-Kul *oblast*, and 20 percent of the seventy-five hundred teachers in the region were to receive in-service training. However, at the time the pilot started, the regional teacher-training institute was only able to provide courses for approximately 9 percent (seven hundred) teachers per year. Of all other *oblasts* that were screened during the pilot selection process, the Issyk-Kul Department of Education demonstrated an unambiguous political willingness to change the current system of in-service teacher training. Moreover, it was determined that the staff in the Department of Education of Issyk-Kul *oblast* had the capacity, provided it received some additional training, to implement the pilot project (Foundation for Support of Educational Initiatives 2005).

The pilot project departed in significant ways from more common strategies that NGOs, including Soros Foundation–Kyrgyzstan, typically choose. The project was not designed as an incubator that was first tested outside of existing government structures and then later mainstreamed or institutionalized. The integration into existing government structures was from the onset a key feature of the project design and constituted a condition that was clearly stated to the Department of Education of Issyk-Kul. The department complied by issuing an order *(prikaz)* that obliged departments of education at the district level *(rayon)* to support the participation of teachers in the voucher-based training program and to grant them all necessary assistance. The district-level departments of education also signed an agreement in which they consented to providing training facilities free of charge and to cover transportation costs for teachers. Furthermore, it was agreed that PEAKS would fund the voucher system in the first project year (2005–6) and then hand over the financing of the pilot to the Department of Education in the second, when the Department of Education of Issyk-Kul *oblast* would assume full responsibility for financing in-service teacher training through the voucher-funding mechanism.

The ailing professional–development system in the post–Soviet era

The post-Soviet professional-development system had been crumbling for over a decade without real alternatives to replace it. Teachers flocked to courses offered by NGOs, but these were not integrated into the ailing government-sponsored system. There was little contact, and even less overlap, between what the NGOs and the government-sponsored courses had to offer. The NGOs focused on teaching methodology (interactive methods, student-centered methods), whereas the government-sponsored courses exclusively emphasized broad and outdated content knowledge. The NGOs prepared teachers to serve as trainers, whereas the government-sponsored courses were taught by university professors and educational authorities, often far removed from pedagogical practice. The voucher-based training system attempted to merge them into one reformed system by opening the door to nongovernmental training providers. These trainers would, for the first time, not offer their courses in their own facilities or in partner schools but in government-sponsored teacher-training institutes.

Timing was essential to the merger. Over the years Soros Foundation–Kyrgyzstan, Save the Children UK, Save the Children US, and other NGOs had recruited and prepared a sufficiently large cadre of trainers with national reputations. They were accredited teacher trainers, recognized both by the NGOs themselves and by the Ministry of Education. Meanwhile, the innovation gap between the NGO-sponsored and the government-sponsored courses increased to the extent that teachers became unmotivated to participate in the latter. The NGOs, in turn, recognized that their programs in effect substituted for, rather than reformed, the existing structure. The substitution was particularly expensive for the largest professional-development provider, the Soros Foundation– Kyrgyzstan, and was not, in the long run, financially sustainable. New training capacity had been built, but a population of dissatisfied teachers had been produced. The need for substantial finance to sustain innovative professional-development courses was obvious. This provided a window of opportunity for piloting a new teacher-training system in close cooperation with the Ministry of Education.

However, numerous problems had to be dealt with. First, the content and methods presented in professional-development courses lagged drastically behind the innovative practices implemented in schools. It was important for the pilot project to transfer the experience of innovation-minded teachers into the professional development of regular teachers. Second, what was taught in the courses did not correspond to the curricular changes made at the central level. In fact, few teachers knew about the changes that donor after donor had demanded—and the Kyrgyz Academy of Education had finally carried out, with funding from the ADB. Arguably, many of the standards introduced were too limited, vague, or abstract to affect pedagogical practice. Teachers learned not to bother with what was changed on paper and continued to rely on outdated, hand-copied lessons plans *(programma)* that included examples of exam questions. Students and parents were equally assessment driven and bought exam questions, compiled in a book, on the open market. Learning to pass the test, with the help of private tutors if necessary, was seen as the most effective strategy for making it through school. Third, the nationwide apparatus for in-service teacher training was too expensive to preserve and had ceased to operate fully in several regions. A great bulk of the funding was devoted to upgrading and rehabilitating infrastructure at teacher-training institutes, leaving little for actual training. Fourth, the few remaining teacher-training institutes were vertically organized, if at all, and therefore only accountable to themselves. The regional teacher-training institutes, also referred to as teachers' upgrading institutes, only have to pass on statistical information on enrollment to the Kyrgyz Academy of Education in the capital. They have little incentive to evaluate the quality of their courses, let alone improve their course program based on feedback from participants.

Finally, the teaching profession has become increasingly unattractive over the past decade and a half. The salary of teachers is too low, and it is customary for teachers to take on additional courses or engage in other activities (such as sales, farming, or animal husbandry) to earn extra money. There is a serious teacher shortage in Kyrgyzstan, and the Ministry of Education struggles to attract and retain teachers. Less than 20 percent of education graduates end up teaching in a classroom. A series of emergency programs were launched, such as paying an additional monthly stipend for new teachers, to lure graduates into teaching. Despite these difficult working conditions, teachers are the ones who implement reforms, decided at central level, funded by international donors, and then handed over to schools. Teachers are frustrated by the enormous demands of students, parents, and administrators in an era of change for which they do not feel prepared.

The voucher system in practice

An intensive search for teacher trainers began in the second half of 2004. An inventory of existing providers was prepared, and quality criteria were established to select carefully among those eligible. The project team distributed a call for proposals to organizations that had a track record in professional development of teachers. The providers had to have programs in place that lasted thirty-six hours, or seventy-two if the courses were intensive. They also had to agree to conduct training outside the capital, in Issyk-Kul *oblast*. The call for proposals yielded an unprecedented response in the education and NGO communities. Of the numerous proposals submitted, fourteen providers, offering a total of thirty-nine different training programs, successfully passed review and were contracted under the voucher scheme. Among the fourteen selected providers were two that, with funding from the PEAKS project, functioned as Professional Development Schools. They offered school-based training to teachers from surrounding schools, and the project team was particularly pleased that they were included. By the end of 2004 the providers were prepared to deliver courses. A second call for proposals was issued at the end of the first project year, enabling new organizations to join the group.

Publicizing the newly introduced voucher system was an important task during the preparatory phase. Seminars and round-table discussions were held, and promotional material was printed to ensure that each and every teacher in the Issyk-Kul *oblast* was informed. The marketing campaign attempted to ensure that teachers were not only aware but also assured of their right to select professional-development courses. After all, the success of the pilot project relied on teachers actually making a choice and enrolling. More pragmatically, the project team needed to ensure that teachers would understand what the piece of paper—the voucher—they were to receive the following year would entitle them to. Part of the campaign was to explain that each voucher represented a monetary value that would be redeemed by the training provider.

Implementation began in 2005 with the distribution of vouchers to 2,456 teachers, based in 183 different schools, in five districts *(rayons)* and two towns throughout the *oblast* (PEAKS 2006b). Each voucher was divided into two blocks of thirty-six academic hours each, allowing teachers to choose either two short courses or one seventy-two-hour intensive course. Once the teacher decided on a course and redeemed the voucher, providers submitted the vouchers to receive payment. Of the 2,546 vouchers that were distributed, 1,672 were redeemed; that is, two-thirds of all teachers in the Issyk-Kul *oblast* had taken the opportunity to enroll in professional-development courses. In the first project year, 63 percent enrolled in courses organized by the government-sponsored regional teacher-training institute, 7 percent enrolled in courses offered by the two professional-development schools, and 30 percent registered for courses provided by NGOs (PEAKS 2006a).

Minor glitches occurred during the first project year. For example, providers lacked funds to make themselves known to teachers. The Soros Foundation–Kyrgyzstan remedied this problem by granting seed money (up to US$200) to cover start-up costs, such as advertising and marketing materials, to attract teachers. Another issue was the sequencing of payment. The voucher mechanism implied that providers would only be reimbursed for their services after submitting the list of participants. Most providers, however, were not able to work on a reimbursement basis. PEAKS resolved this issue by agreeing to a 50 percent advance payment for providers of courses that attracted twenty-five teachers or more. The need for advance payments became obsolete in the second project year, when providers had built sufficient reserves to function on a reimbursement basis.

Evaluation of the voucher scheme

The pilot project was continuously monitored and annually assessed by teams of Kyrgyz and international evaluators. In fact, only 183 of 192 schools received vouchers during the first project year. The remaining nine schools in Issyk-Kul *oblast* were used as a control group and only included in 2006. The findings from the first annual evaluation were used to improve the design of the voucher-based system in the second year. The formative evaluation after the first year, coordinated by Saule Hamzina and conducted by a team of Kyrgyz evaluation experts, gathered statistical information and used qualitative methods (individual interviews, focus-group interviews, document analyses, lesson observations) to assess the impact of the voucher scheme on project beneficiaries, as well as to assemble the opinions of beneficiaries and stakeholders (Hamzina et al. 2006). Approximately three hundred teachers and administrators were interviewed. The project beneficiaries, that is, the training participants, scored the organization of the training as 4.6 on a scale of 1 to 5, with 1 lowest and 5 highest. They found courses with an interactive approach particularly invaluable. Despite the agreement reached with the Department of Education of Issyk-Kul *oblast,* teachers ended up paying for transportation and accommodations themselves. Despite these aggravating circumstances, non-attendance of registered teachers or absences during training sessions—common problems in government-sponsored courses—rarely occurred.

The formative evaluation after the first project year revealed several problems. Despite the comprehensive marketing campaign, many school principals and deputy principals exerted control over the vouchers and coerced teachers into registering for specific courses. A substantial number of teachers reported in the evaluation that they were not able to choose courses freely but had to comply with the choice of their administrators. The manipulation of teachers was discernible on the voucher forms. The project team received vouchers from schools in the same handwriting, while on other vouchers the names of providers or titles of courses the teacher had chosen were crossed out and replaced with different names and titles. Despite these initial problems, over 70 percent of respondents stated that the courses offered under the voucher scheme were more useful than the ones they had previously experienced.

Challenges

Changes in funding mechanisms are influential and comprehensive. They set in motion a whole range of far-reaching changes that some support in principle and that others, for political reasons, oppose. Observers are rarely neutral. Opinions are heatedly expressed, and camps are quickly formed. The pilot project was immediately situated in the larger controversy over whether market forces, such as demand/supply-driven provision of teacher training, should ever enter the sphere of education. Even though there is consensus concerning the inefficiency of the centrally organized, post-Soviet bureaucratic apparatus, few dare to suggest, much less implement, an alternative that would help erode central-level authority.

Besides these principled views on the market mechanism, manifested in voucher models, there were also other challenges the pilot project had to face. Many are endemic to educational reform in Kyrgyzstan in general and by no means restricted to the voucher scheme alone. One of the stakeholders that took a principled approach and rejected the voucher-based teacher-training system was the Trade Union of Teachers of Issyk-Kul *oblast.* The union labeled the voucher scheme "omnivorous" and "consumptive," and accused government officials of bending to the pressure of an international organization, rubber-stamping whatever was presented to them by foreigners.

Political changes and constant replacement of senior-level government officials are recurring themes in Kyrgyzstan, posing great challenges for cooperating with government institutions. Those at the top of the hierarchy, the ministers of education, experience rapid turnover. In the past five years alone the country has seen four ministers of education come and go. Rarely does a minister of education stay in office longer than a year. This has tremendous repercussions for agreements made with government institutions. With every change in decision-makers, previously made arrangements must be renegotiated; standing agreements are rarely honored by successors. In other words, the memorandums of agreement become worthless every few months and need to be constantly renewed. For example, the original agreement, written in 2004, stated that PEAKS would provide 100 percent of the financing for the vouchers during the first project year. During the second project year PEAKS was prepared to cover 60 percent of the cost under the condition that the Department of Education of Issyk-Kul *oblast* fund the remaining cost. It was planned that the third year of project implementation would be completely financed by the *oblast* educational authorities. However, significant political changes occurred in the very first project year, and at the end of March 2006 PEAKS alerted the *oblast* educational authorities that it would abort the pilot project if the original agreement of cost-sharing was not honored. Finally, under public pressure to support the popular voucher pilot, the *oblast* educational authorities agreed to cover 40 percent of the cost in 2006, and 100 percent in 2007.

Continuous political and administrative turnover, however, only partly explains the reluctance of government institutions to share costs in pilot projects that have been initiated by international NGOs. In general, the Ministry of Education and its institutions at the *oblast* and *rayon* level behave passively toward international organizations. As long as funding is channeled into the education sector, there is little resistance to suggested reforms. In fact, the government of Kyrgyzstan, particularly the Ministry of Finance, views international loans and grants as important sources for tax and other types of revenue. On the surface, educational authorities comply with the suggested reforms and even offer assistance in revising policy documents and guidelines. Resistance, subversion, and negligence come at a later stage, when policies and reforms are to be implemented in practice. Against this background the agreement made in the pilot project was unprecedented. Different from other international projects, government institutions were not just spectators, receiving funds for yet another pilot project advanced by international organizations. They were expected to steer, implement, and co-fund the voucher-based reform. The goal was to break the vicious cycle of international dependency.

The pilot project visibly generated reform pressure on the Kyrgyz Academy of Education, which oversees in-service teacher training at the central level. One contested practice is the procedure for accreditation. The Kyrgyz Academy of Education had established a standard set of bureaucratic requirements in which the quality of training programs is not assessed but regarded as secondary. Formal criteria are used only to evaluate whether the training provider is entitled to be included in the voucher scheme. At the same time there is an abundance of training providers, especially in high-demand fields such as English-language teaching, that provide courses without any state license or accreditation. The current accreditation practices are nonsensical and detrimental to providing high-quality teacher training in a voucher-based scheme.

Finally, the voucher pilot also helped shed light on why there is such a lack of government funds for in-service teacher training. The budget that the Department of Education receives from the Finance Department of Issyk-Kul *oblast* is divided into two parts. Most is allocated to preserving the *oblast*-level teacher-training institute itself—building maintenance, transportation, utilities, staff salaries, and overall operational costs. Only a small portion of the budget is left for covering actual services or professional-development courses. The new funding mechanism will drastically change the distribution of teacher-training funds when, perhaps in the distant future, government-sponsored providers are only one option among many. It is questionable whether government-sponsored regional teacher-training institutes would be able to survive in an open market. Not only would they need to develop more attractive professional-development courses, but they would also have to scale up and generate sufficient income from courses to cover their sizeable infrastructure and operational costs.

The future of voucher-based training

Teachers, the beneficiaries of the voucher-based training courses, have responded enthusiastically to the changes the new system set in motion. The new financing mechanism visibly increased both the quality and the quantity of the in-service training programs offered in the Issyk-Kul *oblast* (Deichman et al. 2007; Nizovskaya, Bulgakova, and Abdumanapova 2007; Hamzina et al. 2006; Foundation for Support of Educational Initiatives 2005). As a recent cost-effectiveness study has demonstrated, the pilot project was also a financial success (Ryskeldiev 2007). Finally, the pilot project reso-nated with the donor community, and new donors have come forward and expressed interest in funding the voucher mechanism for the professional development of teachers.

Despite these overwhelmingly positive reactions to the pilot project, there is cautious optimism among the project team. The implementation of the voucher mechanism is demanding from a management perspective. It requires a capacity that the local edu-cational authorities are not able, or perhaps not willing, to provide. Used to having to deal only with school directors or government officials, local officers would now need to reorganize their work routine in fundamentally different ways. Rather than passing on orders, they would be required to coordinate and facilitate. They would have to turn the district office into a hub where all activities surrounding in-service teacher training are administered collaboratively. They would need to become the go-between for teachers, schools, and training providers. Moreover, it would be incumbent upon them to sort out the divergent interests these three groups pursue. What is required is not only a boost in managerial competence among local government officials, but also a change of attitude. Local government officials would need to believe in and act upon a new culture of cooperation and negotiation. This is easier said than done, given the long-held belief in uncontested state au-thority.

The most feasible scenario for the future is the following: Donor organizations adopt the new financing mechanism and help to imple-ment it throughout the country. The new mechanism should be scaled up and widely implemented; positive outcomes can no longer be ignored when a critical mass of teacher-training insti-tutes operates under the new financing mechanism. The pilot project in Issyk-Kul *oblast* has only begun to pave the way for a future in which teachers will determine what they need in terms of professional development, and in which government officials will have redefined themselves as coordinators and facilitators of innovative practice.

References

Deichman, Valentin. 2006. *New school: A space for opportunities.* Conference report. Bishkek: Soros Foundation–Kyrgyzstan.

Deichman, Valentin, Aleksandr Ivanov, Larisa Kiseleva. 2007. *O vvedeniie vachernogo mehanizma finansirovaniia v sistemu povisheniia kvalifikacii uchitelei: Operacionnoie rukovodstvo (Introduction of voucher financing mechanism into the in-service teacher-training system: Operational guidelines).* Bishkek, Kyrgyzstan: Printing House Maxprint.

Foundation for Support of Educational Initiatives. 2005. Narrative report on progress of implementation of the voucher scheme in the in-service teacher-training system in Issyk-Kul oblast. Bishkek: Foundation for Support of Educational Initiatives.

Foundation for Support of Educational Initiatives and Soros Foundation–Kyrgyzstan. 2003. *Proceedings of the international conference "New School—New Teacher."* Vols. 1–2. Bishkek: Foundation for Support of Educational Initiatives and Soros Foundation–Kyrgzstan.

Hamzina, Saule, Yuliya Aleshkina, Ulan Jumashev, Jyldyz Kerimbekova, and Vladilina Terehova. 2006. Otchet o promezhutochnoi ocenke projekta vnedreniia vauchernogo mehanizma finansirovniia sistemi povisheniia kvalifikacii uchitelei (Formative evaluation of the project focused on the implementation of voucher financing mechanism in the in-service teacher-training system). Available in Russian at the educasia.net website.

Nizovskaya, Irina, Evgenija Bulgakova, and Zuhra Abdumanapova. 2007. Otchet po itogovoi ocenke projekta vnedreniia vauchernogo mehanizma finansirovaniia sistemi povisheniia kvalifikacii uchitelei (Final evaluation report of the project focused on the implementation of voucher financing mechanism in the in-service teacher-training system). Available in Russian at the educasia.net website.

PEAKS (Participation, Education, and Knowledge Strengthening). 2006a. Attachment 4: Pilot teacher-training voucher system in Issyk-Kul Oblast. Background information. Bishkek: PEAKS Office.

———. 2006b. Attachment 5: Interim assessment survey of the voucher pilot implementation in 2005. Bishkek: PEAKS Office.

Ryskeldiev, Ulan. 2007. Finansoviie aspektov projekta vnedreniia vauchernogo mehanizma finansirovaniia sistemi povisheniia kvalifikacii uchitelei (Financial aspects of implementing voucher-based system of financing of in-service teacher-training). Available in Russian at the educasia.net website.

7

Circulating "Best Practices" in Mongolia

Natsagdorj Enkhtuya

Many observers have marveled at how reforms travel across national boundaries. Their worldwide proliferation has provoked the question of whether the diffusion of student-centered teaching, vouchers in teacher education, privatization in higher education, and other reforms should be interpreted as signs of globalization in education (see Steiner-Khamsi and Stolpe 2006). However, though there is an emergent body of research on traveling reforms, little has been written on reforms that circulate within a single country.

How should we interpret the circulation of best practices among institutions in one country? Is the handover from one NGO to another yet another indicator that there is a global consensus on how to run projects effectively? Or is it the local context that matters—institutions, experts, and stakeholders—who advance the same kinds of projects? This chapter deals specifically with cross-institutional borrowing, which is the transfer of so-called best practices from one institution to another. Cross-institutional borrowing seems to run counter to organizational theory, wherein every institution attempts to differentiate itself from competitors, if for no other reason than to establish its own visibility, credibility, and legitimacy. As this chapter demonstrates, there are close personal and institutional ties among educational development organizations in Mongolia, and cross-institutional borrowing is more the rule than the exception.

This chapter presents several features of the project School 2001, originally designed, funded, and implemented by the Mongolian

Foundation for Open Society (MFOS), and later adopted by others. Several project features of School 2001 (such as the notions of school adoption and peer mentoring/training) were subsequently borrowed by other institutions, including DANIDA in 2000; the Ministry of Education, Culture, and Science (MOECS) in 2002; and the World Bank in 2006. DANIDA and the World Bank succeeded in implementing the features of school adoption and peer mentoring/training in their respective projects: the Rural School Development Project (RSDP), funded by DANIDA, and in the Rural Education and Development project (READ), funded by the World Bank.

From global network programs to locally developed projects

From 1998 to 2001, MFOS implemented the School 2001 project, an in-service training program that involved seventy-two schools. School 2001 was considered a large project in a country with a small population size (2.5 million) and a total of approximately six hundred schools. This meant that one out of every eight schools was directly involved in the project. School 2001 was considered unique within the OSI network, the context of in-service training providers, and reform in Mongolia. Within OSI, it marked a departure from an exclusive focus on network programs developed centrally in the OSI-NY office, to an emphasis on local development, monitoring, and evaluation. Within the context of in-service training providers in Mongolia, it emphasized student-centered learning and also pioneered a particular reform strategy that was practitioner driven, emphasizing project ownership, peer training, and peer mentoring. In particular, the "school adoption" reform strategy, whereby practitioners from partner schools mentor and train teachers at the new partner schools as well as surrounding schools was viewed as an effective and sustainable teacher-development strategy. Finally, within the overall reform context in Mongolia, School 2001 attempted to give voice to practitioners and empower them to participate in the ongoing standards-based curriculum reform that the Ministry of Education had launched in 1998 with minimal input from schools.

As discussed in Chapter 1, there have been three distinct phases—strategic, conceptual, and organizational development—within OSI and its national foundations. Each has had a major influence on education programming. In Mongolia, these strategic shifts included moving from implementation of the centrally designed global network programs, to locally designed educational development programs (referred to as mega projects), to prioritizing advocacy and policy think-tank projects. (For an overview of the three organizational stages in Mongolia's national foundation, see Table 10).

During the first organizational stage (the stage of global network programs), OSI-NY consulted with international consultants to develop RWCT, Debate, and SbS. OSI-NY also offered these programs as comprehensive training packages to all national foundations of the Soros Network. The national foundations were given technical-assistance funds to adapt the packages to local contexts. MFOS adopted several network education programs, including the early childhood development program SbS, the youth program Debate, the civic-education project Street Law, the school program RWCT, and the English-language program. For example, SbS introduced child-centered methodology and enforced the creation of a developmentally appropriate learning environment for pre- and primary-school students. The Debate program was implemented at both secondary school and university levels, encouraging open discussion and public dialogue among youth and adolescents. The RWCT project emphasized student-centered and cooperative-teaching methods.

In the early stage these network programs were administered by the Children and Youth programs in the OSI-NY and then handed over to international professional associations. The network programs in education typically consisted of a set of attractive training modules, useful teaching materials, and rigorous training standards developed by American and European experts. The modular training ensured that the quality of professional-development courses was sustained over time and that courses were offered exclusively by trainers who had been certified by OSI or, later, by international professional associations overseeing these programs. Since 2004, when MFOS ceased to exist and the education programs of MFOS were spun off, they have been administered by the newly founded NGO Mongolian Education Alliance (MEA).

The mega projects, which marked the second stage of OSI educational programs, were different from the global network programs, which originated in New York and were closely monitored by the

Table 10. Organizational stages of OSI projects in Mongolia

DURATION IN MONGOLIA	PROJECTS IN MONGOLIA	DEVELOPMENT AND IMPLEMENTATION
GLOBAL NETWORK PROGRAMS (in over thirty countries)		
1996 onward	English Language Program RWCT SbS Debate Grants for School Program Education Advising Centers Street Law National Scholarship, etc.	Developed and monitored by the OSI-NY office, disseminated to all national OSI foundations, and locally adapted *Implementation:* 1996–2004 MFOS; 2004 onward MEA
MEGA PROJECTS (in five countries only)		
1998–2001	School 2001	Developed in-country and monitored by the OSI-Budapest office's Education Support Program *Implementation:* 1998–2001 MFOS; 2004 onward network of schools and follow-up activities coordinated by MEA
EDUCATION POLICY CENTERS (in over thirty countries)		
2004 onward	Advocacy and public awareness projects with an emphasis on governance issues (transparency, freedom of information, media coverage of elections, campaign financing, ethnical norms of politicians, etc.), economic issues (shadow economy, nomadic pastoralism, economic freedom index, etc.), and social issues (social-sector privatization, education policy, public expenditures in education, etc.)	Partly developed in OSI-NY or OSI-Budapest; partly developed in Mongolia *Implementation:* Open Society Forum (OSF)

OSI-NY office (see Table 10). In contrast, these mega projects were initiated based on a local needs assessment and monitored in the countries of implementation. They were intended to move beyond the professional development of teachers and instead identify, and subsequently respond to, underserved areas of educational reform. The term *mega project* refers to the volume of the budget and design and to the fact that these projects typically have several components. The Mongolian mega project School 2001, for example, began with sixteen project components (professional development of teachers, textbook development, educational TV, mobile libraries, newsletter, computer literacy, grants for schools, and so forth), which were reduced to eleven after one year. The original budget for School 2001 was US$1 million per year over a three-year period, but the actual expenses amounted to $US1.5 million.

Naturally, there was close cooperation between School 2001 and the network programs—SbS, RWCT, and Debate in particular. This is unsurprising, given that the same office administered both programs. School 2001 was the first nationwide project with coordinators in all six regions of the country and the capital, Ulaanbaatar. The School 2001 administrative staff helped the networks disseminate their training programs to the provinces, and the trainers from the network programs, in return, were used in the partner schools of School 2001 as trainers and mentors. School 2001 viewed itself as a school-based reform movement. It attempted to support bottom-up curriculum reform; that is, practitioners, rather than government officials and university professors, developed standards-based curricula for language subjects (Mongolian, Russian, English), history, geography, arts, and social sciences. In retrospect, however, the curriculum reform was led by the ministry, and input by practitioners was minimal. Only a few methodologists and trainers from School 2001 were invited to participate in the curriculum reform of 2002. However, though the effect on policy and curriculum reform was clearly limited, School 2001 has had an enormous impact on educational practice in preschools, schools, and universities.

OSI changed its strategy at the turn of the millennium. During the third phase, OSI funded the establishment of education policy centers and began to invest in direct policy support and advocacy work both in the United States and overseas. In Mongolia, the Open Society Forum (the successor to the MFOS) now acts as a policy center for issues related to the public, finance, and social sectors—

including education. Currently, the contours of a fourth stage are increasingly visible. OSI has started to direct its attention to educational initiatives in countries outside its traditional post-socialist region, and now funds projects in Africa, Central and Latin America, and West and Southeast Asia. This fourth stage has had repercussions for Mongolian NGOs. Though they initially received funding from OSI, they are now required to generate income on their own or seek funding from other donors.

The three different types of reform strategies or educational programs—global network, national development, social-sector policy—reflect various stages of organizational development within OSI. All three types of programs exist side by side in Mongolia. The educational programs, including network programs, are administered by the Mongolian Education Alliance. Meanwhile, the Open Society Forum coordinates advocacy and policy work in the social sector, including in education.

The School 2001 reform strategy

The two prominent features of School 2001 that were subsequently borrowed by other institutions in Mongolia were (1) school adoption and (2) horizontal support and mentoring (see Erdenejargal, Enkhtuya, and Steiner-Khamsi 2002).

School adoption

One of the two key characteristics of the School 2001 reform strategy was school adoption, a staggered model of partnership in which the number of schools joining the project increases over time. In each partner school, a core team participated in School 2001 training workshops and prepared to train and mentor their peers at the school level and at neighboring schools. The core teams consisted of the principal, a head teacher (assistant principal), and three teachers (from the social-sciences and humanities departments). In the first year core teams were recruited from schools as well as a few pre-service teacher-training institutions. Figure 1 illustrates the adoption processes over the three-year cycle.

In the first year one school adopts two schools in the same province. In the second year these two schools each adopt two new schools. In the third year the four schools each adopt two new

Figure 1. The school adoption strategy in School 2001

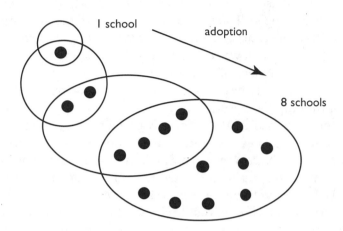

schools. The network of adopter and adopted schools remains intact over the three-year period, so that the schools continue to co-operate closely with one another (see Table 11).

Table 11. School 2001 Partner Schools

SCHOOL 2001 PARTNER SCHOOLS, PROJECT YEARS 1–3	
Year 1 (September 1998–June 1999)	19 partner schools
Year 2 (September 1999–June 2000)	39 partner schools
Year 3 (September 2000–June 2001)	72 partner schools

Mongolia is divided administratively into twenty-one provinces *(aimags)* and the capital, Ulaanbaatar. Starting in Ulaanbaatar and six *aimags*, the project had covered every province by the second year. The number of partner schools doubled, more or less, each year, reflecting the adoption pattern. Schools that had already been enrolled as partner schools adopted, that is mentored and trained, teachers at new schools. (For the increase of School 2001 partner schools over the course of the three-year project, see Table 11).

The staggered model of school-based reform helped generate a high-level of project identification and ownership by the participating schools. Becoming a School 2001 partner school implied both privileges (access to national training workshops, funds for establishing a resource, and training center at the school) and responsibilities (school-based training at one's own school and the adoption of two other schools). The staggered approach to including project participants also helped to legitimize practitioners as experts. When School 2001 started, it was customary in Mongolia that only methodologists, government officials, or university professors offered in-service training to teachers. Teachers were not regarded as capable of training their peers.

In contrast, School 2001 deliberately promoted practitioners from year one schools to expert status in relation to practitioners who only joined the project in year two. Similarly, practitioners who joined the project during year three looked for training, mentorship, and guidance from practitioners from year one and year two schools. By the end of the second year, School 2001 was considered not simply a project that emphasized student-centered teaching and practitioner-driven curriculum development but rather a reform movement that comprised a rapidly growing number of schools. In Mongolia, the feature of school adoption was sometimes referred to as the "avalanche model," starting out with a small number and ending with numerous participating schools. Enthusiasm for the project was so great that School 2001 partner schools adopted additional schools on their own. The number of these "shadow partner schools" (Erdenejargal, Enkhtuya, and Steiner-Khamsi 2002, 21) grew significantly during the second and third project years.

Horizontal support

The project pursued a counter-hierarchical approach in order to empower practitioners. Most projects at the time trained government officials, administrators, and professors in the expectation that they would pass on what they acquired to practitioners. In School 2001 the opposite strategy was selected. Although these high-status groups were included in the project, they were not the focus. Rather, they were informed about School 2001 only to enable them to better support teachers, that is, practitioners. In the first project year, for example, principals were invited to just one national workshop, whereas the core-team teachers attended four. Also, professors of education at participating teacher-training institutions were invited to join the project only in the second and third year, after regular teachers had established their reputation as experts. Along with this horizontal approach, also referred to as peer training and peer mentoring, the School 2001 project introduced school-based training.

Similar to the other countries presented in this book, Mongolia once had a well-developed in-service teacher-training infrastructure. Each teacher was entitled to intensive professional development every five years, usually held in the capital. The socialist system of professional development collapsed in the 1990s. This was followed by a reduction in funding for in-service preparation of select teachers for the extension of the curriculum from ten to eleven years (see Steiner-Khamsi 2005). Once regular teachers were left without any professional development at all, NGOs became involved. First was DANIDA, followed by MFOS, Save the Children UK, and in the past few years other NGOs, such as World Vision. School-based teacher training was not only cheaper than bringing teachers to the capital for professional development, but also it was more sustainable because it forged a strong network of mutual support among neighboring schools. This was particularly important for schools in remote rural areas, which had difficultly accessing information and material from the provincial centers or the capital.

School 2001 was evaluated, at least twice a year, by a team of consultants from Teachers College, Columbia University, New York. Their reports, translated into Mongolian, were made available to the project participants and served as a foundation for continuous improvement in the design and implementation of the project. The evaluation report written at the end of the second project year, for example, highlighted the enormous amount of time that core teams invested (see Steiner-Khamsi et al. 2000). Core-team teachers from year one schools visited teachers in their own school or other schools an average of fifty-eight times to provide advice and mentoring on interactive and student-centered teaching methods. By June 2000, that is, the end of the second project year, 2,167 teachers in Mongolia had attended one or more workshops offered by core team teachers in School 2001 partner schools. On the average, seventy teachers from surrounding schools attended school-based training offered in School 2001 schools.

The borrowers

There is a tendency in Mongolia to extend the duration of international projects, either because they are successful or because a donor fears being accused of withholding funds from the education sector. School 2001 was designed as a three-year project—a deliberately short time span reflected in its title. Rather than doing more of the same over an extended time period, MFOS sought to convince the Ministry of Education to institutionalize a few of the features of School 2001, notably peer mentoring and peer training, as well as practitioner-driven curriculum reform. A first attempt to influence curriculum reform in 2002, funded by the ADB and administered by the MOECS, failed. The 2002 curriculum reform for the extended curriculum, from ten to eleven years, was implemented with minimal input from practitioners. It appears, however, that a new curriculum reform of 2007 has explicitly requested practitioner input. It remains to be seen whether the request, put forward by the ADB and MOECS in 2007, actually materializes. In contrast to resistance to the advocacy for more practitioner input in curriculum reform, prescribed by School 2001, the demand for peer mentoring and peer training, organized at school level, found great resonance among government institutions and international organizations. Receptivity to school-based professional development is most likely grounded in the recognition that such training is more cost effective and sustainable than centralized or regional in-service teacher training.

The MOECS was first to embrace the feature of horizontal support and school adoption promoted by School 2001. At a donor meeting held in Paris, May 15–16, 2001, the government of Mongolia submitted a list of proposals for external assistance in the period 2001–4 (Government of Mongolia 2001). The line ministries prepared the project and technical-assistance proposals for their sectors. The proposals for the education sector were budgeted for US$56 million, US$20 million of which was requested for the reconstruction and rehabilitation of schools. One of the few proposals dealing with the quality of education was a comprehensive school-based professional-development program for teachers that MOECS chose to label "School 2004."

MOECS suggested to the donors that they continue funding School 2001, so that by the year 2004 all schools in Mongolia would be adopted, mentored, and trained by another school. The proposals put forward by the government of Mongolia were in large part disregarded by the donors, including recommendations to draw more attention to rural school development and to fund school-based professional development throughout the country. School 2004 was not realized. The concepts of school adoption and horizontal support, however, were later successfully implemented by DANIDA and the World Bank.

DANIDA was the first donor in the early transition period to focus on the professional development of teachers, particularly in rural schools. From 1992 until 1999, DANIDA strengthened primary schools in rural areas that were at risk of being shut down due to dwindling enrollment and lack of funding to rehabilitate dilapidated facilities. In 2000, DANIDA took its commitment to rural school development to scale by launching the RSDP. RSDP was financed from DANIDA funds made available to a Danish-Mongolian NGO (Danish Mongolian Society) and coordinated jointly by two universities: the Mongolian State University of Education in Ulaanbaatar, and the Copenhagen International Centre for Educational Development. The first phase of RSDP lasted from 2000 to 2004, and involved forty rural schools. The second phase began in 2004 and will end in 2008 (Jadamba and Baltzerson 2005).

There are a few similarities between the RSDP and School 2001 that deserve special mention. RSDP applies a cascade model similar to School 2001. It trains a core team of practitioners at each partner school, who, in turn, mentor and train their peers in their own and at neighboring schools. The second round of partner schools, enrolled in 2005, were paired with the first round of partner schools that had been involved since 2000. The schools from the first phase act as mentors or adopters of the schools from the second phase. Both core features of School 2001, school adoption and horizontal support, are to some extent discernible in RSDP, funded by DANIDA. Naturally, there are also many differences between the two projects, mostly because they cater to different target groups. For example, RSDP exclusively targets schools in remote rural areas. In contrast, School 2001 typically selected the best-performing schools in urban, semi-urban, and rural areas and prepared them to become in-service and resource centers for the surrounding schools. RSDP also emphasizes, to a much greater extent than School 2001, community involvement and, among other activities, attempts to revitalize the dormant school councils. Despite the differences between RSDP and School 2001, there are sufficient similarities in the professional-development component to suggest that cross-institutional borrowing actually occurred.

The READ project explicitly draws from project features that were successfully implemented in School 2001. READ, a project of MOECS, is financed by a grant from the World Bank and is implemented by MEA. It began in January 2007 and will end in January 2009. The project emphasizes literacy for six to eleven year olds and provides books for participating classrooms. MEA is the same NGO that also sustains the network of former School 2001 schools, and it is able to build on experiences and the network of trainers prepared in these schools. Naturally, there are differences between School 2001 and READ, such as a greater emphasis on parental involvement, a focus on primary schools in rural areas, and a large allocation of project funds to purchase books for children. By the end of the project, every primary school class in 393 rural schools will have a classroom library. A classroom library consists of 160 books. Some are Mongolian children's books; others are translations of books published elsewhere. Project ownership is a key feature of READ. For example, school children from ages six to eleven are included in the management and maintenance of the classroom libraries; they take turns serving as assistant librarians.

The most prominent features of READ—school adoption, and horizontal support—have been borrowed from the School 2001 design. The project started in five *aimags* and by September 2007 operated in all *aimags*. By the end of the project, a total of 393 schools in rural districts and villages (*soum*-centers and *bagh*-centers) will have been included in this project. Based on previously positive experiences with school networking and school-based training, READ advances training and mentoring by practitioners in the form of peer training and peer mentoring. In each *aimag* an initial school is selected, along with five core schools. The five core schools in each *aimag* train and mentor their surrounding schools, called cluster schools. These networks of schools, consisting of one core school and up to six surrounding cluster schools, are expected to cooperate closely with one another. Teachers assist one another

Figure 2. Networking of schools in READ

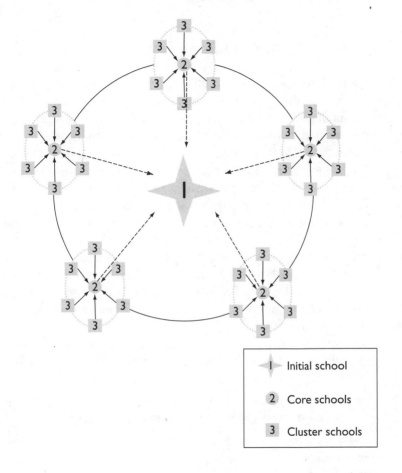

	Initial school
2	Core schools
3	Cluster schools

in training and mentoring on issues related to promoting literacy. Figure 2 illustrates the relationship between initial schools, core schools, and cluster schools.

The duration of the READ project is only twenty-four months, too short to implement adoption cycles fully. Therefore, stable networks with one initial school, five core schools, and four to six cluster schools per core school have been established. These networks last for the duration of the project. The initial schools act as a "school adopter," responsible for mentoring and training core schools. The core schools, in turn, adopt cluster schools. Well aware of the downfalls of cascade models in professional development,

READ preserves and strengthens the networks of schools throughout the project.

More than a cascade

The two key features of School 2001, school adoption and horizontal support, initially come across as typical of the cascade model; that is, a small group of individuals at school level (core-team members) are trained as trainers for teachers at their own school and surrounding schools. Typically, the quality of training deteriorates at each subsequent level because the training at the next level rarely extends over more than one training session. This is not the case with School 2001 for two specific reasons: institutional agreements were made between schools, and their network activities were funded by the project. Thus, a great bulk of the School 2001 budget was earmarked for transportation and accommodation, enabling the networked schools to visit and support one another in their reform initiatives. In fact, School 2001 explicitly distanced itself from the cascade model of professional development used in government structures.

In the government-sponsored in-service teacher training (see Figure 3), there are three cascades: a university professor teaches

Figure 3. The cascade model
of government-sponsored in-service training

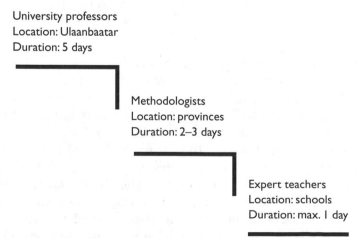

University professors
Location: Ulaanbaatar
Duration: 5 days

Methodologists
Location: provinces
Duration: 2–3 days

Expert teachers
Location: schools
Duration: max. 1 day

five-day workshops in the capital, Ulaanbaatar, in which method-ologists, hired by the provincial education authorities (education and culture departments), participate. Upon completion of their training in Ulaanbaatar, the methodologists return to their prov-inces and offer an abbreviated version of the training (two to three days) to expert teachers from schools, typically department heads or leaders of the methodology units at the school level. Upon re-turn from the province-level workshops, these expert teachers, in turn, train regular teachers at their schools. In practice, the third cascade—training regular teachers by expert teachers—is rarely implemented or ends up being merely an information session on what the expert teachers learned in the province-level professional-development workshops.

Cascade models are common and, with good reason, heavily criti-cized (see Wedell 2005). The trainers (methodologists, expert teach-ers) receive relatively brief input that they are then supposed to pass on to project participants at the next level. As a corollary, the more cascades that exist, the shorter the workshops become. Train-ers are not learning to develop their own training program but simply replicate what they have acquired in an abbreviated fash-ion. The quality of the training deteriorates with each cascade that is added. To make things worse, government-sponsored mod-els use trainers in the first and second cascade who are far re-moved from educational practice. By the time expert teachers participate in workshops, all pedagogical content has evaporated, replaced with extremely broad and abstract ideas on core prin-ciples of education; the relation between education and social, political, and economic change; and the role of the educated citi-zen in today's Mongolia.

The professional-development programs implemented by NGOs, such as RSDP and READ, and the workshops offered by UNICEF, Save the Children UK, and World Vision, are quite different from the government-sponsored in-service training. It has become a well-established practice among NGOs to prepare and certify practitio-ners as trainers. In some of the NGO-sponsored programs, notably in the programs coordinated by the MEA, a rigorous certification procedure was put in place for practitioners who became trainers in SbS, RWCT, and School 2001. The certification program for fu-ture trainers includes extensive exposure to professional develop-ment, class observations, model lessons, model training, and continuous feedback and mentoring by experienced trainers. In School 2001, for example, certified trainers participated in up to twenty workshops, both as participants and as co-moderators, over a period of three years. This is in stark contrast to other professional-development programs where the future trainers attend brief sessions and are then expected to teach the acquired content to regular teachers.

Cross-institutional borrowing

Even though elements of the two key features of School 2001—school adoption and horizontal support—were borrowed by other institutions, the network of reform-minded schools continues to exist, seven years after School 2001 ended. Their experiences are included in *Open Schools,* the monthly newsletter that the MEA disseminates throughout the country. Those teachers from School 2001, RWCT, and SbS partner schools who became certified as trainers continue to offer professional-development workshops. They are hired as part-time trainers, mostly by NGOs, but also by provincial education authorities and universities. Both RSDP and READ have included a few of the former School 2001 partner schools in their projects, thereby revitalizing the network.

To reiterate the question that was raised in the introductory section of the chapter: How should we interpret the circulation of "best practices" among NGOs in one country (in this case Mongolia)? Three explanations are the most plausible: (1) early actors in the NGO sector set a standard of best practices that subsequent donors and implementers adopted in order to gain support from, and access to, an already established network of innovative schools or forces; (2) referring to successful reform strategies, applied in Mongolia or elsewhere, helps an organization secure funding for its own operations; and (3) there is a tight network of innovators in the educational development sector, a "personnel union" of sorts among Mongolian NGOs.

First, projects do something to the community they target. For better or for worse, projects rarely have no effect at all. As mentioned earlier, NGOs in Mongolia filled the vacuum in in-service teacher training that resulted from a lack of government funds for the professional development of regular teachers. They supplied the educational system with their own content and methods, materials, and international trainers. As opposed to government-sponsored in-service training, the NGOs prepared practitioners to serve as trainers and mentors (horizontal support). Moreover, the NGOs pursued training strategies they deemed sustainable; networking surrounding schools and introducing school-based training were not only seen as more cost effective, but also as more sustainable than professional development offered at the central or regional level.

What teachers expect from professional-development courses became visibly influenced by their experiences with NGO-sponsored training. Teachers raised their standards and demanded that government-sponsored programs be more pedagogical, interactive, and relevant. Government-sponsored training was heavily criticized for presenting lecture-style workshops on broad educational concepts that have little relevance for practice. The fact that the workshops—or rather, conferences—were held for audiences of one hundred to two hundred teachers, brought them under attack for sacrificing quality for the sake of reaching as many teachers as possible. The bar for professional development was raised once a critical mass of teachers was exposed to the alternative courses offered by NGOs in Mongolia.

In other words, the NGO programs set standards for best practices and created a demand for practice-oriented professional development. This meant programs offered to small groups of participants, accompanied by peer mentoring and school visits, and preferably organized at the school level. NGOs, including OSI, sometimes apply a narrow notion of sustainability. A project is only considered successful if it is later supported by other financial sources. In the ideal-case scenario, the project is continued with government funds, or, if those are not available, with money from new donors. On the other hand, a project is considered a failure if it is not continued in some form. This definition of sustainability suffers from the short time frame that NGOs apply to situate their work, a problem common to OSI national foundations. In Mongolia, for example, MFOS was repeatedly given notice that it needed to phase out all operations in the next few years. The OSI board in New York instructed MFOS for the first time in 2000—only four years after it began operation—to start thinking of exit strategies for the year 2002. The exit was postponed for another two years, but finally happened in 2004.

Despite the external pressures that NGOs, particularly OSI national foundations faced, it is important to evaluate projects retrospectively and to assess their long-term impact on the target group. In Mongolia it was teachers who, having over the previous decade become accustomed to interactive professional-development programs offered by practice-oriented trainers at the school level, pressured MOECS to revamp its in-service training program. Additional pressure to reform in-service training was introduced by charging fees to participants, often in return for professional-development credits (issued by universities) or other forms of accreditation (issued by provincial education authorities). Thus, teachers were given a choice among different providers but had to pay for their own professional development. For the first few years teachers were motivated to pay for in-service training courses because promotions, and by default raises, were directly linked to professional development. Starting in 2006, however, teachers became disenchanted with the system of fee-based professional development. They were dissatisfied with the "product" they paid for, and they realized that professional development, promotion, and salary increases were not as closely tied together as anticipated.

Second, the idea of school networking has been recognized as a powerful tool for disseminating innovative practices in other countries in the post-socialist region. Experiences with school networking were presented at international and regional conferences, and promulgated by international consultants and regional specialists. Kyrgyzstan, Uzbekistan, and Tajikistan, for example, implemented a professional-development-school model in which, similar to School 2001, some schools served as in-service and resource centers for other schools. Positive experiences with the PEAKS project were amply shared in the OSI network, partly because OSI was (along with the Academy of Educational Development, Aga Khan Foundation, Abt Associates, and Save the Children UK) one of the consortium and implementation partners of the Central Asian PEAKS project. By comparing their experiences with projects in other parts of the region, Mongolian education experts felt reinforced by an international stamp of approval for their belief in school networking as an effective reform strategy or best practice to disseminate innovation.

Third, there is a pragmatic reason for the circulation of project features in one country: the personnel union of educational NGOs in Mongolia. There are many Mongolian experts engaged in international cooperation—perhaps only surpassed by the number of NGOs that they establish.[1] The number of experts engaged in the education sector, on the other hand, is quite small. This latter group gathers regularly at donor and NGO meetings or at government-sponsored events. Some collaborate closely for the duration of a project or serve permanently on each other's advisory boards or boards of experts. Since there are only a few Mongolian NGOs that have the capacity, with regard to language and skills, to collaborate internationally, competition is replaced by close collaboration. The situation could change rapidly if external assistance to Mongolia were reduced or the number of NGOs working in the education sector mushroomed. It is the same handful of Mongolian experts, directly involved in either the design, implementation, or monitoring of School 2001, who also borrowed elements of the two main features for new projects funded from other sources, notably RSDP and READ.

It would be wrong to assume that international donors imposed the concepts of school adoption and horizontal support. School 2001 was established as one of the five mega projects, which implied that it had to be based on a thorough needs assessment and designed locally. This is not to mitigate the important role that international donors play in sustaining local initiatives. The ability to continue the network of innovative schools over a period of ten years has depended to a great extent on financial resources from various sources or, to put it differently, on cross-institutional borrowing. What is proposed here is quite different from Ruth Mandel's assessment in Kazakhstan, Kyrgyzstan, and Uzbekistan where, according to Mandel, NGOs purposefully distance and differentiate themselves. She sees this competition as a survival strategy, reflecting attempts by NGOs to create their own niche in a huge field of externally funded projects. Each NGO establishes its own profile, expertise, and network, for which it subsequently seeks funding from international donors (Mandel 2002). Mandel's assessment is not reflected in Mongolia. Even though NGOs compete for the same sources of international funding, they don't do it by creating their own distinct reform strategies. Rather, they learn or borrow best practices from one another in order to make the case that the proposed reform strategy has proven successful. The three reasons discussed above account for the fact that in Mongolia the best practices of one NGO continue to circulate with the support of funding secured by other NGOs.

Note

[1] There are more than five thousand NGOs in Mongolia. However, only approximately 5 percent work exclusively in the education sector. Many of them are donor-oriented NGOs (DONDOs); this means they exist only on paper and become active if and when they are able to secure international or other external funding.

References

Erdenejargal, P., N. Enkhtuya, and Gita Steiner-Khamsi. 2002. *Reform strategies of the Mongolian School 2001 educational development program.* Ulaanbaatar: MFOS.

Government of Mongolia. 2001. Project and technical assistance proposals, 2001–2004. Mongolia Consultative Group Meeting, Paris, May 15–16. Ulaanbaatar: Government of Mongolia.

Jadamba, B. and J. Baltzerson. 2005. Information: Rural School Development Project. Ulaanbaatar: Mongolian State University of Education/Danish-Mongolian Society.

Mandel, Ruth. 2002. Seeding civil society. In *Postsocialism: Ideals, ideologies, and practices in Eurasia,* ed. Chris M. Hann, 279–96. London: Routledge.

Steiner-Khamsi, Gita. 2005. Vouchers for teacher education (non) reform in Mongolia: Transitional, postsocialist, or antisocialist explanations? *Comparative Education Review* 49(2): 148–72.

Steiner-Khamsi, Gita, and Ines Stolpe. 2006. *Educational import: Local encounter with global forces in Mongolia.* New York: Palgrave Macmillan.

Steiner-Khamsi, Gita, N. Enkhtuya, Tanya Prime, and Sarah Lucas. 2000. *Year 2 evaluation of the School 2001 educational development program.* Ulaanbaatar: MFOS.

Wedell, Martin. 2005. Cascading training down into the classroom: The need for parallel planning. *International Journal of Educational Development* 25(6): 637–51.

8

The Latecomer Syndrome

*Beyond Project Implementation
toward an Education Policy Think Tank in Tajikistan*

TATIANA ABDUSHUKUROVA

Compared to other former Soviet republics, Tajikistan's transition from Soviet rule to a democratic society was significantly delayed by economic crisis, the loss of subsidies and trade with Moscow, and a disastrous civil war (1992–93) followed by a four-year period of civil unrest. This prolonged civil conflict disrupted lives and severely damaged infrastructure. Economic decline worsened already high levels of poverty and increased unemployment. A sharp reduction in public spending limited the government's ability to provide basic services such as education and health for its citizens (ADB 2000, 14). Only since the peace accords were signed in mid-1997 has Tajikistan's government been able to turn its attention to an economic, social, and educational development agenda by articulating the goals of democratization and economic liberalization and by welcoming financial assistance from international agencies.

As the security situation stabilized by the end of the 1990s, Tajikistan experienced an influx of international aid aimed at supporting peacebuilding, promoting democracy, and reconstructing civil society. From 1998 to 2004, foreign aid commitments rose from US$40 million to US$913 million (Aid Coordination Unit of Tajikistan 2006). Although the share of foreign aid to GNI shrank from a high of 16.8 percent in 2001 to 9.9 percent in 2003, it still exceeded the average in the former Soviet republics (USAID 2006, 31).

In the following years, Tajikistan continued to rely heavily on foreign aid, requiring increased responsiveness to the agendas and priorities of funding agencies. Not only did Tajikistan's education reform begin to share basic features of the post-socialist reform package with other post-Soviet countries (especially Central Asian republics), but it also experienced problems typically associated with foreign aid dependency throughout the developing world. As Joel Samoff has explained, far too often externally funded education reform processes remain driven by "the agendas and procedures of the funding and technical assistance agencies, with constrained national participation, limited national control, and very little sense of national ownership" (1999, 269). Although nearly every education-sector study in Tajikistan recognized the lack of necessary policy skills and proposed additional training, national participation in the design and implementation of education reforms remained only symbolic. In fact, the rhetoric of local policy capacity building seemed to have been accompanied by stagnating policy capacity in many domains, especially in the area of education.

In context with the increase of foreign aid dependency in Tajikistan, OSIAF-Tajikistan was one of the first international NGOs to become actively involved in policy-related areas. OSIAF-Tajikistan has emphasized key open society issues, such as human rights, migration policy, local governance, public health, and education reform. While most international organizations focused exclusively on service provision and delivery of humanitarian aid, OSIAF-Tajikistan's strategy targeted policymakers at the institutional level by building local policy capacity, essential for continuing self-sustaining political, economic, and social reforms. This chapter examines the work of one of the OSIAF-Tajikistan's spin-off organizations, the Education Reform Support Unit (ERSU), which works as a policy think tank in the education area. Following discussion of the education reform context in Tajikistan, this chapter examines the power and limits of ERSU as an independent, locally run organization in an environment heavily dominated by international donors and strict government control.

Donor assistance and the post-socialist education reform package

Tajikistan entered the post-Soviet era with a relatively well-educated population and a developed education infrastructure, inherited from the Soviet Union. At the time of the collapse of the Soviet Union in 1991, Tajikistan's education system provided almost universal general education and ensured gender parity at all levels. Since independence, however, Tajikistan has struggled to maintain achievements in education under new political and socioeconomic conditions, while grappling with a whole range of new tasks such as strengthening state independence, revising national history, and reviving the culture and traditions of the Tajik people.

Political instability in the 1990s had a negative impact upon education. The total damage resulting from the civil war was estimated at up to US$7 billion, and IMF and World Bank reports showed tremendous harm to the educational sector (Rashidov 2000, 82). A severe lack of financial resources during the 1990s made it practically impossible to provide basic education for all children, let alone undertake a fundamental reform of the education system. As a result, previously high literacy rates have been declining, school enrollment rates decreasing, and student dropout rates escalating. Furthermore, capital infrastructure has rapidly deteriorated; pedagogical materials, equipment, and textbooks have fallen into short supply; curricula have stagnated; and many qualified teachers have left schools.

To cope with these challenges, numerous international donors entered the country and a growing number of local NGOs emerged to voice the needs of civil society. In the past ten years the Republic of Tajikistan has received financial assistance for education reform from many international organizations, including the World Bank, ADB, UNICEF, UNESCO, USAID, OSIAF-Tajikistan, Aga Khan Foundation, and German Technical Cooperation Agency. According to the Balance of Payment statistics (IMF 2006), the largest financial assistance in 2004–5 came from the ADB and the World Bank through loans and grants (a total of US$25 million and US$12.1 million accordingly). Cumulatively, the total amount of loans provided added up to US$307.17 million from the World Bank, and US$100.61 million from the ADB (Ministry of Finance 2006). In 2006–7, Tajikistan received a US$18.4 million grant from the World Bank for the implementation of the FTI[1] to ensure accelerated progress toward the MDG of universal primary education by 2015.

Driven by international donor agencies, Tajikistan's education reform became strikingly similar to education reform strategies in other Central Asian countries, covering both the problems of infrastructure (for example, rehabilitation of school buildings, supplying school furniture, and textbooks), and education quality (for example, revision of school curriculum, development of courses and teaching/learning materials, reform of pre-service and in-service education of teachers and school principals, and involvement of local community and parents in school management). What was included in this post-socialist education reform package, however, is as important as what was omitted. Similar to other Central Asia countries, the majority of international donors in Tajikistan failed to involve local education stakeholders in education policy development, limiting the role of local NGOs to implementation of externally designed education reform projects. Without exception, international donors have justified their dominant role in Tajikistan's education development by explaining that local policymakers struggle with a severe lack of policymaking skills (such as analytical and strategic planning capacities), while the NGO sector has neither "a real voice" (OSI 2002, 11) nor the "organizational capacity" (USAID 2000, 156) to engage actively in education policy formulation.

Indeed, social partnerships among the government, the NGO sector, and international donor agencies remain problematic. Primary reasons include a lack of mutual understanding and trust, a primitive legal system, limited access to government information, lack of awareness concerning NGO activities, weak coordination among NGOs, and an absence of mechanisms and experience with lobbying for social projects. Furthermore, the efficiency and effectiveness of the NGO sector is negatively affected by widespread corruption within local governments, as well as the incompetence of many local officials and their unwillingness to permit activities outside the scope of government-approved work (USAID 2005).

One of the weakest features of Tajikistan's NGOs is their dependence on international donors. Many NGOs still see their donors as customers and "sail under the flags of convenience" (Lynch 1998, 9), tailoring their programs to donor priorities rather than the needs of an identified constituency (USAID 2005). The majority operate under broad mission statements, undertaking multiple activities. The result is poor implementation and growing distrust from international donors. The long list of NGOs operating in Tajikistan (2,750 as of January 1, 2006)[2] does not mean that all of them are active. "Dead souls" account for approximately one-third of those registered, and this is one of the main factors contributing to the growing distrust of the NGO sector by the government.

Given the constrained relationship among the government, international agencies, and the NGO sector, education development in Tajikistan reflects what has come to be "a standard approach to understanding education systems, their characteristics, and their problems in the developing world." Foreign experts spend a short period consulting relevant local officials, reviewing available data, visiting selected sites, and recording their impressions. The information then becomes a foundation upon which the provision of international education assistance, and subsequent analyses and policy decisions rest (Samoff 1999, 255). Although experienced, well-informed foreigners and their national collaborators can learn a lot in a short time, broad-scale studies with tight deadlines risk broad-scale misunderstandings:

> Standard methodology and presumed global patterns become substitutes for systematic and detailed empirical observation. Single events become modal patterns, coupled events become time series and trends, and off-hand remarks become definitive characterizations. (Samoff 1999, 255)

As a result, education reform strategies do not emerge organically from the character and demands of the national education system as understood by its major constituencies or from the needs and interests of its policy and decision-makers. Instead, they reflect the assumptions, orientations, and priorities of international donor agencies. Not surprisingly, these "ahistorical, uncontextual short-order studies" (Samoff 1999, 255), serving as the basis for education reforms, are rarely used by local education managers, administrators, curriculum developers, teacher educators, principals, teachers, students, and parents. In fact, donor-driven education reforms generally result in "constrained national participation, limited national control, and very little sense of national ownership" (Samoff 1999, 249). Over the longer term, neither the country nor the international agencies are well served by the lack of social partnership among the government, international agencies, and local education stakeholders (including NGOs).

It is in this complex context of international aid relationships that OSIAF-Tajikistan initiated the development of local policy capacity in order to increase the potential role of NGOs as agents for public lobbying and advocacy in an environment heavily dominated by international donors. The strategy focused on developing local policy capacities in "sectoral and institutional terms" (Samoff 1999, 267); that is, developing the institutional frameworks for regular interaction among researchers and policymakers within Tajikistan, for cooperation among researchers and policymakers across national borders, and for the sustained dialogue required for more effective international partnership.

Developing national education policy capacity: The "Tajik strategy"

OSIAF-Tajikistan was established in1996. However, the political situation at the time did not allow for full-scale operation, particularly in the area of education. OSIAF-Tajikistan only began implementing education programs in 2000, much later compared to OSI/ Soros Foundations in other post-socialist countries. This "late start" defined, to some extent, a particular "Tajik strategy" in the education area. By the end of the 1990s, most OSI/Soros Foundations in Central and Southeastern Europe had already closed, and many foundations in Central Asia, Caucasus, and Mongolia were requested to think of exit strategies, including spinning off some of their programs as independent NGOs. In the education area, the emphasis of OSI/Soros Foundations across the region shifted from international network programs (that is, pilot projects developed by OSI-NY and implemented by national foundations) to systemic reforms in national education policy contexts (that is, mega projects and policy research developed by local NGOs). In particular, the ESP of OSI-Budapest encouraged national foundations across the region to establish education policy centers in order to address the need for open, evidence-based policy analysis, advocacy for equity, and effective, sustainable development in education policy processes. These policy centers took on the role of independent voices in maturing democracies, and some of them became key players in education policy development in their countries (for example, Center 2000 + in Romania and the Centre of Public Policy PROVIDUS in Latvia).[3]

As a latecomer in the OSI/Soros Foundation Network, OSIAF-Tajikistan benefited from the experiences of other OSI national foundations. Instead of focusing exclusively on pilot projects in the initial stages of its operation (the approach of OSI/Soros Foundations in other post-socialist countries), OSIAF-Tajikistan established two operational units from the very beginning—the project implementation unit (focusing on pilot projects), and the policy analysis unit (focusing on national policy research and advocacy). This type of concentrated effort was expected to have more impact in the professional, financial, and organizational context of the education system in Tajikistan. In both operational areas capacity building constituted the main strand of activities. The goal was to prepare sufficient human resources for continuing, initiating, and implementing education reforms by in-country specialists on a self-sustaining basis.

Ensuring state support for national policy capacity building

The operational programs of OSIAF-Tajikistan attracted considerable interest and support from the local education community and the Ministry of Education, thanks to their focus on the most urgent needs of Tajikistan's education system in the context of political, economic, and societal development. OSIAF-Tajikistan's priorities largely corresponded to the education goals articulated by the government, which stated that Tajikistan's development toward a more democratic society would largely depend on introducing new technologies, building in-country expertise, providing access to professional information, and encouraging lifelong learning (Ministry of Education 2002). OSIAF-Tajikistan made vigorous attempts to help the Ministry of Education approach reforms in a systemic and efficient way; establishing a close partnership with ministry officials was vital.

Following two policy and education strategy seminars with ministry officials and other education stakeholders, as well as direct consultation with ministry officials, the Ministry of Education expressed its willingness to work closely with OSIAF-Tajikistan in its education reform efforts. Furthermore, the ministry expressed readiness to tackle the difficult issues of restructuring the education system to make it more sustainable. A Memorandum of Understanding between the government of the Republic of Tajikistan (signed by the Ministry of Education of the Republic of Tajikistan) and OSIAF-Tajikistan was signed on September 20, 2000. A key section of the memorandum described the creation of a group of education policy specialists in Tajikistan through the establishment of ERSU:

> Together and on an equal footing with the Ministry of Education, [OSIAF-Tajikistan will] establish an Education Reform Support Unit (ERSU) of six persons (3 + 3) under the Ministry of Education with the aim of conducting research and analyses of education system issues, including developing a plan for structural reform of secondary education. Members of the Education Reform Support Unit will be selected through open competition by both the Joint Selection Committee of OSIAF-Tajikistan and Ministry of Education of the Republic of Tajikistan. (para. 3.1.2.)

Following the Memorandum of Understanding, ERSU was established to pursue three goals. First, ERSU aimed to support systemic education reform initiatives that would identify and address specific needs of education development in Tajikistan. Second, ERSU would serve as an analytical watch dog, working to ensure that numerous outside education initiatives contributed meaningfully and positively to a coherent, primarily Tajik education framework, rather than serving the donor agenda. Third, ERSU would become a reform catalyst, initiating and facilitating informed discussions on important education issues, helping to shape public opinion, and mobilizing stakeholders to support the overall educational development process in Tajikistan. Given these complex goals, it was originally planned that ERSU would be established in two stages. The first stage would focus on developing human resources (including a series of intensive training sessions to foster national policy capacity) and on creating the necessary resource base (including collecting and analyzing quantitative and qualitative data on the current state of the education system of Tajikistan). The second stage would deal with a formal institutionalization of the unit within the current structure of the Ministry of Education.

Developing national human resources (the first stage)

The staff of the newly created ERSU was selected on a competitive basis by the search committee, which included three representatives of the Ministry of Education and three representatives of OSIAF-Tajikistan. Out of twenty-eight applicants, seven were hired, and the selection process was finalized by the end of May 2001. The newly created ERSU team included education experts, economists, and political strategists. Initial capacity building was provided by the Research Triangle Institute of North Carolina. All members of ERSU were trained in basic elements of policymaking, overall education system reform issues, and leadership skills. More specifically, the ERSU team developed expertise in statistical analysis, financial analysis, program design, education policy (including policy planning, development, implementation, and evaluation), as well as content-specific areas of higher-education reform, school curriculum, and textbooks.

Underpinning this collective application of educational policy tools and practical techniques was a theoretical and conceptual understanding of development itself, including development ethics and the lessons learned from past experiences in international development worldwide. Chief among these was that sustainable education development would be possible only if education reforms had national ownership and were firmly based in the political, economic, and social realities of Tajikistan. Instead of relying on "short-order studies" by external experts for developing Tajikistan's education development strategies, ERSU initiated the first large-scale data collection from multiple sources, including the Ministry of Education, the Ministry of Finance, various donors and international NGOs, *oblast* (region) education departments, and district *(rayon)* education departments. Additionally, ERSU designed a series of questionnaires that filled certain quantitative data gaps and collected qualitative information regarding parent, teacher, and school-director opinions, as well as concerns about the nature and character of present-day education, and their vision for the future of education in Tajikistan. Finally, ERSU developed a simple demographically driven enrollment, input, and cost-policy tool that provided the capability to discuss various policy options for the development of Tajikistan's education system with local educational stakeholders, ministry officials, and international donors.

The ERSU team made its debut at the National Education Development Conference in the fall of 2002. The main goal of the conference was to chart a meaningful and achievable way forward— one *not dependent on donor assistance*. Unless the donors plan to remain forever, it is in Tajikistan's best interest to come up with a plan it can carry out alone. The underlying principle was that international donors could contribute to the development and implementation of the plan but should not be the driving force behind it. The conference featured a number of working papers produced by the ERSU team during its first year of operation. One was a *descriptive* account of the current education system, "Analyses of the Status of the Educational System of the Republic of Tajikistan" (ERSU 2002a). Another was an *analytical* account of the education system, "National Model of Education of the Republic of Tajikistan" (ERSU 2002b), that critiqued and quantified key problem areas of the education system and highlighted the opinions and needs of parents, teachers, school directors, and *rayon* education officials. These working papers provided conference participants with a foundation upon which to move forward—a common understanding of the issues, and a shared vision for the future development of education in Tajikistan.

Failing to institutionalize within state structures (the second stage)

Despite the value of the nationally developed education sector reviews, the ERSU team still found itself in an awkward situation following the national conference. On the one hand, both state officials and international donors seemed to appreciate the enormous efforts made by the ERSU team to collect and analyze the most recent data from a wide spectrum of education stakeholders and to involve diverse stakeholder groups in envisioning the future development of education in Tajikistan. On the other hand, both state officials and international donors expressed their reservations regarding formal recognition of the ERSU team and its research findings. State officials were particularly wary of an open critique of the existing education system, unsuited to Tajikistan's conservative policymaking culture. Meanwhile, international donors' plans for education development did not necessarily correspond to the findings of locally produced education-sector reviews. In fact, both state officials and international donors referred to the ERSU studies on a regular basis—often without formal recognition of ERSU—but only to the extent that these findings reinforced their own education development agendas.

Clearly, state officials were not ready to recognize formally a new player in Tajik education policymaking. While drawing on ERSU expertise on an individual basis (through personal communication), ministry officials decided against implementation of their original plan to institutionalize ERSU within the Ministry of Education. The education policy environment was still heavily dominated by Soviet-era thinking; that is, the government always knows best and has the sole authority to critique, express ideas, and make decisions about education policy development. The establishment of any new policy structure (even if institutionalized within the existing state structure) would seem to question state authority and competence in education policy development. In addition, the post-Soviet policy environment was dominated by the reemerging oriental mentality that values respect for superiors in age and rank. This prevented any substantial contribution from younger, better-educated, professional education experts. In this context ERSU was perceived as an "institutional misfit," capable of generating potentially useful data about the education system but incongruous with the traditional cultural norms and traditions of Tajikistan's education policymaking.

Instead of institutionalizing ERSU within state structures, officials decided to create their own Education Policy Department within the Ministry of Education. This department would draw primarily on trusted members of the Ministry of Education in order to appear less threatening to state authorities. Not a single ministry official, including members of the ERSU selection committee who had signed the Memorandum of Understanding just two years before, seemed to remember that ERSU had been established to foster capacity building for the Ministry of Education. The Education Policy Department[4] drew on people from within ministry structures who were neither versed in education policy process nor familiar with education policy tools. Similar to other state bureaucracies in Tajikistan and other Central Asian republics, state officials—even in education policy—were not chosen based on their education and professional experience. Rather, they were nominated according to the clan principle, as members of certain regional kin networks[5] (Schatz 2004; Collins 2006).

Establishing a nongovernmental education policy think tank

Having realized that the original plan of institutionalizing ERSU within governmental structures was neither timely nor appropriate, OSIAF-Tajikistan decided to pursue an alternative strategy by registering ERSU as an independent education policy think tank. In 2002 (approximately two and a half years after the team was organized), ERSU was officially registered as an education policy NGO—PULSE. Unlike other policy think tanks in Central and Southeastern Europe, ERSU became a spin-off of OSIAF-Tajikistan without ever having been a part of the OSI/Soros Foundation Network. This presented a dilemma for three reasons. First, the close association between ERSU and OSIAF-Tajikistan led many governmental officials and representatives of international agencies to believe that ERSU had already secured sufficient financial support from OSIAF-Tajikistan. This created serious obstacles for ERSU in fund-raising and financial sustainability. Second, many government officials became wary of any NGOs associated with the OSI/Soros Foundation Network, due to its perceived role in the wave of "color revolutions" across the former Soviet Union. These included the Rose revolution in Georgia in 2003, the Orange revolution in Ukraine in 2004, and the Tulip revolution in Kyrgyzstan in 2005. Finally, the potential interference of newcomers with clan politics made them unwelcome in Tajikistan's conservative policy environment. As a result, ERSU was initially pushed out of various education commissions, committees, and working groups organized by government officials and international organizations.

In spring 2005, the Ministry of Education underwent radical changes that proved instrumental in bringing official recognition to ERSU as a professional group whose opinions were highly sought by different education stakeholders in Tajikistan. The appointment of a new minister of education changed the culture of policymaking, shifting a traditional preoccupation with clan-based politics to a more professional policymaking culture. With a background as a university professor, the new minister of education, Farkhod Rakhimov, had a strong desire to push forward a variety of education reforms. However, he faced tremendous difficulties. He acknowledged that one of the main problems was a lack of professional expertise within the Ministry of Education in evidence-based education policymaking. The minister of education also recognized that the newly created ERSU was the only source of such expertise in Tajikistan. Knowing most of the ERSU team members personally, he initiated regular communication with ERSU, consulting it on various education issues and utilizing its data. Recognizing the value of local policymaking capacity, the minister offered all ERSU team members, individually, senior positions within the Ministry of Education. Although such an offer was compelling, only one ERSU team member accepted and became head of the Department of State Education Policy. In other words, changes in policymaking culture as well as the relationship with the minister of education himself were key in bringing recognition to ERSU as a new player in Tajik education policy.

Although the new relationship between ERSU and the Ministry of Education is far from perfect, it has clearly improved. In particular, ministry officials have learned to recognize the value of nationally produced education-sector reviews and policy analyses, which provide a more contextual, in-depth, and nuanced interpretation of the current state of education in Tajikistan. Following the publication of "Analyses of Higher Education System in Tajikistan" (ERSU 2006) and discussion of the document at a national symposium, the government followed ERSU policy recommendations, thus initiating major reform in the area of higher education. As a deputy minister of education mentioned in a personal communication on November 29, 2005, "It was the first time that local experts raised a problem to the governmental level and, truth be told, pushed for reform in higher education." Having recognized the professionalism and expertise of the ERSU team, ministry officials have begun regularly to consult ERSU for information and advice on certain issues. Furthermore, members of ERSU are now included as education experts in various working groups organized by the Ministry of Education, World Bank, and ADB, focused on developing the

"National Strategy of Higher Education System" and the "Comparative Analyses of Higher Education System of Central Asian Countries."

From governmental officials to school representatives, ERSU is recognized for its efforts to foster social partnerships among various education stakeholders. In the context of Tajikistan's hierarchal mentality and centralized culture, ERSU remains the only organization that provides an institutional structure for regular interaction among government officials, schools, international agencies, and NGOs in education reform. One mechanism for this interaction is the regular organization of education conferences and workshops, providing an opportunity for ERSU to share, discuss, and evaluate the results of its education policy studies with various education stakeholders. Another mechanism is the publication of *School and Society,* a journal published by ERSU since 2004, which remains the only source of information in the education field. As education expert Jamily Kholova wrote in a personal communication, December 14, 2005:

> ERSU's greatest contribution is involving a wide spectrum of education stakeholders in education reform processes. Teachers and school directors across the country are aware of the results of ERSU education studies. ERSU members communicate with people on a grassroots level and share information through their journal *School and Society*.

Powers and limitations
of the local education policy NGO

An active and organized policy community involving a range of bodies drawn from civil society is essential to effective development in education. Undoubtedly, OSIAF-Tajikistan's support for local education policy capacity was instrumental in creating a more professional education community in Tajikistan. The establishment of ERSU has not only strengthened local capacity for the production of more contextual and meaningful education sector reviews, but also contributed to greater national ownership of education reforms. Furthermore, the establishment of ERSU has provided institutional structures for fostering social partnerships among civil society, state structures, and international donor organizations. Not only are such social partnerships mutually beneficial, but they are also an essential condition for developing a healthy civil society and ensuring sustainable education development.

While ERSU has filled a vacuum in Tajikistan's education policy sector, its future prospects remain uncertain for several reasons. Similar to other Central Asian republics, the NGO sector has not developed the capacity to generate sustainable funding sources, and most organizations remain heavily dependent upon the donor community (USAID 2005). Although ERSU is able to secure small grants from other donor agencies, its main financial support continues to come from OSIAF-Tajikistan. Local philanthropy is still not a significant source of funding for NGOs and is limited by heavy tax burdens and lack of incentives for potential individual and corporate donors (USAID 2005). In addition, ERSU needs to strengthen its administrative capacity to be able to work effectively with various funding agencies. Although Tajikistan is crowded with international donors who would be interested in supporting local education policy efforts, most NGOs (including ERSU) still have insufficient management and reporting capacities to conform to donor requirements. More important, the potential of a deteriorating political climate may present a further impediment to financial sustainability and effectiveness of ERSU and other local policy think tanks. The government may crack down on NGO activities and take steps to severely restrict or prohibit their activities, fearing "the transportability of the Orange and Rose revolutions" (Herman 2006, 35). Repressive leaders in some former Soviet Republics (especially Central Asian) could couch their harassment in legal terms, accusing NGOs of violating finance laws or other types of regulations and then relying on compliant courts to rule in the government's favor (Herman 2006; Shea and Moore 2006). The primary challenge in these countries would be minimizing government interference.

Given this complex set of obstacles, there are three possible scenarios for the future development of ERSU. One of the most pessimistic is that ERSU could fail to become self-sustaining. Lacking financial incentives, it could simply disintegrate, with team members absorbed by various local and international organizations operating in Tajikistan. The positive side of this scenario is that each ERSU expert could influence decision-making processes from within by working in other local and/or international institutions. On the other hand, ERSU experts may not be as effective in education policy research and advocacy individually as they are collectively. Furthermore, they are likely to lose their independence as they conform to the internal rules and education development agendas of the institutions they represent. To some extent, ERSU has already begun disintegrating. One former member has joined the Ministry of Education, and another has left for a regional UNDP office in Dushanbe. Although these individuals have kept their professional ties with ERSU, this trend could continue if opportunities for attracting external support remain limited.

The second scenario involves an alteration of institutional structure should ERSU fail to secure necessary external funding for its activities. In this case ERSU would cease to operate as an independent NGO and would be absorbed by the state. While such an arrangement would secure funding for ERSU, ensuring its sustainability, it could also lead to a loss of independence—quite likely in the centralized, hierarchical education policymaking context of Tajikistan.

A final, more optimistic scenario is that ERSU would diversify and strengthen its organizational capacity to access a variety of local and international funding sources. This would allow ERSU to develop further as an independent education policy think tank able to conduct policy research, promote evidence-based advocacy, and encourage policy debates among international donors, civil society, and decision-makers. In terms of the reception to foreign aid in Tajikistan, these efforts could facilitate broader national involvement in analysis, policy, and program decisions, with a correspondingly greater sense of national ownership of the results.

In the politically challenging environment of Central Asia, the way forward for NGOs engaged in policy advocacy is neither obvious nor easy. As international donor support declines, the need for ongoing dialogue and effective social partnerships among different education stakeholders becomes even greater. The international community must also continue to press authoritarian regimes in the region to allow policy-oriented NGOs to organize and carry out their core mission of advancing citizen interests (Herman 2006). While the future of NGOs remains uncertain in most Central Asian republics, nongovernmental policy think tanks (like ERSU) must convince the government of the importance of social partnerships while maintaining independence from the state in order to preserve and utilize their comparative advantage as innovative social actors. Policy NGOs can play effective roles in Tajik society and might in the future provide a way to mediate between the citizens of a more open society and international agencies.

Notes

[1] All low-income countries that demonstrate serious commitment to achieving universal primary completion can receive support from FTI. In Central Asia, Tajikistan is the first country awarded FTI funds. The main goal of the FTI initiative in Tajikistan is to increase efficiency in the provision of educational services in the sphere of general secondary education by updating the education management system, increasing its professional capacity, and improving school infrastructure and teaching/learning facilities.

[2] Following the adoption of the Law on Public Associations (1998) and a substantial reduction of registration fees for NGOs (2001), the number of locally registered NGOs escalated from 111 in 1998, to 1241 in 2001, and to 2,750 in 2006 (Ministry of Justice of the Republic of Tajikistan, 2006). Until March 2001, astronomically high registration fees hindered the development of Tajikistan's civil society. In a country where the average salary is, at most, US$10 a month (when paid at all), the US$165 registration fee for community-based organizations and US$240 fee for national associations prohibited activists from registering their NGOs. In 2001, the government issued Resolution 132—On the Order of Collection and Amount of Registration Fees for the Registration of Public Associations and Political Parties in the Republic of Tajikistan—which slashed the registration fee to US$25 for community organizations and to US$60 for NGOs working at the national level.

[3] In most countries policy centers emerged in 2002 and 2003, after operating as education policy programs within the respective OSI/Soros national foundations for a few years. Being a part of OSI/Soros Foundations allowed these policy centers to gain the necessary knowledge in both public policy issues and organizational matters. At the time of their separation from the OSI/Soros Foundations, these spin-offs were well equipped with the managerial, project, and research skills necessary for their independent existence.

[4] Later renamed the Department of Analysis and Reform in the Educational Sphere.

[5] Clans are informal organizations based on kin and fictive kin ties. They may penetrate and transform formal regimes in several ways through clan-based appointments and patronage, by stripping state assets to feed clan networks, and by crowding out other mechanisms of representation. As they undermine formal institutions, clans create an informal modus operandi, best understood as "clan politics" (Collins 2004).

References

Aid Coordination Unit of Tajikistan. 2006. Foreign aid in Tajikistan. Available online.

ADB (Asian Development Bank). 2000. Women in Tajikistan: Country briefing paper. ADB, Programs Department East and Office of Environment and Social Development.

Collins, Kathleen. 2004. The logic of clan politics: Evidence from the Central Asian trajectories. *World Politics* 56(2): 224–61.

———. 2006. *Clan politics and regime transition in Central Asia.* New York: Cambridge University Press.

ERSU (Education Reform Support Unit). 2002a. Analyses of the status of the educational system of the Republic of Tajikistan. Working paper. Dushanbe, Tajikistan: ERSU.

———. 2002b. National model of education of the Republic of Tajikistan. Working paper. Dushanbe, Tajikistan: ERSU.

———. 2006. Analyses of higher education system in Tajikistan. Working paper. Dushanbe, Tajikistan: ERSU.

Herman, Robert. 2006. Advocacy in the Europe and Eurasia region: Progress, promise and peril. *The 2005 NGO Sustainability Index for Central and Eastern Europe and Eurasia.* Washington DC: United States Agency for International Development, Bureau for Europe and Eurasia, Office of Democracy, Governance and Social Transition.

IMF (International Monetary Fund). 2006. The balance of payment statistics. IMF country report 06/62. Dushanbe, Tajikistan: IMF.

Lynch, James. 1998. The international transfer of dysfunctional paradigms. In *Learning and teaching in an international context: Research, theory, and practice*, ed. D. Johnson, B. Smith, and M. Crossley, 7–33. Bristol: University of Bristol, Center for International Studies in Education.

Ministry of Education. 2002. *Education For All (EFA) 2000 assessment—country report—Tajikistan.* Dushanbe, Tajikistan: Ministry of Education.

Ministry of Finance. 2006. Foreign aid statistics. External Debt Department. Dushanbe, Tajikistan: Ministry of Finance.

OSI (Open Society Institute). 2002. *Education development in Kyrgyzstan, Tajikistan, and Uzbekistan: Challenges and ways forward.* Education Support Program. Budapest, Hungary: OSI. Available online.

Rashidov, Abdulbashir. 2000. *Education for all: Tajikistan.* Dushanbe, Tajikistan: Ministry of Education.

Samoff, Joel. 1999. Education sector analysis in Africa: Limited national control and even less national ownership. *International Journal of Educational Development* 19: 249–72.

Schatz, Edward. 2004. *Modern clan politics: The power of "blood" in Kazakhstan and beyond.* Seattle, WA: University of Washington Press.

Shea, Catherine, and David Moore. 2006. Civil society under threat: Common legal barriers and potential responses. *The 2005 NGO Sustainability Index for Central and Eastern Europe and Eurasia.* Washington DC:

United States Agency for International Development, Bureau for Europe and Eurasia, Office of Democracy, Governance and Social Transition.

USAID (United States Agency for International Development). 2000. Tajikistan. In *The 2000 NGO Sustainability Index for Eastern and Central Europe and Eurasia.* Available online.

———. 2005. *The 2004 NGO Sustainability Index for Central and Eastern Europe and Eurasia.* Bureau for Europe and Eurasia, Office of Democracy, Governance and Social Transition. Washington DC: USAID.

———. 2006. *The 2005 NGO Sustainability Index for Central and Eastern Europe and Eurasia.* Bureau for Europe and Eurasia, Office of Democracy, Governance and Social Transition. Washington DC: USAID.

9

Invisible and Surrogate Education

Filling Educational Gaps in Turkmenistan

ERIKA DAILEY AND IVETA SILOVA

Turkmenistan stands out in this book—and possibly in global experience—as a country where education reform has not been merely hampered by the many objective challenges common to the post-socialist transformations in the region. Until 2007, it has been deliberately propelled backward toward illiteracy and isolation from the world for political ends. The unexpected death in December 2006 of "president for life" Saparmurat Niyazov (Turkmenbashi, "leader of the Turkmen"; later Beyik Turkmenbashi, "great leader of the Turkmen") (r. 1991–2006), who instituted retrograde measures and was one of the world's most notorious dictators, has provided an equally unexpected opportunity to slow and possibly reverse the backward slide. In one of the most surprising developments in the region's educational history, the man now championing educational reform—President Gurbanguly Berdymukhamedov—was a senior education official who, under Niyazov, oversaw the education system's demise.[1]

President Niyazov's zeal in imposing one-man rule and rapidly creating a unique post-Soviet identity for Turkmenistan, which had

An education expert living in Turkmenistan contributed invaluable information to and commentary on the draft. Although that person cannot be credited by name for fear of reprisals, the authors gratefully acknowledge the contribution.

never before existed as an independent state, enforced—despite the enlightened efforts of many educators—an educational approach that was isolated, virtually devoid of critical thinking, and even anti-intellectual. Under Niyazov, the educational priorities were on vocational skills, political indoctrination, and uniformity of thought. In this inhospitable climate, parents, teachers, educational administrators, and civil society more broadly were forced to become the informal surrogate of the Ministry of Education, trying to develop long-term survival strategies for the education of the country's new generation—approximately one-third of the population is under the age of fifteen—and attempting to fill educational gaps left by Niyazov's rule.

Because of the repressive political environment, educators in government schools have been able to function less as an engine of reform than as enforcers of retrograde education policies. Under Niyazov, civil society served largely as the guardians of remnants of the Soviet educational legacy and, in limited cases when educators were introduced to foreign influences, as conduits for more progressive educational trends. Likewise, as the government of Turkmenistan had until recently resisted most forms of international technical assistance and, until Niyazov's death, virtually all calls for reform, international donors played only a very limited role in providing state education structures with access to contemporary teaching methods and curricula and in supplying scholarships abroad, "life boats" ferrying the most talented, motivated, well-resourced, or privileged to alternative educational opportunities. Nevertheless, some international donors have devised an array of tactics for maintaining various levels of educational support that the situation would allow.

This chapter examines Turkmenistan's unique educational context and the improvised approaches used by civil society and international donors to preserve the country's cultural and intellectual legacy since Turkmenistan's independence. Following an overview of educational development during the President Niyazov's rule, the chapter analyzes the prospects, challenges, and inadvertent consequences of two distinct strategies used by international donors in Turkmenistan—government-approved educational initiatives and initiatives implemented beyond government oversight.

A country of extremes:
Education reform in post-Soviet Turkmenistan

Turkmenistan is in many ways a country of extremes. Occupying the far southeast portion of the Soviet Union and of the Russian empire before it, Turkmenistan derives from a clan-based society, numbering today around five million, excluding an untallied diaspora, mostly in Afghanistan, Azerbaijan, Iran, the Russian Federation, Ukraine, and Uzbekistan. Its people survive in witheringly hot conditions in the oases of the Kara Kum Desert (in Turkmen, Garagum) mostly through fishing along the coast of the Caspian Sea, cotton monoculture, and hydrocarbon extraction and transport. It has one of the largest natural gas reserves in the world, yet the vast majority of its people live in poverty, with life expectancy plummeting and fetal mortality rates among the highest in the world.

During his twenty-one years in power—first as Communist Party leader of the Turkmen Soviet Socialist Republic and then as Turkmenistan's first president—Saparmurat Niyazov maintained strict control over public expression and access to information reminiscent of the heavy-handed propaganda of the Soviet period. He banned all political alternatives, subsumed control of all three branches of government under the presidency, and created a cult of personality based on himself and his parents rivaling that of the Kim dynasty in North Korea. It is arguably the extreme political environment that has had the most profound, and profoundly damaging, effect on the development of education in Turkmenistan.

Since independence, Turkmenistan's education system has suffered from many of the same challenges facing other countries in the post-Soviet space, such as declining expenditures, decaying infrastructure, ethnic discrimination, and corruption. However, the extreme level of political control in Turkmenistan has redirected its educational system from the natural trajectory of post-Soviet educational reform, moving it virtually backward toward ideological indoctrination and isolation from information and intellectual discourse elsewhere in the region and globally. With the possible exception of neighboring Uzbekistan, Turkmenistan's government is the only one considered in this volume that has deliberately reduced educational opportunities and indeed banned some substantive content in favor of ideological control.

Turkmenistan's educational deterioration is the result of several developments, some of which are typical of most post-Soviet countries, while others are unique to Turkmenistan. Similarly to other former Soviet republics of Central Asia, independent Turkmenistan experienced budgetary cut backs, layoffs, and deterioration of infrastructure that have severely challenged the country's capacity for educational development. The educational system suffered the loss of skilled teachers, school administrators, and scholars to government lay offs, emigration, "brain drain," ethnic discrimination, increases in teacher workloads, and budget cuts. The situation was exacerbated by school overcrowding, textbook shortages, risky behavior among teenagers, and other strains on the country's social fabric that have compromised the quality of education.

A unique dynamic at play was the "constant and unsystematic reform in Turkmenistan since the 1990s" that has muddied popular and executive understanding about policy goals and largely eliminated the possibility of the development of a coherent educational strategy (Turkmenistan Helsinki Initiative 2004, 1). Fundamental to shaping Turkmenistan's educational development—and the principal tool of the system's dismantlement—was the introduction on May 3, 1993, of the Bilim (knowledge) education program. It was the launch of the Bilim program that formally marked the system's retrogression, which, according to a report by the Turkmenistan Helsinki Initiative resulted "in a total crash of the educational system as such" (2004, 1). A misnomer, the Bilim program precipitated the wide-scale "Turkmenification" of the education system, reduced the number of years in secondary education to nine and the number of years in higher education to two, introduced strong ideological control of the official school curriculum, and initiated major restrictions on access to information and knowledge. The elimination of most minority-education schools and their replacement by Turkmen-education analogues, extreme reductions in the number of classes taught in Russian, severe reductions in higher-education enrollment, lay offs of educational professionals, and decreases in the hours, staff, and holdings of libraries followed. This left very few educational opportunities for non-ethnic Turkmen or for Turkmen educational professionals.

"Turkmenification" policies

As part of the process of post-Soviet nation-building, President Niyazov made it a priority to promote the Turkmen language and ethnicity and an idealized form of Turkmen history and culture in place of a more multicultural and russified Soviet culture. The ban on opera and ballet is perhaps the clearest example of President Niyazov's efforts to promote "Turkmenification" by doing away with exposure to "non-indigenous" culture. Changes along these lines also affected the educational system. In 1992, Turkmen became the sole official language of Turkmenistan. A year later President Niyazov announced that, along with the language conversion, Turkmenistan would transition to a Latin-based "Turkmen National Alphabet." Presidential Decree No. 812, April 12, 1993, On the Adoption of the New Alphabet for the Turkmen Language, stipulated that the alphabet would be put into force and usage starting January 1, 1996 (Clement 2004, 6). By 1996, the Cyrillic script was replaced with the Latin for use in the Turkmen language. However, the lack of adequate Turkmen-language classes and textbooks to help the older population of Turkmen speakers and all generations of non–Turkmen speakers gain fluency impeded the transition and fueled poverty and out-migration among the country's minority population. The change in alphabet created a dramatic reduction in the number of available written materials, notably school textbooks and library holdings. Responsibility for publishing new textbooks devolved from the Academy of Sciences, which was closed in 1998, to the Ministry of Education, Supreme Council for Science and Technology, and individual educational institutions, resulting in part in vastly reduced numbers of publications. Since first-grade students were no longer taught Cyrillic beginning in 1996, when implementation came fully into force, the majority of students have been cut off from books about their own history, culture, and intellectual heritage—a particular loss for a population as relatively small in number as ethnic Turkmen.

Along with the enforcement of linguistic "Turkmenification" across the educational system, opportunities to study foreign languages also were severely cut. For example, while the study of Turkish and English had grown since the Soviet era with the introduction of tuition-based Turkmen-Turkish primary and secondary schools, the government dramatically reduced the number of schools and classes in which the language of instruction was a minority language such as Russian, Kazakh, or Uzbek. Opportunities to study Western languages, such as English, French, and German, moved largely from the purview of state schools and institutes of higher education to the care of private educational centers and foreign embassies and study-abroad programs, bringing more policing of the movements of foreigners and local residents with whom they had contact.

Reduction in years to learn

As the government's efforts to isolate local residents grew, so did the number of measures adopted to eliminate or reduce educational opportunities. Whereas other post-Soviet Central Asian Republics moved to increase the years of schooling and expand higher-education enrollments, Turkmenistan began to shut down. In 1993, President Niyazov introduced a sweeping education reform that reduced mandatory secondary education from eleven to nine years for all but the Turkmen-Turkish schools (ten years), the Pushkin Russian school (eleven years), and the Anadolu Turkish school (twelve years). As a result, until February 2007 all but a small number of students from elite families had been stripped of the opportunity to attain anything more than an incomplete secondary education and, for some in particularly under-resourced schools, basic literacy in Turkmen. Further, the government catastrophically reduced higher-education enrollments. According to UNICEF (2007), university enrollment rates fell from approximately 10 percent in the early 1990s to 3 percent in 2004, while it generally increased in other countries of the former socialist bloc. Moreover, President Niyazov reduced the five-year university education of Soviet times to a two-year internship program followed by two years of university study.

These deceptively simple administrative changes have had a profoundly negative effect on students' educational prospects. Since a nine-year education is not accepted as a high-school diploma anywhere in the world apart from Turkmenistan and its similarly repressive ally, Belarus, most students in Turkmenistan had become ineligible to receive a higher education abroad. President Berdymukhamedov expressed his commitment to education reform by ordering that secondary education be extended to ten years and higher education to five years. While enrollment in higher-education institutions did increase at the beginning of the 2007–8 academic year, the increase—by 540 students—was modest. It is unclear when or even whether Berdymukhamedov's order will fully reverse the downward trends and allow for growth from pre-Niyazov levels.

Ideological control of the curriculum and mandatory study of the Ruhnama

The Bilim reforms of 1993 heralded the beginning of the gradual narrowing of subjects available in Turkmen schools and institutes of higher education. Among the most influential was the elimination of certain courses of study at the primary and secondary level, such as physical education and the study of minority languages, literatures, and history. However, the case of Turkmenistan did not reflect the process of "nationalization" of education common to many former Soviet republics (including Central Asian republics), whereby governments strove to eliminate all Soviet content from school curricula and replace it with the new "national" content. In fact, the government of Turkmenistan reduced or totally eliminated the amount of time assigned for studying the works of Turkmen national poets and writers in the curriculum (Clement 2004). As the Turkmenistan Helsinki Initiative (2004) explained, the classic works of Turkmen literature by Berdi Kerbabayev, Rakhim Esenov, Beki Seitakov, Turkish Dzhumageldiyev, Khidir Deryayev, and Nurmurad Sarykhanov were among those purged from the curriculum. Instead, school and university curricula were subsumed into the cult of personality of President Niyazov through the introduction of such subjects as the History of Neutral Turkmenistan, the Politics of Independence of Saparmurat Turkmenbashi the Great, and the so-called literary heritage of Saparmurat Turkmenbashi, consisting of a collection of his poems and biographies of the president and his parents.

Furthermore, the Turkmenistan Ministry of Education encouraged "the policy of mastering all school disciplines through the prism of Niyazov's works," especially his two-volume book *Ruhnama* (book of the soul or spiritual book). In practice, this meant that the *Ruhnama* eclipsed intellectual and cultural expression for political purposes, much as Mao Tse Tung's *Little Red Book* did in the People's Republic of China. *Ruhnama*, ostensibly written by Saparmurat Niyazov and referred to officially as the "holy" *Ruhnama*, became mandatory reading for schooling and employment alike. It also effectively supplanted the substantive curriculum, as clearly illustrated by an example of problem-solving from the mathematics textbook for the second grade developed by the Ministry of Education:

> Gulnara was reading the book "Ruhnama." She read six pages on the first day. On the second day, she read four pages more than on the first day. On the third day she read five pages less than on the second day. How many pages of "Ruhnama" did Gulnara read on the third day? (5)

Restrictions on access to information and knowledge

Under Niyazov, the government of Turkmenistan also imposed restrictions on access to knowledge that were consistent with its broader policies of full state control of information. In Turkmenistan, all media are run by the state. Extraterritorial broadcasting from the BBC, Deutsche Welle, and Radio Free Europe/Radio Liberty are jammed by radio waves but are accessible via satellite television. Websites are blocked to prevent independent information from reaching citizens through surrogate means. The state silences independent reporting from inside Turkmenistan by refusing to grant visas to the majority of foreign journalists who request to visit, and by beating, intimidating, arbitrarily detaining, arresting, deporting, and imprisoning local stringers. On May 2, 2006, the U.S.-based Committee to Protect Journalists ranked Turkmenistan as the third "most censored" country in the world (2006), and Reporters withough Borders named Turkmenistan one of fifteen "enemies of the Internet" (2005).

Under Niyazov, the government carried out purges of library holdings, with countless books being destroyed, sometimes in mass book burnings.

> In the early '90s, many school teachers subscribed to Russian periodicals such as *Biology at School* or *History at School,* etc. It was a way of learning new methods of teaching and of adopting up-to-date pedagogical experiences for a number of teachers. However, subscription to foreign periodicals is banned nowadays in Turkmenistan, depriving teachers of the possibility to upgrade their skills. (Turkmenistan Helsinki Initiative 2004)

To summarize, a number of changes that had taken place since 1993—"Turkmenification" policies, reductions in the years to learn, cuts in budgetary allocations to the education sector, corruption, ideological control of the curriculum, and restrictions to access to information—have created major gaps in Turkmenistan's educational system. As the Turkmenistan Helsinki Initiative put it, "Current Turkmen graduates cannot be called illiterate; yet, they can already be called uneducated" (2004, 10). Unfortunately, no comparative statistical data are available on the relative academic achievements of Turkmenistan's students over time or as compared to students from other countries.

International responses to educational gaps in Turkmenistan

Local educational stakeholders (teachers, parents, and the students themselves), nongovernmental groups, and international donors have developed distinctive strategies for filling educational gaps created by Niyazov's retrogressive policies. Programs have generally developed on the regional, municipal, and community levels (depending on available human and financial resources), as well as abroad, but to a more limited degree on a national level. Until recently, the financial burdens for these responses have been shouldered by families, individual educators, and foreign donors, rather than by the government, and this inherited financial responsibility has impeded many in Turkmenistan from taking advantage of available educational alternatives.

Government efforts to control nongovernmental educational initiatives outside of the traditional scope of state schools have created significant challenges for international support to in-country educational initiatives. Nevertheless, international agencies such as UNICEF, EU's TACIS program, and individual embassies such as those of France, Germany, Turkey, the United Kingdom, and the United States have all run successful programs. In addition, some educational assistance has been provided to educators and students from Turkmenistan by international organizations such as USAID, the Academy for Educational Development, Counterpart Consortium, the International Research and Exchanges Board (IREX), American Councils for International Education (ACCELS), and OSI.

Among the most popular, the U.S. government has funded grassroots training for the civil sector through Counterpart Consortium, which maintains centers in various parts of the country and provides access to the Internet and information resources through the American Corners. Part of the EU's warming relations with Turkmenistan under Berdymukhamedov will include the announced establishment of European Corners.

Some of the most common and successful alternatives to government schools in Turkmenistan have come in the form of "shadow education"—parent-led studies, private schooling and tutoring, self-study, and home schooling. Others have been institutionalized in state structures (such as the Turkmen-Turkish schools), nongovernmental institutions (such as free or low-cost vocational training and enrichment programs), or private enterprises (such as a number of independent, private commercial educational centers). Some substantive learning is available by Russian cable television, the Internet, IREX, and ACCELS. By and large, attempts to introduce online distance education have been limited by the extremely low levels of Internet connectivity in Turkmenistan and by government surveillance of Internet activity.

Generally, international organizations have had two options when pursuing their goals in Turkmenistan: to work directly with the government (by implementing government-approved and government-controlled educational initiatives); or to provide educational resources, teacher training, Internet-based and satellite-based educational resources, and scholarships abroad. Each approach has its merits, but both have some inadvertent ill consequences that warrant closer examination in order to understand the complexities of international educational assistance in an authoritarian environment.

Government-approved educational initiatives

President Niyazov inculcated wariness of foreign aid but did authorize some forms of collaboration with international donors to implement educational initiatives locally, notably with the United Nations, EU, and some foreign embassies. Resistance on the policy and implementation levels from the president's office and the traditionally conservative Ministry of Education have kept some of these initiatives relatively modest in scope and thwarted others.

One of the exceptions is the network of Turkmen-Turkish primary and secondary schools (sponsored by the Gülen community),[2] which actually expanded during Niyazov's rule, while two of five known foreign-sponsored schools—notably the French and German schools—eventually closed.

At the time of President Niyazov's death in December 2006 there was only one exclusively Russian-language school left in Turkmenistan (although a limited number of schools offer some coursework in the Russian language). The Pushkin Russian School in Ashgabat was run under the aegis of the Embassy of the Russian Federation in Turkmenistan. At the same time, the number of Turkmen-Turkish schools reached sixteen by the 2006–7 academic year. Local education stakeholders consider the quality of education offered by Turkmen-Turkish schools superior to that offered in state schools because of the triple-language instruction (English, Turkmen, and Turkish) and hybrid curriculum. Matriculation is fee-based—in the early 2000s, for example, parents in Turkmenistan had to pay US$1000 a year for the education of one child (Balci 2003)—which makes these schools "elite" to the extent that they serve only the children of parents who can afford to pay the tuition fees or bribes necessary to ensure enrollment or who have the personal connections to secure coveted spots.

Given that the government of Turkmenistan had until Berdymukhamedov's revisionist policies virtually prohibited internationally sponsored curricular reform altogether, why did it allow a network of Turkmen-Turkish schools to function in the country? Some of the reasons include the importance of personal connections with President Niyazov and the conformist, pro-state attitude of the Gülen community in Turkmenistan. For example, Bayram Balci explains that the Gülen community is very active in Turkmenistan because two of its members served as advisers to President Niyazov himself (the adviser on energy issues and the deputy minister of textiles, Ahmet Calik, and the minister of education, Muamer Turkyilmaz). In addition, the Gülen community is known for its supportive attitude toward the authoritarian government of Turkmenistan. For example, the Gülen community often employs the "strategy of seduction" toward the Central Asian governments, including Turkmenistan, to guarantee its presence in the country (Balci 2003, 165). Commonly, this means that the Gülen community offers its support for the government's policy and post-Soviet ideology in exchange for the undisturbed existence of its schools across the region. For example, Gülen's followers teach their students to love the new independent state, the president, the flag, the new institutions, the *Ruhnama,* and the new heroes who have been chosen by the new regimes (Balci 2003). Furthermore, some schools supported by the Gülen community are known to curry favor by translating some of the president's books and distributing them in Turkey. In Turkmenistan, the general director of the Turkmen-Turkish schools directorate, Seyit Embel, translated the *Ruhnama* into Turkish (Mamedov 2005). As Balci points out, the Gülen schools thus become "ambassadors to Turkey for these Central Asian regimes" (2003, 165), promoting their culture and history in Turkey and, inadvertently, legitimizing these authoritarian regimes abroad.

While a close collaboration with the government has allowed these international organizations to operate on a much wider scale, the goals of their programs have occasionally been compromised because of the government's selective implementation of the initiatives. For example, UNICEF and the Ministry of Education jointly initiated a Global Education Program in 2002 to introduce the "child-friendly learning approach" in Turkmenistan's schools. The concept of global education is to educate the "whole person" by addressing the intellectual, emotional, physical, moral, and spiritual dimensions of the learner in a comprehensive approach. According to UNICEF, the aim of the Global Education Program is "to prepare the individual for meaningful life in an increasingly complex, fast changing, multicultural and interdependent world" through introducing "interactive learning methods that encourage co-operation, discussion and active participation" (2003). The Ministry of Education of Turkmenistan selected eighteen pilot schools— three from each province *(velayat)* of Turkmenistan and the capital, Ashgabat—to pilot the concept and methods in schools.

A close collaboration with the government has allowed UNICEF to implement the program on a country-wide scale, yet it has involved complex politics and required many compromises in program development and implementation. First, all project participants were hand picked by the Ministry of Education instead of through collaboration involving UNICEF, ministry officials, international experts, and the schools themselves. This resulted in the selection of a number of "trusted people" who presumably would inform the state authorities of any "misconduct" by their local and international colleagues, such as attempts to criticize or undermine existing education policies and practices. Second, international experts were allowed to come to Turkmenistan to lead teacher-training workshops, but they were never allowed to enter state schools to observe teachers as they attempted to implement new teaching and learning methodologies in their classrooms. Given the lack of monitoring and evaluation by outside experts, the new methodologies were implemented only selectively as some project participants attempted to adapt new educational concepts for indoctrination purposes in schools. For example, informal interviews with project participants revealed how they attempted to recast the concept of "school-community interaction" by requiring students to report on their parents' and grandparents' knowledge of and respect toward the *Ruhnama.* Instead of reaching the original goal of "enriching and diversifying the range of learning/teaching methods employed in schools" (UNICEF 2003), the project has, apart from some positive effects, inadvertently resulted in providing the state with a wider variety of educational tools for ideological indoctrination of students and tighter policing of families and communities.

In an authoritarian, one-man state, some form of collaboration with the government is essential to implementation of broad programming. Many foreign stakeholders have used the government's go-ahead to then promote reforms that the government resisted. But providing assistance to a regime that until recently has refused to provide anything but the most minimal budget for educational expenditures and that was indeed actively dismantling the educational system as a whole and corrupting its curriculum for reasons of political indoctrination runs the risk of compromising or appearing to compromise some of the original program goals (as in the case of UNICEF's Global Education Program) or of appearing tacitly to endorse the values of the regime (as in the case of the Turkmen-Turkish schools and Russian universities still requiring knowledge of the *Ruhnama* for enrollment). Under President Berdymukhamedov, donor-to-government cooperation in the educational sphere has so far taken a dramatic positive turn. It is not yet clear how the lag time between the issuance of reformist policies on the presidential level and their actual implementation will affect the success of the promised reforms or the image of donors assisting the government.

Educational opportunities not run by the government

The unduly high levels of control the government of Turkmenistan generally demands in the educational sector far exceed international norms. Until recently, the choice before donors wishing to promote education in Turkmenistan therefore has been stark: either fund government-run opportunities, precondition funding on reform and be willing to abandon initiatives if compliance is not attained, or seek government approval to run programs independently but be ready to proceed even if the government does not acquiesce. Until the death of Niyazov some international donors chose not to work through the government because of its obstructionist bent, instead prioritizing work directly with informal networks of educators and students or helping students study abroad. Such efforts have included teacher training, NGO development, and scholarship programs abroad that help provide access to information, knowledge, and literature.[3]

While there are clear benefits to collaboration with Turkmenistan's education stakeholders, there are also practical challenges even when the government "approves" programs to be run by non-state actors. For example, government interference in freedom of association, assembly, and movement limits the scope of all educational initiatives not run directly by the government, such as scholarships abroad. As a result, these programs can benefit only hundreds of students in a given year rather than the tens of thousands in the Turkmen state school system. Furthermore, some educators and students who have sought but been denied government permission, such as NGO registration, have been subjected to arbitrary interrogations, house raids, and restrictions on their freedom of movement to intimidate them into ceasing their activities. For example, some students who have attempted to travel for education abroad—even when the programs were government sanctioned—have been subjected to arbitrary interrogations and threats to them and their families. The Turkmenistan Helsinki Initiative reported that some teachers participating in English language competition activities organized by ACCELS were publicly called "traitors" and threatened with dismissal from their jobs by local education authorities (2004, 7). Notwithstanding governmental harassment, however, the growing demand for such programming suggests that the educators and beneficiaries believe that content integrity of alternative educational initiatives outweighs the personal risks.

Some of the government's repressive practices further hamper the operation of some internationally initiated cultural, academic, and professional exchanges. The clearest example is the state's restriction of some people's right to leave the country for any reason, whether for temporary employment, emigration, or study. The "exit visa" regime existed as part of the Soviet legacy until January 2002, when it was abolished, but it was reintroduced in March 2003 after the November 2002 coup attempt. In 2004 this system was lifted again, and since then the majority of the population can leave the country freely without government permission. However, in 2006 a human rights defender estimated that some seventeen thousand individuals remain on an unacknowledged travel black list. While the purpose is presumably to prevent travelers from leaking negative information about the country abroad, some students wishing to complete their studies and receive professional training have also suffered the negative impact of the black lists.

Another institutional obstacle to study abroad programs was established by Presidential Decree No. 126 (June 1, 2004), which invalidated all higher education degrees received abroad after 1993 and mandated the dismissal of their recipients from government employment (International League for Human Rights and Turkmen Initiative for Human Rights 2006). As President Niyazov stated, "Those Turkmen students who are being educated abroad and are not studying *Ruhnama,* are no longer our people" (quoted in Turkmenistan Helsinki Initiative 2004, 8). As a result, university students were threatened by their rectors that if they studied abroad they would not be reinstated upon return to Turkmenistan (Clement 2004).

The largest practical impediment to study-abroad programs was the nine-year secondary-school system itself. The fact that Turkmenistan's students could receive only nine years of education precluded their admission to universities elsewhere in the world, for whom ten years of secondary education is a standard minimum requirement. In a promising move, President Berdymukhamedov announced in July 2007 that foreign-earned degrees would once again be recognized in Turkmenistan. But as of this writing, Turkmen and Russian universities that conducted entry examinations in

Turkmenistan continued to require students to pass exams in the *Ruhnama,* in Turkmen, as a condition for entry.

At the moment, these alternative programs offer opportunities for Turkmenistan's students to gain knowledge, skills, and degrees that they, until recently, have been unable to receive in their home country. But the high cost of such opportunities per student and the small number of spots available keep the number of beneficiaries small in proportion to the overall population. And, troublingly, the programs that can only be conducted abroad have the unintended negative consequence of facilitating "brain drain" for some of the country's most promising students and educators, highlighting the contradictions inherent in international educational assistance provided in an authoritarian context.

The complexities of international educational assistance in an authoritarian context

As in many repressive and authoritarian states, parents, teachers, and students in Turkmenistan have been forced either to accept the inadequate and failing educational system or to draw on personal, community, or international resources to devise educational opportunities the state cannot or will not provide. The government has largely managed to "fend off the NGO incursion" and create an "NGO-free zone" comparable in its scope and intensity to North Korea (DeMars 2005, 164). However, some international NGOs, foreign embassies, and private businesses have managed to devise an array of responses for filling educational gaps in Turkmenistan. These responses vary from providing financial support to various forms of "shadow education" to institutionalizing educational alternatives in the mainstream education system (such as the network of Turkmen-Turkish schools) to providing grassroots training for the civil sector and professional-development opportunities and study-abroad programs for teachers and students.

Notwithstanding the strategy employed by foreign donors—either working in collaboration with or funding work independently of the government—international education assistance has clearly offered new opportunities for Turkmenistan's educators and students to gain knowledge, skills, and degrees that they are unable to receive in educational institutions in their country. However, implementation of these educational alternatives has highlighted the inherent complexities and inevitable contradictions of NGO roles in an authoritarian regime. As this chapter illustrates, a close collaboration with the authoritarian government can lead to selective implementation of educational initiatives and inadvertently result in legitimizing the authoritarian regime itself. At the same time, the alternative strategy of providing international assistance directly to Turkmenistan's educators and students (both with and without governmental approval) may involve not only practical limitations of program implementation (such as limited outreach to program participants), but also personal risks to local program participants for their involvement in educational activities not run by the state (such as threats and arbitrary interrogations). In this complex environment some of the international stakeholders may have imperiled their participants, failed to make an impact on a large scale, or failed to achieve their own missions altogether. Yet to varying degrees all have contributed to the larger process of post-Soviet transformation in Turkmenistan by filling educational gaps in a rapidly deteriorating educational system.

President Gurbanguly Berdymukhamedov's intention to restore the education system in Turkmenistan seems beyond doubt. Indeed, the day after his inauguration on February 14, 2007, he signaled a sea change in education policy by issuing a presidential decree extending secondary education to ten years, and university education from two to five years. Since then, President Berdymukhamedov has announced the reopening of the Academy of Sciences, ordered teachers to be hired and even brought back from retirement, and commissioned the writing of forty-two new textbooks to be available for the 2007–8 academic year (Turkmenistan Initiative for Human Rights 2007). On March 17, 2007, President Berdymukhamedov signed a decree limiting the use of the national state oath in public places, including educational establishments in Turkmenistan. Accordingly, schoolchildren who would have started the usual school day with a solemn recital of the state oath, swearing loyalty to the motherland and Turkmenbashi the Great, now use it only once, at the school graduation ceremony. Moreover, the words "Turkmenbashi the Great" were changed to the "President of Turkmenistan." Such changes might seem superficial, but they represent a concrete step toward reducing the cult of personality in the education system.

Physical training and the study of social sciences have been restored to the national curriculum. And two- to three-year vocational colleges and professional schools began enrolling secondary-school graduates again in September 2007. What has most attracted the attention of the academics, schoolteachers, and students is the fact that the president raised their monthly salaries and stipends by 40 percent beginning in September 2007. Such reforms, particularly the salary increases and the creation of extra job vacancies, encourage many qualified professors and scientists who either became victims of regular lay offs or sought more profitable jobs in other fields to consider returning to teaching.

President Berdymukhamedov's proposed reforms are a promising development and may in time lead to the restoration of Turkmenistan's system to a pre-1993 level or better, although it is not yet clear how the government will finance these broad-reaching infrastructural improvements. President Niyazov's negative impact on education has been so profound that it will take intensive and sustained effort to overcome. Priorities should include significant new government expenditures in the sector; a less repressive political climate to allow for curriculum enrichment, critical thinking, and access to information and knowledge; and improved economic prospects to reverse "brain drain." While the future course of Turkmenistan's educational development is improved but uncertain, it is clear that efforts to preserve and advance the nation's cultural and intellectual legacy will require a new dynamic among the state, civil society, and international donors.

Notes

[1] President Berdymukhamedov served for the better part of a decade under Niyazov as deputy chairman of the Cabinet of Ministers of Turkmenistan responsible for education, culture, health, sports, tourism, and other civil sectors. As acting head of state following Niyazov's death, Berdymukhamedov ran essentially unopposed on a platform of education, pension, and agricultural reform predicated on a commitment to Niyazov's legacy. While the Berdymukhamedov administration seems reformist by comparison with Niyazov's, it continues to derive its political legitimacy from the perpetuation of Niyazov's legacy rather than a rejection of it. This is apparent even in the sector that is likely to benefit most from the new regime's liberalizations:

education. President Berdymukhamedov has fueled Niyazov's cult of personality, overseeing the adoption of a law on the presidency (2007) that requires
the president of Turkmenistan to perpetuate Niyazov's legacy. Although it is
not explicitly stipulated in the law, this obligation can be presumed to encom-
pass his educational legacy as well.

[2] Fethullah Gülen's Islamic reform movement originated in the teaching
of Said Nursi (1873–1960), who emphasized the importance of scientific
knowledge in raising religious consciousness. The Gülen community's movement builds on the idea that education is key to raising a generation both
deeply rooted in Islam and able to participate in the modern, scientific world
(Agai 2003).

[3] More specific information about the nature of these activities is withheld here to preclude undue government scrutiny of the programs that might
impede their implementation or jeopardize their participants.

References

Agai, Bekim. 2003. The Gülen movement's Islamic ethic of education. In
    Turkish Islam and the secular state: The Gülen movement, ed. Hakan
    Yavuz and John Esposito, 28–68. Syracuse, NY: Syracuse University
    Press.

Balci, Bayram. 2003. Fethullah Gülen's missionary schools in Central Asia
    and their role in the spreading of Turkism and Islam. *Religion, State
    and Society* 31(2): 151–77.

Clement, Victoria. 2004. *Trends in secular and religious education in
    Turkmenistan.* Seattle, WA: National Bureau of Asian Research.

Committee to Protect Journalists. 2006. North Korea tops CPJ list of "10 most
    censored" countries. *CPJ Special Report 2006.* May 2. Available online.

DeMars, William. 2005. *NGOs and transnational networks: Wild cards in world
    politics.* Ann Arbor, MI: Pluto Press.

International League for Human Rights and Turkmen Initiative for Human
    Rights. 2006. Alternative report to the UN Committee on the Rights of
    the Child. Available online.

Mamedov, Nazar. 2005. Ethnocultural practices in post-Soviet Kyrgyzstan and
    Turkmenistan: A comparative perspective. M.A. thesis, Central Euro-
    pean University.

Reporters without Borders. 2005. The fifteen enemies of the Internet and
    other countries to watch. November 17. Available online.

Turkmenistan Helsinki Initiative. 2004. Education in Turkmenistan. Avail-
    able online.

Turkmenistan Initiative for Human Rights. 2006. Education in Turkmenistan.
    Available online.

———. 2007. New textbooks to be issued. Available online.

UNICEF. 2003. Towards child-friendly learning with global education. Avail-
    able online.

———. 2007. TransMONEE database. Available online.

10

Quotas for Quotes

Mainstreaming Open Society Values in Uzbekistan

JACQUELINE ASHRAFI

After achieving independence in 1991, Uzbekistan's government pledged to set the country on a path to democracy and a free-market economy. Education was viewed as one of the most important mechanisms for achieving political, economic, and social progress. Throughout the 1990s the main goal of education reform was a reorientation from Soviet education practices toward the new demands of an emerging democracy. New education policies announced a major shift away from the Soviet ideological framework to a more Western-oriented one, creating socioeconomic, legal, psychological, and pedagogical conditions for the "moulding of versatile individuals," able to adapt to contemporary society, make conscious choices, master educational and professional programs, as well as become responsible citizens (Ministry of Public Education 1997, 34). Clearly, Uzbekistan's education reform goals echoed education slogans in other countries of the post-socialist bloc, triggering an influx of foreign assistance in education. By the end of the 1990s, education reform in Uzbekistan was strongly supported by numerous international agencies, including the ADB, UNICEF, UNESCO, USAID, EU, the British Council, Save the Children, OSI, and many others. Between 1996 and 2004, OSI alone

"Jacqueline Ashrafi" is a pseudonym for an expert in the field of education in Central Asia. Her real name is withheld to avoid the possibility of reprisals for the views expressed herein.

spent US$22 million on programs supporting the development of open society in Uzbekistan.

Ultimately, Uzbekistan's commitment to international standards of democratic governance proved hollow. By the end of the first decade of independence, many critics argued that "the adoption of democratic institutions was mere window dressing, designed for show rather than for real change" (Freedom House 2003). Like many other post-socialist countries, Uzbekistan adopted "the language of the new allies" but not necessarily the practices associated with it (Silova 2006; Steiner-Khamsi 2004). Increasingly, the education system became characterized by a conservative management style, with all major decisions still made at the ministry level and transmitted downward through regional and district institutions for implementation in schools. School curriculum and textbook-development systems remained highly centralized, alternative textbooks were not accepted, and the teaching profession was not respected. There was also a lack of access to information and limited resources available to teachers and students. The education system aimed at the ideological indoctrination of students, presenting a real threat to the development of a democratic society and market economy in Uzbekistan. In fact, many critics claimed that post-communist Uzbekistan was even more retrograde than before (Freedom House 2003).

Uzbekistan has increasingly become one of the strongholds of authoritarianism in the former socialist bloc. The Rose revolution in Georgia served as a warning to the governments of Central Asia about the power of well-organized civil societies. Uzbekistan's authorities began to create major obstacles for local and international NGOs in the aftermath, effectively stifling their work. In December 2003, Uzbek president Islom Karimov made a speech announcing it was time for Uzbek society to stop looking for outside help and that internal resources should be mobilized for development as an independent state.

Karimov's speech marked the beginning of a state crackdown on the NGO sector. All grants received from international donor organizations now had to be approved by a specially created committee, all events had to be preliminarily approved, and all international NGOs were required to re-register with the Ministry of Justice and to reopen their accounts in two officially designated banks, the National Bank of Uzbekistan or Asaka Bank. On January 28, 2005, the harassment of NGOs intensified as President Karimov promised that "democracy and various so-called open society models," along with other "alien" ideas espoused by NGOs, would not be tolerated (Press Service of the Republic of Uzbekistan 2005). This was interpreted literally, according to the Uzbek proverb, Ask someone to bring you a hat, and he will bring you a head. By the end of 2005, most international NGOs (including OSIAF) had been suspended or evicted, and more than 60 percent of all active local NGOs had been closed down (OSI 2005). Given the tightening of the authoritarian regime in Uzbekistan, the general consensus was that "Western policies meant to support development of political and economic openness in Uzbekistan had failed" (International Crisis Group 2006, 1).

In the increasingly repressive environment of Uzbekistan, one would not expect to find evidence of international NGOs promoting democratic values. Yet, some international NGOs left remarkable legacies, helping to maintain civil society values and educational opportunities in the expectation of future change to a new government. This chapter examines the contribution of two education programs funded by OSIAF—the textbook-development program, and the in-service teacher-training program—that were miraculously able to survive after the closure of OSIAF in 2004. Following the analysis of the education reform context and the role of international NGOs in education reform during the transformation period, this chapter reflects on the strategies used by OSIAF in mainstreaming open society values through education, despite the increasingly authoritarian nature of Uzbek government.

Post-socialist education reform package: The unique "fifth model of education"

Since Uzbekistan's independence in 1991, education has become a priority in state policy. The direction of education reform was set by President Karimov himself when he criticized the shortcomings of American, British, Japanese, and Soviet education systems and insisted that Uzbekistan should develop its own unique "fifth model of education." The Law of the Republic of Uzbekistan on Education and the National Program for Personnel Training (the Program)[1] were adopted in 1997. The Program defined some of the shortcomings of the existing personnel training system in Uzbekistan. It pointed out "the discrepancy in the requirements of democratic and market transformations, lack of technical and informational conditions for effective education, lack of skilled pedagogical staff, poor equipment, scientific literature and didactic materials, as well as the failure of close interaction, or mutually beneficial integration, between the systems of education, science, and production" (36). The Program pointed to the seventy-year heritage of Soviet education for the lack of linkage between education and the labor market, and it proposed the establishment of a system where these ties would be strengthened.

The proposed reform envisaged three stages of education development. During the first stage (1997–2001) the major tasks included revision of educational standards and curriculum, creation of a new generation of textbooks, and retraining of personnel. This was to be done with comprehensive assistance and "in collaboration with international donor organizations and funding" (40). The second stage (2001–5) called for a complete transition to a compulsory twelve-year education system, with nine years of general secondary education followed by three years of specialized education. The latter would take place either in professional colleges, where students would receive a general education as they pursue study in a number of different careers, or in academic lyceums, where students would broaden their knowledge of certain specialized fields (for example, law, economics, medicine).[2] Graduates of both types of institutions would have the same rights in terms of university access. The third stage (2005 and subsequent years) aimed to "improve and further develop personnel training on the basis of accumulated experience, and in terms of the broader socioeconomic development of the country" (41). Despite claims of its uniqueness, the proposed reform included features found in most other Central Asian republics—extension of education to twelve years, development of new curricula and textbooks, revision of educational standards, teacher training, and so forth—constituting a post-socialist education reform package.

Implementation of the new education reform, however, had some features unique to Uzbekistan. One example was the construction of new elite schools—colleges, lyceums, and gymnasia—which led to the emergence of exclusionary practices. In particular, the reform envisioned the construction of a very limited number of elite schools, calculated on the prediction that 10–15 percent of all graduates would enter higher education, while the remaining 85–90 percent would enter the labor market without any professional skills. While the majority of post-socialist countries (including most in Central Asia) have tried to expand access to higher education in order to become more competitive, Uzbekistan has attempted to limit access, fearing that an increase in the number of educated youth could potentially threaten the regime. Since independence, higher-education enrollment in Uzbekistan has actually been reduced by half, from 15.2 percent in 1990 to 7.9 percent in 2002. Meanwhile, it has increased substantially in most other countries of the former socialist bloc (UNICEF 2005).

In addition, the location of most colleges and lyceums was limited to certain geographic regions, thus preventing many students from obtaining high-quality education. In most cases the locations of different colleges and lyceums were chosen based on the place of residence of Uzbek historical figures. For example, the great poet Alisher Navoi was born and lived in the Navoi region; therefore, most educational establishments in Navoi specialize in literature and languages. Similarly, the great scientist and mathematician Al-Khorezmi lived in the Khorezm region, which means most lyceums specializing in mathematics were built in Khorezm. Clearly, these geographic restrictions have prevented many children from attending elite schools, adding to inequality in the education system and depriving the poorest children—and young women in particular—of their right to quality education.

While these are just a few examples of the divergence between officially articulated education goals (emphasizing democratization of education) and the reality of school practices (increasingly exclusionary, centrally controlled, and politically indoctrinating), there are many other instances where the language of reform has proved to be simply rhetoric. In most cases the reorientation of the education system toward democratization did not move beyond lip service. The "flag of convenience" (Lynch 1998, 9) was hoisted to secure international funding and subdue fear of "falling behind" other local education stakeholders. Once international funding was obtained, the money was often used for other purposes, from domestically developed reforms aimed at increasing state control, to political indoctrination. During the first decade of the transformation process there emerged an immense gap between what the government signaled to international organizations and what it conveyed to its own domestic constituents.

It is precisely the gaps between "policy talk," "policy action," and "policy implementation" (Tyack and Cuban 1995) that local and international NGOs attempted to fill in through their work. The unique feature of the Uzbek context was that these NGOs had to learn to play by the rules and master the language of local reform in order to have an impact. Based on both positive and negative experience, the assessment of government reform initiatives, and extensive discussions concerning the future of education, many local and international NGO representatives came to believe that close collaboration with the Uzbek government would be in everyone's best interest. It also ultimately proved to be the only option.

OSI/State relationship:
From close collaboration to complete alienation

OSIAF of Uzbekistan was established in 1996 to support programs focusing on legal, political, educational, communication, and human rights issues. Education formed the cornerstone of OSIAF initiatives, aiming to support innovation, increase knowledge of human rights and economics, and introduce new child-centered methodologies in order to foster the development of an open society.[3] From the very beginning it was crucial for OSIAF to establish good relations with the Uzbek government and local authorities to ensure that all programs ran smoothly. Given firm government control, hierarchical decision-making, and the politics of fear in Uzbek society, few individuals dared to engage actively with international NGOs without prior approval from state authorities. For example, if OSIAF organized an event (workshop, training, conference), the minister of education had to issue and sign an order allowing teachers to participate. OSIAF was forced to establish a legal basis for cooperation with the government, resulting in numerous Agreements of Cooperation between the Ministry of Higher and Secondary Specialized Education and the Ministry of Public Education.

OSIAF support for education reform had to be formulated within the official education agenda of the Uzbek government, in strict compliance with the Program. This was a fairly easy task, since the official language of education reform in Uzbekistan reflected many Western education policies and practices. According to the Program, one of "the most important prerequisites for radical reform of the training system" was "the dynamic movement of the Republic toward the construction of a democratic legal state and open civil society" (38). More specifically, the aim of the Program was "the fundamental reform of the education system, the complete reversal of its ideological routine, elaboration of the national educational system for training of highly qualified personnel up to the level of advanced democratic states, while meeting the requirements of morale and morals" (39). Was there a place—not to mention a legal basis—for OSIAF work in Uzbekistan? Definitely. The OSIAF mission was to assist the government in building an open society and market economy, with responsible, independent-minded citizens. Thus, OSIAF was able to develop a strategy to both meet the requirements of government reform initiatives as well as its own mission.

For several years OSIAF managed to implement its educational programs without interference from the government, working in compliance with existing state legislation and in accordance with state-articulated goals and objectives. For example, in order to organize a single training for teachers, OSIAF had to obtain a special decree *(prikaz)* from the Ministry of Education to release teachers from their obligations at schools. In textbook publishing, approval depended on compliance with government regulations on the requisite number of quotations from President Karimov. While some of these regulations seemed neither reasonable nor rational, strict compliance was the only way many NGOs, including OSIAF, could contribute to education reform in Uzbekistan.

Despite having cooperated, OSIAF still came under increasing government control and was eventually closed in 2004. In an official letter from state authorities (signed April 14, 2004), OSIAF was—particularly through its educational programs—accused of promoting values "alien to Uzbek society," and "contradicting national morals." Among numerous far-fetched accusations, two were directly aimed at OSIAF education programs. First, the letter stated that "there were three unlicensed resource centers established for teachers and students of higher education institutions, contradicting the law of the Republic of Uzbekistan . . . according to which all NGO educational activities must be authorized."[4] In fact, there were no laws on NGO licensing at the time the resource centers were established. It was only in March 2004 that the Cabinet of Ministers

issued decree #100, on the creation of a special committee responsible for licensing NGOs, and it was not until one year later that
the commission was actually established. Furthermore, Uzbek authorities disregarded the fact that the higher-education resource
centers were created jointly by OSIAF and higher-education institutions in accordance with Article 6 of the Agreement of Cooperation between the Ministry of Higher and Secondary Specialized
Education and OSIAF (signed January 11, 2002).

Second, OSIAF was accused of "buying and disseminating literature in social sciences and humanities, containing information
perverting the essence and content of socioeconomic and political
reforms conducted in Uzbekistan." The letter made particular reference to the electronic library (consisting of nine CDs published
in 2001 and disseminated to higher-education establishments), arguing that the library "contained materials contradicting the national interests of Uzbekistan and discrediting state policies." Once
again, OSIAF activities were based on the Agreement of Cooperation (especially Articles 2, 4, 7, 10, and 13), and OSIAF's role was
only to assist the government in implementing reforms by providing access to literature and information. In fact, all textbooks were
purchased based on official letters of request from the ministry.
Access to the electronic publishing materials (EBSCO) was provided based on a request from the Ustoz Foundation (a governmental NGO which retrains teachers) in context with its efforts, in
cooperation with UNESCO, to provide access to information.[5]

While speaking the language of government bureaucracy had been
a successful tactic for NGO work, by 2004 it was no longer effective. Following the 2003 Rose revolution in Georgia and the 2004
Orange revolution in Ukraine, the Uzbek government began to ha-
rass and prosecute local and international NGOs openly. It began
systematically to wipe out the NGO sector and destroy any trace of
nongovernmental initiatives by removing books from the libraries,
closing down resource centers, and giving NGO property to state
institutions. Despite the closure of OSIAF in April 2004, some education initiatives survived and continue to function independently.
Two programs—textbook development and teacher training—merit
particular attention. These are examples of education initiatives
that are least likely to survive state crackdowns on the NGO sector due to their explicit focus on promoting open society values in
education. Why did these initiatives survive in Uzbekistan? What

programmatic features were central to ensuring their continued existence? How were open society values made mainstream?

Quotas for quotes: The textbook-development program

Since the beginning of the 1990s, Uzbek education reform prioritized the development of "a new generation of textbooks." Throughout the 1990s old textbooks were wearing out, and there were very limited resources for printing new ones. The situation in Uzbekistan was particularly critical due to a shift from Cyrillic to the Latin alphabet in 1996. Uzbek students suffered most from the information vacuum. Only essential textbooks were published in the Latin alphabet, while remaining learning materials (reference books, manuals, and so forth) remained only available in Cyrillic. Even worse, there were practically no books or newspapers published in Latin script, and the Internet was neither easily available nor affordable for the majority of the rural population. In any event, most young people could read neither Russian nor any other language aside from Uzbek. Throughout the transformation period, textbooks remained the only source of information for most students. The legacy of Soviet ideology remained, with most textbooks (including government-published "new generation textbooks") stressing the existence of "one truth" and the importance of "official knowledge," while discouraging critical thinking.

Textbook revision is generally considered one of the most sensitive areas of education reform, especially in authoritarian countries aiming at political indoctrination of students. However, the Uzbek government has encouraged the involvement of international agencies as a way to attract additional funding to produce its "new generation" of textbooks. The Program reflected the "international language" of textbook reform and provided an easy entry for international agencies in textbook development. In particular, the Program stated that "in a democratic society, not only children, but every individual is brought up to be a free-thinker" (10). Furthermore, it criticized existing school curricula and textbooks, arguing that "sciences that teach basic morals, social, economic and legal knowledge, are not given a proper place" (8). OSIAF, as well as other donors (especially the ADB and the British Council), fit into the picture perfectly. International organizations collectively supported the publication of new textbooks and attempted to introduce international bidding procedures while encouraging an open market in textbook publication. The ADB provided a US$40 million loan for curriculum and textbook development, competitive textbook publishing, and modern equipment for publishing houses. The loan enabled the British Council to render technical assistance for the development of national standards, curriculum, and textbooks. OSIAF focused on building knowledge and skills in textbook development for authors and publishers, teacher training in new methodology, and a more interactive use of textbooks in schools.

More specifically, OSIAF focused on textbook development in two subject areas central to promoting open society values—civics and economics. The goal of the textbook-development program was to produce a series that, unlike existing materials, would encourage critical thinking, raise awareness of legal rights, and promote a sense of citizenship among students. The strategy supported a competitive process of textbook development, democratic selection procedures, and involvement of teachers in piloting new textbooks. These were bold ideas for Uzbekistan. They challenged the centralized structure of decision-making in the education system, while questioning the belief that the role of the textbook was simply to transmit "official knowledge."

In an education system where no alternative textbooks are allowed, OSIAF goals could be achieved only by working within the existing system, downplaying the genuine mission of the foundation, and playing by the rules. Official program documents had to downplay the focus on "democratization," "active citizenship," and "critical thinking," yet ensure that these principles were retained in the implementation process (for example, through training sessions and workshops for textbook authors) and program outcomes (for example, the actual textbooks themselves). In addition, OSIAF had to abide by official rules in textbook publishing, including meeting the quotas for quotations from President Karimov's speeches and the number of references made to his works. For example, any law/civic education textbook had to include at least fourteen quotations from Karimov. Generally, state authorities would be more likely to approve a school textbook if it strictly complied with or—better yet—exceeded the official quotas.

Without compromising its mission, OSIAF complied and produced a series of textbooks on civic education for secondary-school students. While featuring abstracts from the president's speeches, making reference to his work, and including his portrait, the books also covered a myriad of comprehensive topics promoting the values of open societies, democratic governance, human rights, and citizenship, teaching students to become independent, critical thinkers. This dual orientation—visibly promoting the values of the existing regime while advancing the values of the open society—was key in securing state approval for publication. Within the centralized education system of Uzbekistan, state approval means the new textbooks will continue to exist, if only because there is no funding to create others. Since their initial publication in 1999, a series of civics education textbooks produced by OSIAF has been reprinted annually by the government. The OSIAF contribution to textbook development was no longer mentioned, however—further indication that civics education textbooks will long outlive the organization itself, continuing to advance open society values in an increasingly authoritarian regime.

Institutionalizing within state structures: In-service teacher-training programs

Teacher training comprised another important component of education reform in Uzbekistan, which, similar to other areas, was largely neglected by the government. Although the Ministry of Public Education had officially expressed its commitment to more participatory and active teaching/learning in schools, practical implementation was stalled for several reasons. In particular, the language of the teacher-training reform was so obscure that most teachers could not understand it. In Uzbek, active teaching/learning methodology was translated as "new technologies" *(yangi tehnologiyalar)*, and ministry officials made no effort to explain to school administrators, teachers, and parents what this actually meant. Encounters with teachers from different regions revealed that new technologies were generally misunderstood as information technologies (computers, Internet connections, and so on), and many teachers naively used this as an excuse to retain old teaching practices—emphasizing teacher-centered instruction, relying on rote memorization, discouraging parental involvement (with the exception of the regular extortion of bribes), and maintaining hierarchical decision-making. Not only did ministry officials fail to explain what the new technologies were, but they also fell short on developing implementation strategy and securing sufficient funding for teacher-training reform.

Aiming to fill the gaps between policy talk, policy action, and policy implementation, several international organizations (OSIAF, UNICEF, Save the Children UK, among others) undertook initiatives aimed at training teachers in interactive teaching/learning methods. OSIAF contributed to these efforts by introducing teacher-training projects such as RWCT, Street Law, School Improvement, Debate, and others. These projects advanced the idea that the means to democratic citizenship resided not only in studying the content of subjects like civics or political science, but also in the daily conduct of classroom instruction—opportunities that are provided for cooperative work, decision-making, critical thinking, opinion formation, and debate. All these ideas seamlessly fit under the slogan of "new technologies," becoming part of Uzbekistan's teacher-training reform.

Unlike other international organizations, which relied on local NGOs as alternative service providers for in-service teacher training, OSIAF chose to work within state in-service teacher-training structures to ensure practical implementation of active teaching/ learning methodology in schools. In addition to working directly with schools, OSIAF trained a whole cadre of professionals from state in-service training institutions that provide regular teacher-training services to all teachers.[6] Furthermore, OSIAF worked with the Central In-Service Training Institution, responsible for upgrading professional skills among education managers at all levels, from heads of ministry departments to school directors. Institutionalization within state structures (that is, inclusion of OSIAF training modules in state curriculum in state in-service teacher-training institutions) meant that all teachers and education managers would be exposed to active teaching/learning methodology, participatory management, and democratic leadership at least once in five years, as required. Furthermore, it meant that OSIAF's teacher-training programs would remain unless replaced by some radical new reform in education.

While program institutionalization within state structures was an effective strategy in Uzbekistan's centralized education environment, there were several problems with this approach. First, there was a high turnover of personnel due to retirement and low salaries. If you train older teachers, what are the chances they will stay long enough to train others? If you teach younger methodologists, what are the chances they will be motivated to stay within the state education system instead of searching for better-paying jobs elsewhere? Teacher salaries constitute just 44 percent of the average in the industrial sector, and 38 percent of the average in financial, credit, and insurance institutions. Moreover, what is the likelihood that trained teachers will actually use the new, active teaching/learning methodologies in their classrooms? Will they have a supportive environment to implement change, given outdated textbooks and limited access to the Internet? Will school directors be open to allowing teachers to use active teaching/learning methods? In Uzbekistan's authoritarian environment, to what extent will a school director allow teachers to discuss issues openly, criticize the existing situation, and encourage meaningful parent participation? In addition to obstacles resulting from working in a hierarchical, centralized education system, program implementation could be impeded by a culture in which the younger generation obeys the older, women are submissive to men, and professional hierarchies are oppressive.

Mainstreaming OSI values in an authoritarian environment: Looking into the future

Since the collapse of the Soviet Union in 1991, Uzbekistan's government has initiated major reforms in the education sphere. While the official language reflected components typically found in other post-socialist countries—particularly the reorientation from Soviet to Western values—practical implementation of these ideas could not be further from officially articulated goals. Throughout the last decade the education system has become more centralized, hierarchical, corrupt, and unequal. Inevitably, an immense gap between what the government signaled to international organizations and what it implemented domestically has emerged. It is precisely the gaps between "policy talk," "policy action," and "policy implementation" (Tyack and Cuban 1995) that local and international NGOs attempted to fill in through their work. Use of the "global semantics" of education reform by state authorities created an entry for many local and international NGOs to initiate education programs aimed at democratization of the education system.

A unique feature of local and international NGOs working in Uzbekistan was that they had to master the language of the Uzbek government in order to have an impact on the education system. In particular, the OSIAF experience was that education programs were more likely to survive if they became institutionalized within state education structures, eventually losing their association with the OSIAF. For this to happen, OSIAF had to master the language of government and play by the rules. For example, the textbook-development program had to comply with the state quota on presidential quotations, while covertly introducing the values of open society and democratic citizenship. Similarly, the teacher-training program could be institutionalized within the state in-service teacher-training institutions only by officially emphasizing its focus on "new technologies," while vigilantly preserving instruction on the means to democratic citizenship through reform of the daily conduct of classroom instruction. Ultimately, the further OSIAF programs were dissociated from the foundation (for example, by dropping all references to OSIAF), the more chance they had to survive and serve as a window for promoting open society values and building a more democratic society.

Although some of OSIAF's education programs outlived the foundation itself, their future remains uncertain. Undoubtedly, institutionalization of the OSIAF's education programs within state structures created unique opportunities for education change. However, it simultaneously created new problems for survival without the compromise of original objectives and values. Once OSIAF education programs became institutionalized within the state structures, the government could manipulate program implementation by modifying program content or selectively implementing program components. In a system where laws were well written yet rarely implemented, education became one of the areas in which one could be particularly creative to make the world better. At the same time, it remained one of the areas where the real impact would not be visible for a very long time, possibly not until a new generation uses the rule of law to build a democratic society.

Notes

[1] References to the page numbers in the Program appear in parentheses in the following paragraphs.

[2] The second stage was prolonged until 2010 because the set tasks have not been accomplished in a timely manner. The main problem was connected with the inability to build and renovate secondary schools and construct new building for colleges and lyceums in such a short period of time.

[3] Education programs included Civics and Economics Education, School Improvement Program, RWCT, Street Law, Interactive Teaching Methods, English Language, Textbook Development, Faculty Development, Resource Centers, and Youth/Debate.

[4] Reference was made to the regulations contained in On the Licensing of Certain Types of Activities (May 25, 2005), and Decree #222–11 of Oliy Majlis (Parliament), List of Activities to Be Licensed (May 12, 2001).

[5] EBSCO Information Services is a worldwide company providing information access through print and electronic journal subscription services, research database development and production, online access to more than one hundred databases and thousands of e-journals, and e-commerce book procurement.

[6] One of the Soviet legacies is Uzbekistan's commitment to regular in-service teacher training. According to the education legislation, each teacher has to undergo in-service teacher training once every five years. Currently, however, the in-service teacher-education system itself (central and regional training centers) is physically incapable of serving *all* teachers over the period of five years. It is estimated that the current capacity of state in-service teacher-training institutions allows enrollment of only 60–65 percent of teachers every five years.

References

Freedom House. 2003. Nations in Transit. Available online.

International Crisis Group. 2006. Uzbekistan: In for the long haul. Available online.

Lynch, James. 1998. "The international transfer of dysfunctional paradigms." In *Learning and teaching in an international context: Research, theory, and practice,* ed. David Johnson, Bob Smith, and Michael Crossley, 7–33. Bristol: University of Bristol, Center for International Studies in Education.

Ministry of Public Education. 1997. Law of the Republic of Uzbekistan on Education. Tashkent, Uzbekistan: Ministry of Public Education.

———. 1997. National Program for Personnel Training. Tashkent, Uzbekistan: Ministry of Public Education.

OSI (Open Society Institute). 2005. Crackdown on NGOs in Uzbekistan. *Eurasian Civil Society Monitor.* Briefing 1. November. Available online.

Press Service of the Republic of Uzbekistan. 2005. Press statement. January 28. Available online.

Silova, Iveta. 2006. *From sites of occupation to symbols of multiculturalism: Reconceptualizing minority education in post-Soviet Latvia.* Greenwich, CT: Information Age Publishing.

Steiner-Khamsi, Gita, ed. 2004. *The global politics of educational borrowing.*
    New York: Teachers College Press.
Tyack, David, and Larry Cuban. 1995. *Tinkering toward utopia: A century of
    public school reform.* Cambridge, MA: Harvard University Press.
UNICEF. 2005. TransMONEE database. Available online.

Conclusion

Centralist and Donor-Dependent Governments

What's Left for NGOs to Do?

GITA STEINER-KHAMSI

This book is not about the role of NGOs in educational development in general. Rather, it deals with one international NGO in particular: the Soros Foundation Network in Caucasus, Central Asia, and Mongolia. During the important, early years of transition, the Soros Foundation was arguably the largest and most influential network in the post-socialist region. It was there before other donors and NGOs had set up their branch offices. An investigation of the particular challenges faced by the Soros Foundation Network promises to shed light on the larger issue of how NGOs work under the conditions of centralist and donor-dependent governments.

Caucasus, Central Asia, and Mongolia: A region?

Naturally, the authors of this book pay great attention to the country-specific conditions under which they operate. We will now take a step back to review similarities and differences across the region to draw conclusions from the chapters they have written. This perspective raises the question of whether or not Armenia, Azerbaijan, Georgia, Kazakhstan, Kyrgyzstan, Mongolia, Tajikistan, Turkmenistan, and Uzbekistan should be considered countries of the same region, an area approximated by the term *the Caucasus and Central Asia.*

To the east is Mongolia, the most sparsely populated country in the world. Eight times larger than Great Britain, the country is home to 2.8 million people, one-third of the population of Greater London. Now an independent country, Mongolia was a close ally of the Soviet Union and distanced itself from the Chinese brand of state socialism. Individuals who grew up under communism know Mongolia best as a country that, according to Lenin, "bypassed capitalism" (Shirendyb 1981; see Steiner-Khamsi and Stolpe 2006, 53ff.). The People's Revolution in Mongolia in 1921 was evidence that the four developmental stages of Marxism-Leninist theory—feudalism, capitalism, socialism, communism—do not apply to non-industrialized countries. At the Second Congress of the Comintern (Communist International) in 1920, Lenin pointed out that "with the aid of the proletariat of the advanced countries, backward countries can go over to the Soviet system and, through certain stages of development, to communism, without having to pass through the capitalist stage" (Shirendyb 1981, 20).

In the 1930s a population of cattle breeders, serving Buddhist-Lamaist monasteries, was reconstructed as a "working class" being oppressed by a "feudal class." Mongolia was used to demonstrate to all "backward countries" that a direct move from feudalism to socialism, bypassing capitalism, was indeed possible. As the second socialist state in the world—and the first in Asia—the Mongolian People's Republic was committed to working with the Soviet Union to form the foundations of the socialist world system. As opposed to today's notion of development/underdevelopment, the socialist conception was ideological. It mattered a great deal for the socialist world how advanced a particular member country was on the socialist path of development. Despite the fact that Mongolia was poor, the bypassing-capitalism narrative helped situate the country as an exemplar of successful political, social, and economic development under socialist auspices. At the end of the 1970s the Mongolian People's Republic was said to have established official relations with over forty former colonies in Africa, Asia, and Latin America (see Rathmann and Vietze 1978, 352).

Today, the Asian influence is clearly discernible in Mongolia. The largest donor is the Government of Japan, followed by the ADB. In the U.N. classification system, Mongolia is conspicuously missing from the Caucasus and Central Asia region. Instead, it is categorized as a country of the East Asia and the Pacific region, for reasons which remain unclear (see Steiner-Khamsi and Stolpe 2006, 90ff.).

The five former Central Asian Soviet republics—Kazakhstan, Kyrgyzstan, Tajikistan, Turkmenistan, and Uzbekistan—lie in the center of the Caucasus and Central Asia region. These countries are all well-endowed with natural and mineral resources that help offset, in some countries more than others, the economic hardship people experienced during the first decade of transition. Kazakhstan and Turkmenistan export fossil fuel, Kyrgyzstan and Tajikistan sell hydroelectricity to neighboring countries, and Uzbekistan's economic growth is, apart from agricultural production (cotton), based on the export of gold, natural gas, and ferrous metals. In the fifteen years since the dissolution of the Soviet Union, these five newly independent republics have grown apart.

Kazakhstan began to experience explosive economic growth in 2000, led mainly by the oil sector. The real GDP grew close to 10 percent each year since 2000 and has reached a GDP per capita of US$9,400. The largest of the Central Asian countries, Kazakhstan has started to dissociate itself from the other four countries in the region. Recognizing this development, USAID and UNICEF have ceased to refer to these five countries as one region, instead referring to it as Kazakhstan and the Central Asia region.

An El Dorado for multiculturalists and multilingualists, Kyrgyzstan acknowledges both Russian and Central Asian languages as languages of instruction in schools. The political tensions among several of the Central Asian states, however, have made schools for ethnic minorities unpopular. The number of schools offering instruction in Central Asian languages has been shrinking since the 1990s, not only in Kyrgyzstan, but throughout the region.

In Tajikistan, the "de-multiculturalization" or ethnic "un-mixing" was initially involuntary. The civil war (1992–97) left over half a million people internally displaced. Almost all of the ethnic minorities that fled Tajikistan during the civil war—Kyrgyz Tajiks, Turkmen Tajiks, Uzbek Tajiks, and Russian Tajiks—did not return. A second emigration wave has been labor related. According to the Migration Policy Institute (2006), Tajikistan may be the largest emigrant labor supplier per capita in the world. Estimates show that approximately 18 percent of the adult population (600,000 Tajiks) leaves the country each year in search of seasonal work. The most popular destination is Russia, which draws about 80 percent of all Tajik labor migrants, followed by smaller numbers going to Uzbekistan and Kazakhstan. The IMF estimates that Tajikistan receives between US$400 million and US$1 billion in remittances annually, or between 20 and 50 percent of its total GDP. The UNDP and other multilateral organizations are in dialogue with government officials, seeking ways to channel the remittances, the main drivers of economic growth, into poverty-alleviation programs and toward achieving the MDGs (UNDP 2005).

Turkmenistan and Uzbekistan have taken a peculiar stance toward international donors and NGOs. Only U.N. organizations and a select few non-Western donors are allowed to operate. The United States has taken the lead, supported by its allies, in criticizing these two countries for human rights violations. Turkmenistan was never open to the West, and Uzbekistan abruptly cut off contact after a decade of openness. The change in foreign relations occurred in 2005 after the government of Uzbekistan came under serious attack for mistreating citizens that it deemed to be "enemies of the state." Throughout the region, as well as in Belarus and Iran, the Soros Foundation has been closely associated with the Rose revolution in Georgia (2003). In the wake of the peaceful color revolutions in Georgia (2003) and a year later in Ukraine (2004), the mission of the Soros Foundation Network, particularly its commitment to building a strong civil society and an open society, became highly politicized. In Uzbekistan, in particular, Soros is viewed as an imminent political threat, and the OSIAF-Uzbekistan was the first international NGO to have its registration revoked in 2004. For this reason, the chapters on Turkmenistan and Uzbekistan are different from the others in this book. In Turkmenistan the Soros Foundation was never given access, and in Uzbekistan it was forced to leave behind human and material resources built up during the eight years it had operated (1996–2004).

Similar to the five former Central Asian Soviet republics, the three former Soviet Baltic states, and former Yugoslavia, the three countries in the Caucasus drifted apart once pan-socialist (and in the case of the Caucasus, Soviet) agreements dissolved. The ethnic land dispute over the Nagorno-Karabakh region escalated to a full-fledged war between Armenia and Azerbaijan from 1988 until 1994, leaving tens of thousands dead and wounded, and hundreds of thousands internally displaced. In "disuniting" they have also become more outward looking. Georgia, Armenia, and Azerbaijan see themselves as part of the European "educational space" (Nóvoa and Lawn 2002) and are in the process of bringing their higher-education systems in line with European reforms. The governments of all three signed the Bologna Declaration and have participated in meetings of the member states since 2005. By the year 2007, forty-five countries were endorsed as members of the Bologna Process, including all former socialist countries in Central, Southeast Europe (except for Kosova) and Eastern Europe. Harmonizing higher-education systems is comprehensive. The six original actions to which the member states subscribe are adoption of a system of easily readable and comparable higher education degrees, adoption of a system essentially based on two cycles (bachelor and master's level), establishment of a system of credits, promotion of mobility, promotion of European cooperation in quality assurance, and promotion of the European dimension in higher education (Bologna Process Secretariat, 2005a). The original action plan was supplemented with four new ones, added at meetings in Prague (2001) and Berlin (2003). States joining the Bologna Process must have ratified the European Cultural Convention. The convention seems to function as a gatekeeper for non-European countries. For example, even though the government of Kazakhstan applied for membership in the Bologna Process at the same time as the three countries in the Caucasus, it was relegated to observer status because it had not signed the European Cultural Convention (Bologna Process Secretariat 2005b, 3). For now, the three countries in the Caucasus constitute the eastern border of European harmonization in the areas of culture and higher education policies.

How do we justify compiling nine case studies, representing countries in the Caucasus, Central Asia, and Mongolia, under the same book cover? There are three features that are unique to this region and distinguish these nine from other post-socialist countries: First, they are comparative latecomers within the Soros Network and, in that capacity, regularly met and exchanged experiences among themselves. Second, they are donor dependent, or to be more accurate, they were donor dependent at the time the Soros Network set up national foundations in this region. However, the collapse of the Soviet Union meant they were downgraded from being treated as poor (socialist) second-world countries to (capitalist) third-world countries. Third, their governments are viewed as highly centralist. These three features deserve further explanation.

Latecomers within the post-socialist Soros Network

In its effort to establish new national foundations in the post-socialist region, the Soros Network moved east. The first national foundation was established in Hungary in 1984, followed by others over the course of the next few years in Central and Southeastern Europe, and then in Eastern Europe as well. By the time the national foundations opened in the Caucasus, Central Asia, and Mongolia, the Soros Network already had educational network programs and experienced staff in place at the older national foundations. The transfer of existing programs, as well as the dispatch of consultants from Estonia, Latvia, Lithuania, Slovakia, Ukraine, and Romania, was seen as a means to help jump start operations in the new region. George Soros and the board of directors of OSI firmly believe in the limited lifespan of national foundations. They see OSI funding as seed money for initiatives that help create open societies that, after a period of inception and consolidation, should be carried on with funding from other sources. This belief has great repercussions in terms of day-to-day activities.

By the time the national foundations in Caucasus, Central Asia, and Mongolia started operation, the older foundations were in the process of phasing out, spinning off various programs, or exiting altogether. Soros phased out programs that were seen as obsolete, either because they were sufficiently mainstreamed or were being continued by other nongovernmental or private providers. English-language teaching is an example of a network program that was phased out in many national foundations at an early stage because of the proliferation of private language schools or because governments prioritized English-language instruction as part of educational reform. Other programs, such as those in arts and culture or education, were spun off either to professional associations (for example, the International Step by Step Association), or to newly founded local NGOs. Typically, OSI provided a financial cushion or transitional grant until the new associations or NGOs succeeded in securing funding in the form of grants or fees for services. The national foundations in the Caucasus and Central Asia began operating at a time when their counterparts to the west were starting to close down. The closing of older national foundations sent a signal that Soros Foundation headquarters in New York acts upon its belief that assistance should not last forever and that innovative practices, initiated by NGOs, should become institutionalized.

After the millennium, Soros urged the new foundations to pre-pare themselves gradually to shut down and to seek matching funds as a first step toward exiting. From the outset, sustainability of project initiatives, beyond the limited duration of the national foun-dation, was a primary concern in the new region. The newly founded national foundations had to work themselves out of busi-ness by handing over their programs to government institutions. The hand-over strategy differentiates the Soros Network from other international NGOs such as Save the Children UK, Aga Khan Foun-dation, or World Vision, which are given a more permanent mis-sion in the countries where they operate. Phasing out the national foundations in EU accession countries and establishing new na-tional foundations in the Caucasus, Central Asia, and Mongolia meant the new foundations were regarded as, and became, an OSI region. They frequently met in regional meetings, exchanged expe-riences, and borrowed reform strategies from one other.

Unsurprisingly, the national foundations in the Caucasus and Central Asia aimed at institutionalizing their initiatives within gov-ernmental structures as quickly as possible. Having cooperative learning or RWCT taught by regular teacher educators, either in in-service or pre-service teacher education, rather than by their own trainers, was interpreted as a successful strategy for ensuring sustainability. Thus, what other NGOs negatively label cooptation—the government using NGO-developed material and resources with-out giving credit to the NGO—was, in the early years of the national foundations, seen as a desired outcome (see Najam 2000). There was little concern for copyright or intellectual property rights within the Soros Network as long as OSI practices were mainstreamed and institutionalized. In the last few years, however, spin-offs of the network programs (especially SbS and RWCT) have revised this approach. SbS also pursued a comprehensive reform approach to early childhood education that affected pedagogy, developmental psy-chology, classroom architecture, teaching/play material, and required close collaboration with parents. This could only be sustained by means of a curriculum reform in preschool-teacher-education insti-tutions. Curriculum reform became, for SbS, an important target that determined whether the program was successfully implemented or not.

A review of the chapters presented in this book conveys the priority attached to having OSI-initiated projects integrated into government-sponsored structures. The limited time perspective also explains the strong belief in capacity building. A great bulk of OSI funding has been allocated for the professional development of teachers, school administrators, government officials, textbook authors, publishers, teacher educators, university lecturers, and all other groups that have a stake in educational reform. Building capacity in the country rather than relying and depending on international experts from the United States and Europe has been a key sustainability strategy for the Soros Network. The expectation is that these national experts will continue to use their newly acquired skills, and use them for educational reform in their countries even when external funding dries up. Capacity building of OSI staff is taken seriously as well. Staff in the national foundations gather several times each year for regional and international conferences and are funded for professional-development courses that strengthened their skills in project management, needs assessment, program evaluation, and educational policy studies. These skills are seen as core requirements for professionally designing, administering, and monitoring educational projects. During the exiting stage of a national foundation, the commitment to capacity building grows even stronger. The boards of national foundations realize that their staff will soon need either to establish their own local NGO and seek external funding or find employment in other organizations. The belief in professional development of the staff is not an expression of employer's guilt. Rather, equipping employees with the necessary skills is a powerful tool for placing former OSI employees in positions of responsibility in which they can continue to support, and possibly steer, educational reform in their countries.

After 2002 the Soros Network expanded in two directions. Incentives were created to establish educational policy centers that would move beyond project work and instead function as think tanks. These think tanks conducted studies and evaluations of educational reforms and functioned as advocacy NGOs. They initiated activities such as donor watch, advanced anti-corruption legislation, and supported strategic litigation. Funding for these educational policy centers was not only made available to the existing OSI national foundations in the Caucasus, Central Asia, and Mongolia, but also to the spin-offs in Central, South East, and Eastern Europe. Another development that began to take shape at around this same time was the commitment of George Soros and the OSI board to go global. The Soros Network now began to operate in parts of the world beyond the post-socialist region.

From Second World to Third World

In 1991, Stephen P. Heyneman, now professor of international education policy at Vanderbilt University, was a senior education specialist at the World Bank, responsible for education policy and lending in twenty-seven countries in Europe and Central Asia. As president of CIES he was in charge of organizing the annual conference in 1992. Fifteen years later, in an interview with past presidents of CIES, he recalled the fall of the Berlin Wall and the wave of independence movements that ultimately broke apart the Soviet Union. Having worked for years in the region, he knew the newly appointed ministers of education in each country and sought ways to invite them as presenters and honored guests. A few months before the conference, and only a few weeks after events had culminated in the region, he met with Anthony Richter, then a regional director at OSI-NY. An agreement was reached within hours that OSI would invite the ministers. Heyneman recalls:

> The formal break-up of the Soviet Union was in the fall and we had our conference in the spring. The Soviet Union broke up into fifteen republics. I had been working in some of them through the World Bank and had connections with them. I thought it would be a magnificent event if we as a society could reach out to each of these new countries, independent for a few months only, and invite them to our conference. ... In the end, our conference, during my presidency, opened up on a stage where they had fifteen ministers of new countries. All I did was announce them: "Colleagues, I would like to introduce you to the ministers of education of these new countries." I read the list of countries: Uzbekistan, Tajikistan, Turkmenistan, etc. The audience went crazy. Everyone applauded. It was very interesting. (Heyneman 2006)

Having only seen the gray-shaded territory of the USSR on their maps, scholars and professionals in international, comparative, and development studies in education in the United States and the West barely knew where to locate these new countries. At first, there was a sense of beginning and revolutionary change, but the initial excitement diminished once it became apparent that people in the region suffered severe economic hardship. Infrastructure collapsed in the first years after the transformation. Access to safe water became a problem, domestic air travel came to an almost complete standstill, and coal for heating and electricity became rare commodities. Prices for fuel, coal, and electricity soared once the market was liberalized, and residents could not afford to pay for basic utilities. Not only villages, but towns as well were literally in the dark, bringing new meaning to the old slogan, Communism brings light. What people in the early 1990s were experiencing seemed like a return to pre-modern or pre-Communist times. The dissolution of agricultural collectives and collectives for animal husbandry not only generated unemployment but also eliminated an important financial resource for preschools, schools, and boarding schools in rural areas. The unequal living standards between urban and rural areas triggered a massive migration to towns and, in particular, capital cities. Scholars hastily settled upon a label—transition—to describe what had gone wrong.

Socialist countries in the region covered in this book had prided themselves on having universal provision of education and healthcare. Ironically, it was only when Education for All was declared in 1990, that access to schooling was becoming an issue for them. Development banks, notably the ADB and the World Bank, insisted on "rationalization," "concentration," "optimization," or structural adjustment programs in order to make the educational systems more cost effective. Cost effectiveness in the region meant reducing the number of small schools in remote rural areas and encouraging the establishment of large schools in regional centers. This policy proved a disaster for populations in rural areas because they could not afford to send their children to regional schools that were too distant from their homes.

Another common reform was to confine complete secondary schools (grades one to ten; later grades one to eleven) to regional centers. This meant taking the two upper grades away from schools in more remote rural areas, reducing them to grades one to eight schools (later grades one to nine). In Mongolia, parents were incensed when the Ministry of Education, with funding from the ADB, introduced its "rationalization" reform. Under tremendous pressure from parents, principals gave preferential treatment to eighth-grade graduates from their own school and quickly filled the few available seats in the ninth and tenth grades with their "own" students. Faced with this situation, parents from regular district schools soon realized that the only way to secure a place in a ninth or tenth grade was to enroll their child in a regional school before eighth grade. The regional schools with complete secondary education started to fill up rapidly after fifth grade, and the situation became intolerable for all parties involved. A counter-reform movement from "below" emerged. In an act of subtle subversion, the directors of the regional education and culture departments approved every single school request to reinstate grades nine and ten. By 2004, the reform imposed by structural adjustment policies was reversed. As one of the directors of the regional education and culture departments quite sensibly remarked: "What were they [the central government] thinking, when they closed down grades 9 and 10? The parents were running down our office to undo this unjust reform" (Steiner-Khamsi, Stolpe, and Gerelmaa 2004).

A vicious circle of underdevelopment in rural areas was perpetuated. In the early 1990s families left the countryside for towns in search of work and better living conditions. A few years later a mass exodus of families occurred because the infrastructure (schools, hospitals) had either collapsed or was deteriorating. While the first migration wave was labor related, the second was policy induced. Ten years later development banks are attempting to undo the damage of structural adjustment reforms. In Kyrgyzstan and Mongolia, for example, the World Bank funds educational projects for rural school development. Since 2005, several countries have been approved for the EFA FTI, and millions of dollars are spent to reintroduce universal access to and completion of primary school.

The quality of education has declined drastically in the past fifteen years. Instructional time for students in the Caucasus, Central Asia, and Mongolia is shorter than for students in any other part of the world. In Tajikistan, for example, the school year lasts thirty-four weeks, compared to the international average of thirty-eight to forty-two weeks per year. When it comes to a regional comparison, Mongolia, Azerbaijan, and Tajikistan have the shortest instructional time, and Turkmenistan, Kyrgyzstan, and Georgia the highest (Steiner-Khamsi 2007). But compared to other regions, students in the Caucasus, Central Asia, and Mongolia do not go to school nearly as much as students in other regions. Exceptions are Central and Eastern Europe, where instructional time is also low but increasing.

Arguably, instructional time is only a quantitative measure of the quality of education. A qualitative analysis reveals that the curricula in the educational systems of the region are cluttered with too many subjects, with too little time allocated to teach them. To make things worse, teachers are prepared to teach only one or two subjects. Because of the overburdened curriculum, however, they end up teaching several, including some for which they have not been trained. Another quality measure relates to the working condition of teachers in the region. Except for Mongolia, teachers in the other eight countries are paid below the national average (Anderson and Heyneman 2005; Steiner-Khamsi 2007; World Bank 2006). The statutory teaching hours *(stavka)* are, depending on country and grade level, sixteen to twenty-four hours a week. But for teachers to make a living, they must teach multiple *stavkas,* engage in private tutoring (see OSI 2006), and engage in all kinds of additional economic activities outside of school. There is very little time left for preparing lessons and providing feedback to students.

The situation in this particular region was at its worst in the mid-1990s. Not only were salaries low, but they were paid late, at times by several months. Teachers in many countries in the region went on strike, which in turn prompted politicians to shame them publicly, accusing them of being greedy and neglecting the job of caring for and educating "our children." The situation for teachers has improved only slightly over the past fifteen years. The teacher shortage is rampant in Kyrgyzstan and Tajikistan. The governments in these two countries issue decrees that, in our opinion, qualify as emergency laws. Details include paying new teachers an additional stipend, provided they stay in service for three years (Kyrgyzstan), or making fifth-year students of teacher education work in schools rather than complete their teacher education degree (Tajikistan). Throughout the region, teacher salaries have been raised, year after year, so that teachers are no longer impoverished, but in some countries they are heavily in debt from loans. In 2007, the average monthly salary for teachers was US$29 in Tajikistan (100 TJS) and US$13 in Kyrgyzstan (530 KGS)—far below the national salary average.

This is not to suggest that external assistance has drastically decreased during the transition period. The countries presented in this book have always been dependent on central funding from Moscow, or in the case of Mongolia, external assistance from other socialist countries. The problem is not so much the level of loans and grants given to the countries in the Caucasus, Central Asia, and Mongolia, but the lower commitment to education. Mongolia is a good case in point to illustrate the shift in priorities. In 1962, the Mongolian People's Republic was accepted as a member of the Council for Mutual Economic Assistance (CMEA), composed of Eastern bloc countries (at the time, the USSR, Bulgaria, Hungary, Poland, Romania, and Czechoslovakia). It received ample external assistance to develop its educational system, and has been aid dependent since the 1960s. The "internationalist" aid from the Soviet Union and CMEA at the end of the 1980s was 30 percent of the GDP, and ten years later the international development aid (ADB, Japan International Cooperation Agency, World Bank, GTZ, USAID, and others) was 25 percent. Aid dependency has not changed, but the priorities for external assistance have shifted, with less funding given to education and the social sector in general. From 1991 until 2004, the government of Mongolia received US$2.6 billion in external assistance (half in loans), heavily concentrated in the economic sector, for transport, industry, construction, electricity, and heating (World Bank 2004). Of all large donors, only the ADB appears to be focused on education. Yet its allocation to the social sector (health, education, social insurance reform) is a meager 9 percent of its overall financial commitment to Mongolia (ADB 2000,7). Armenia, Azerbaijan, Georgia, Tajikistan, and Uzbekistan are aid dependent as well, and categorized, according to the debt sustainability analyses carried out by the IMF and the World Bank, as having a "modest" or "moderate" debt burden. The only exception is Kyrgyzstan, which is in the process of being rated as a "heavily indebted poor country."

Working under centralist governments

The OSI has been criticized in some countries in the region for not being close to the people but rather exclusively focused on influencing large stakeholders, such as governments and donors. Even though OSI provided start-up funds for local NGOs as part of its mission to strengthen civil society, it regarded itself, according to critics, as one of the "big players" when it came to its operations among national foundations. It is accurate to state that the national foundation in this region targeted systemic change in education and therefore had to win approval, or even better, support, from governments. Both a donor and an implementer, the national foundations insisted on being included in donor-coordination meetings, demanded a broader participation in education-sector reviews, and held public events to discuss education-sector strategies. The last are typically prepared by international consultants from multilateral organizations, and merely rubber-stamped by ministries of education.

There are two explanations for this particular Soros reform strategy. First, as mentioned before, national foundations were set up with a limited life span, generating pressure to institutionalize their initiatives within existing government structures as quickly as possible. More often than not, OSI-funded projects were designed as incubator, demonstration, or pilot projects, with the expectation that the government, often with financial support from donors, would carry on and mainstream the OSI initiative. Second, the national foundations worked under politically unstable, centralist governments characterized by rapid turnover of senior officials. With every political change, senior government officials at the central, regional, and local levels, as well as at the school level (principals) are replaced with allies and supporters of the new administration. Schools are treated as government sites and not as public sites, making it necessary to realign the leadership locally whenever there is a change at the central level. It became a routine procedure for national foundations of OSI to prepare a Memorandum of Understanding with their respective ministries of education, in which agreements, such as cost-sharing arrangements, support of a pilot project by providing release time for teachers, administrators, and so on, were put on paper and signed. As with other international NGOs or donors, these agreements have not always been honored, especially if there was a change in political administration. A compilation of Memoranda of Understanding assembled from the national foundations operating in the region would by far exceed the volume of this book, and probably fill an entire bookshelf.

The World Bank regularly evaluates six governance indicators in 212 countries. The ratings are taken from thirty different organizations, mostly commercial risk-rating agencies, NGOs, multilateral-aid agencies, and other public-sector organizations. The report,

Governance Matters 2007, provides time series data for the period 1996–2006 on the following six governance indicators:

- *Voice and Accountability*—measures the extent to which a country's citizens are able to participate in selecting their government, as well as freedom of expression, freedom of association, and a free media;
- *Political Stability and Absence of Violence*—measures perceptions of the likelihood that the government will be destabilized or overthrown by unconstitutional or violent means, including terrorism;
- *Government Effectiveness*—measures the quality of public services, the quality of the civil service and the degree of its independence from political pressures, the quality of policy formulation and implementation, and the credibility of the government's commitment to such policies;
- *Regulatory Quality*—measures the ability of the government to formulate and implement sound policies and regulations that permit and promote private sector development;
- *Rule of Law*—measures the extent to which agents have confidence in and abide by the rules of society, and in particular the quality of contract enforcement, the police, and the courts, as well as the likelihood of crime and violence; and
- *Control of Corruption*—measures the extent to which public power is exercised for private gain, including both petty and grand forms of corruption, as well as "capture" of the state by elites and private interests. (World Bank 2007, 3–4)

A review of the six indicators for the nine countries presented in this book reveals the following findings for the year 2006: *Voice and accountability* are virtually nonexistent in Turkmenistan, and Uzbekistan, but close to the 50th percentile mark in Georgia, and over the 50th percentile mark in Mongolia. *Political stability* is very low, particularly in Uzbekistan, Tajikistan, Kyrgyzstan, and Azerbaijan. It is in the 0–10th percentiles for the data on Uzbekistan and Tajikistan, where political stability is seen as a problem. For the remaining four indicators—*government effectiveness, regulatory quality, rule of law,* and *control of corruption*—Armenia, Georgia, and Mongolia are assessed much more positively than the other countries (Kazakhstan, Turkmenistan, Azerbaijan, Tajikistan, Uzbekistan, Kyrgyzstan) but are still only around the 50th percentile. In contrast, former socialist countries in Central, Southeast, and Eastern Europe that are now part of the EU are in the 90th-100th percentiles, with only a few in the 50th–90th percentiles.

Corruption in education has become a hotly debated issue in the local media of these countries, as well as in educational research (see OSI 2006). Three of the nine countries discussed in this book (Kyrgyzstan, Georgia, and Kazakhstan) successfully introduced standardized university exams to curb bribes given to university lecturers and administrators in return for a seat in a prestigious university. Mongolia and Tajikistan are currently piloting standardized exams. Efforts to combat corruption in education are strongly advocated by civil society organizations working in these countries, and the establishment of testing centers has been funded by the World Bank and USAID.

Ketevan Rostiashvili (2004, 27ff.) presents estimates of how much families in Georgia had to pay to place their child in a university before unified entrance exams were introduced. On average, parents paid up to US$2,100 for private tutoring to have their child prepared for the three to four subjects tested in the university entrance exams. With nearly thirty thousand students entering universities each year, the private tutoring business was worth nearly US$65 million annually. Additionally, parents were requested to pay bribes if their child scored below the required grades. For example, bribes cost, on average, US$8,000–9,000 for admittance to the journalism faculty at Tblisi State University (TSU). The most expensive bribes were for the law faculty at TSU (US$20,000–30,000), but when the new State Technical University opened a competing law-degree program, the law faculty at TSU had to lower their bribes to US$10,000–15,000 per admitted student. Rostiashvili finds that parents paid on average US$5,500 in bribes per child. Approximately ten thousand of the thirty thousand admitted students scored below the required grade and only secured a place thanks to bribes. This means that annually US$50 million were spent on bribes. The findings from this fascinating study on corruption in the higher education system of Georgia, pre-Rose revolution, can be summarized as follows: Parents in Georgia paid US$50 million in bribes and US$65 million on private tutoring in 2003. In the same year, the government's expenditure on education was only US$34 million.

The variety in dealing with centralist governments

The governance features, summarized in the previous section, have a bearing on how NGOs, including national foundations of the Soros Network, function. In analyzing how NGOs define their relationship with governments, Adil Najam (2000) identified four types: cooperation, confrontation, complementary, and cooptation. While his typology might apply to NGOs in other parts of the world, we found a different set of NGO-government relations in the post-socialist region. The case studies reflect a fascinating range of strategies in the post-socialist region to cope with a governance environment that is centralist and, for the most part, donor dependent. We propose the following three terms to distinguish the roles of NGOs, exemplified in national foundations of the Soros Network: *complementary, cooperative, surrogate.*

The complementary role of NGOs

The most common strategy for dealing with a centralist government is to present a corrective to ongoing reforms that is in line with the mission of the NGO. An NGO incubates an innovative practice in an area that is neglected by the government with the expectation that the complementary project will later grow into an institutional practice, inscribed in educational policy. In practice this means that the NGO initiates, designs, and monitors a project that, upon successful completion of the pilot stage, is to be implemented on a large scale. Preferably, it will be funded by the government or, if this is not possible, by other donors. As illustrated in the following examples, strategies for persuading centralist governments to pay more attention to civil society involvement vary.

In Armenia, OSIAF initiated community schools in 2000 with the expectation that other donors, and ultimately the Ministry of Education, would take the pilot project to scale. It established twelve Community TeleCenters throughout the country that were used as learning centers for individuals of all age groups, as well as cultural and recreational centers for the community. These centers integrated information technologies and thereby provided an opportunity for students and community members to communicate by email and to use the Internet. Additional project components, such as e-curricula in the Armenian language, ICT training for teachers, and the creation of an interschool Web portal, maximized the usage of resources made available in the Community TeleCenters.

Armenuhi Tadevosyan examined (Chapter 2) the reception of these centers by the government and other donors. Two projects, in particular, were closely related to what OSIAF had already established in the year 2000. The Armenia School Connectivity Program, implemented by the NGO Harmony and funded by USAID, fully integrated the twelve pilot schools and involved them in all activities of the new project. An important side effect of integration into the USAID-funded project was the ability to reach out to a greater number of schools in the country that were members of the Armenia School Connectivity Program. The newly established computer centers, created in over three hundred schools, used material and best practices developed in the OSIAF-Armenia pilot project. The integration of the pilot project into the larger Armenia School Connectivity Program, funded by USAID, occurred smoothly. However, the subsequent project, carried out by the Ministry of Education and funded by the World Bank, very selectively drew only on networks, resources, and expertise already built in the two previous projects. The similarities in the three projects are striking, and yet the World Bank–funded project insisted on the novelty of its approach and did not integrate the existing network of schools into its project.

In most of the case studies presented in this book, a "policy window" (Kingdon 2003, 165; see also Sabatier and Jenkins-Smith 1993; Howlett and Ramesh 2003) opened, in which the government first signaled a commitment to change. In the Armenian case study, the Financing and Management Reform Project—approved in 1997 and funded by a World Bank loan of US$15 million—targeted community and parental participation in school funding and management, and at the same time assured schools that they could decide how to use the income that was generated at the school level. The OSIAF-Armenia–funded project, Community TeleCenters, built on the promise made by the government, and at the same time put a civil society spin on it. Rather than merely exploiting the parents and the community for financial support of schools, the centers were created to provide services *to* the community and increase their participation in schools.

Elmina Kazimzade (Chapter 3) also highlighted the window of opportunity for OSIAF-Azerbaijan to become actively involved. The "new quality standard of textbook provision" was signed by the government of Azerbaijan and approved by the World Bank for a loan of US$73 million for the period 2003–13. OSIAF-Azerbaijan used this broader legal framework and larger educational reform to "'de-monopolize' authorship, improve pedagogical and technical quality by stimulating competition among publishers, and open up the market to provide a wide range of free textbooks and teaching/learning materials" (Crighton 2001, 19). It was an opportune moment to design a project in line with the mission of the NGO: to train innovative practitioners and academics, based in the country, as textbook authors. Besides building local capacity, OSIAF-Azerbaijan insisted on a practice that was unprecedented in textbook publishing: the textbooks had to first be piloted and then, based on feedback from practitioners, revised before being printed for general use. OSIAF managed to persuade the Ministry of Education to "de-monopolize" the market and to stimulate competition among publishers. It proposed to the Ministry of Education the establishment of a Textbook Approval Board that, functioning as an external and independent body, determines the rules for competition and criteria for textbook evaluation.

In Mongolia, the project School 2001, described by Natsagdorj Enkhtuya (Chapter 7) originated in the context of standards-based curriculum reform. In 1997, the Ministry of Education planned to revise the curriculum with funding made available by the ADB. The MFOS anticipated that the ADB-funded reform would consist only of cosmetic changes, proposed by Mongolian government officials and academics who were far removed from educational practice. As a result, the curricula would be revised only on paper and never make it to schools. To counter this trend, the MFOS generated a movement "from below" and launched a school-based curriculum-reform project that lasted from 1998 until 2001, labeled School 2001. The project offered school-based professional development on student-centered learning, lesson planning, and curriculum design for school hours. The term *school hours* refers to the proportion of the curriculum in which schools were entitled to develop and teach their own content. The project provided schools

with grants to publish their own curricula, such as booklets on local history, local fauna, local art, and so on.

What triggered the interest of the Ministry of Education and
other NGOs and donors was not so much the curricular aspects of
School 2001 but how the project operated. School 2001 was committed to peer training and peer mentoring, that is, teachers training teachers. To do so effectively, the project paired schools and
actively supported and funded school networking. The school networking approach, in which schools "adopted" (trained and
mentored) surrounding schools, as well as new partner schools,
was novel. The school-adoption feature transformed it into a nationwide project in which schools enthusiastically adopted other
schools and promulgated practitioner-driven reform. The sheer
number of schools involved in this reform movement—one out of
every eight school in the country—made it impossible to overlook.

Unfortunately, the curricular objective was not embraced by government officials. The Ministry of Education invited only a few
practitioners to participate in the ADB-funded curriculum reform.
This was merely tokenism, as the practitioners in the working
groups were outnumbered by government officials and academics
who insisted on having curriculum reform strictly under their control. Anticipating such an outcome at the end of the project, government officials in charge of curriculum issues were included from
the beginning as participants and attended, alongside practitioners,
all project activities.

Ironically, though the original purpose of the project—ensuring
practitioner input in curriculum reform—failed, the project was a
great success in other, unanticipated ways. In effect, School 2001
was not only a school-based reform movement for practitioners,
but it also functioned as professional development for government
officials in charge of curriculum reform. The initial purpose was to
some extent unrealized, but what caught on were the ideas of peer
mentoring, peer training, and school-based training. These features
resonated with the Ministry of Education and other donors, notably DANIDA, because the centralist in-service training was too
expensive and ineffective, and alternatives were not apparent.
School-based training filled a vacuum at a time when teachers were
complaining because the Ministry of Education had discontinued
in-service training for teachers. The Ministry of Education was

convinced that school-based training, successfully demonstrated in School 2001, was the way of the future.

In May 2002, the deputy minister of education submitted his proposal, "School 2004," to a meeting of donors, held in Paris. The proposal requested funding for a continuation of School 2001 so that by 2004 every school in Mongolia would be adopted, mentored, and trained by another school. The donors did not approve the proposal. However, a Danish-Mongolian NGO, funded by DANIDA (which had been committed for years to rural school development), adopted several key features of School 2001 and successfully implemented them for its school-based training. Enkhtuya explains the close cooperation among NGOs in Mongolia, which results in the best practices of NGOs circulating with the help of other NGOs.

The Georgia case study, presented by Anna Matiashvili (Chapter 4), captures the struggle over the semantics of decentralization. On one side are international development banks, which tend to reduce decentralization to a matter of finance, and on the other side are civil society organizations, including OSI, which attempt to uncover the social accountability potential of decentralization reform. On this issue, the centralist governments tend to side with the development banks. This is because the ministries of education are provided with ample technical assistance to implement the financial aspect of decentralization and are left on their own when it comes to reforming the governance of education. The development banks are indecisive about whether they want to have a strong centralist government that oversees and administers grants and loans or whether they support a devolution of power to the regional and local level, which could entail less accountability for the borrower (government). The ministries of education themselves are reluctant to delegate decision-making authority to lower levels of administration.

It is important to keep in mind the size of the education sector to understand the importance given to controlling it. In Mongolia, 73 percent of all public servants are employees in the education and health sectors (ADB 2004). In Tajikistan, education salaries make up about 56 percent of the total wage bill of the public sector, which, besides education, includes public administration, defense and law enforcement, health, social protection, and several other areas (World Bank 2005). The political significance of education is not to be underestimated. It is the largest sector in post-socialist countries in terms of individuals employed by the government. Given the tendency of governments and development banks only to advance decentralization of finance, it has become a top priority of NGOs to act as a counter-force and emphasize the neglected aspect of decentralization: participation and governance by community members.

The Georgian case represents a prototypical reform of OSI, also pursued in other countries of the region. The government of Georgia issued the Decentralization Decree in 1999, and a year later signed a cooperation agreement with the OSGF to pilot several models of administrative decentralization in the education sector. The Memorandum of Understanding explicitly framed the OSGF as a pilot that would be used nationwide upon successful completion of the project. The project was enthusiastically endorsed and successfully implemented. However, two unexpected events occurred that annulled the agreement. First, a much bigger donor stepped forward with a US$60 million credit, disbursed over a period of twelve years, provided that the government of Georgia would give financial autonomy to schools. The big donor was the World Bank, and the program to which the government of Georgia committed itself was the Education System Realignment and Strengthening Program. As part of the program, per capita financing was introduced and vouchers issued for both public and private schools. In term of governance, the project was very narrowly defined in that it provided training for school administrators and educational authorities, mostly in the domain of educational finance.

The second key event was the peaceful Rose revolution of 2003, in the wake of which former agreements with NGOs were discontinued and replaced. OSGF was not exempted from this general approach to agreements made with the previous government, even though the Soros Network has been credited or discredited, respectively, for having been closely associated with political events leading up to the revolution. The new government and the World Bank brought in their own stakeholders and experts, disempowering the local capacity built in the previous period. Matiashvili's observations concur with those made by other authors in this book: the centralist government changes orientation and alliances whenever a bigger donor, typically a development bank, enters the field of educational reform. In order to justify a multi-million dollar loan to its own constituents and the public media, the government downplays existing projects and best practices that NGOs already had in place for years. The government pretends that the proposed new project, generously funded by multilateral donors, fills a great need that had not been addressed in the past. The distancing posture and the institutional amnesia have more to do with legitimacy issues surrounding large loans and credits than with the actual outcomes of similar projects already in existence, funded by NGOs or other small donors.

One of the initiatives traveling throughout the region—Turkmenistan excluded—is curriculum reform, induced by the decision to extend general education from ten to eleven, and then from eleven to twelve years. The SFK first became involved in national curriculum reform in 2001, when it realized that the government-sponsored reform entailed, in reality, merely stretching the current curriculum content by one year. There was no talk of revising curricular content, nor was there any mention of systematically using standards or outcomes as a foundation to develop a new curriculum. By the end of the same year, SFK mobilized approximately seventy policymakers, academics, and NGO representatives to discuss how to proceed with curriculum reform in ways that would be pedagogically useful. Saule Kalikova and Iveta Silova (Chapter 5) list the series of eighteen conferences—organized at international, national, and regional levels—workshops, and public events aimed at creating public awareness of and civic participation in curriculum reform on one hand, and generating local capacity for curriculum reform and educational policy analysis on the other. A permanent working group was established that prepared, over a period of two years, policy papers emphasizing the need for an outcomes-based curriculum reform.

This approach, along with demands to move from teacher-centered education to learner-centered and from facts-based to skills-based learning, was endorsed in a government review and incorporated in subsequent decrees. The economic boom in Kazakhstan has made the country donor independent. This has had huge repercussions for international donors, multilateral organizations, and international NGOs that had been operating in Kazakhstan. Their relationship to the government has changed from one defined in terms of donor-recipient, to one in which international organizations are placed in the backseat. NGOs are only called upon selectively, whenever the government requires technical advice and expertise to implement reforms in accordance with what it chooses to perceive as international standards.

The complementary or corrective function of NGOs, as illustrated in the four case studies of Armenia, Azerbaijan, Mongolia, and Kazakhstan, is closely associated with the type of work attributed to "transnational advocacy networks" (TANs). The term was introduced a few years ago in international and comparative education (for example, Mundy and Murphy 2000) and in the social sciences (Appadurai 2000) to capture the response of NGOs and grassroots organization to globalization. These organizations attempt to influence not only world politics, but also, in their capacity as a global civil society, national governments. Arjun Appadurai relates his demand for a "globalization from below" (2000, 16) to George Soros's vision of a global open society (Soros 1998). Established for the purpose of "doing good" (Fisher 1997), international NGOs usually adhere to values of social justice, civic participation (civil society building), and transparency. Arjun Appadurai also had the good cause of NGOs in mind when he proposed that TANs should be viewed as the only international force to counter corporate globalization. Economic globalization is, according to Appadurai, "a run-away horse without a rider" that can only be tamed by successful TANs that "might offset the most volatile effect of run-away capital" (2000, 16).

In the countries of the region, the IMF and the development banks represent first and foremost the interests of global trade. Even though political stability, economic growth, the rule of law, and so on benefit citizens, they are primarily advanced by international financial institutions to facilitate international trade. The decentralization of finance, creation of an open textbook market, privatization of preschools and higher education—to name just a few features of the post-socialist reform package—target a reduction of public expenditure and an increase of market forces in education. Several national foundations of the Soros Network attempted to counter the dependence on global capital, represented by international financial institutions in their countries, by building local capacity and enhancing civic participation. Two of the case studies, on

Armenia and Georgia, best represent how OSI has attempted to broaden decentralization reforms. Governments and development banks narrowly define the decentralization of finance as the ultimate goal and thereby reduce the community to a "cash cow." The role of the community is simply to pay fees and to generate income for schools. In contrast, the national foundations have supported community participation, community schools, community newsletters, and a series of other projects that emphasize the other aspect of decentralization: civic participation. Their goal is ultimately more transparency and more social accountability of governments, seen as prerequisites for an open society.

The cooperative role of NGOs

Counterbalancing negative outgrowths of the post-socialist reform package represents only one of the strategies that NGOs use in a governance environment that is centralist and donor dependent. Another common strategy is to strengthen governance capacity selectively in areas that comply with the NGO's own mission. There are numerous examples from the national foundations of the Soros Network that reflect this particular strategy. A common practice, not addressed in any of the chapters of this book, deserves mention here: professional development courses and fellowship for government officials. Study tours for government officials have, for good reasons, gone out of fashion. More often than not, these study tours fell into the category of "reward travel." They often, like buying jeeps or computers for government officials so they would presumably be better equipped to monitor a project, led to corruption. Instead, OSI supported fellowships that enabled government officials to travel to other post-socialist countries and learn by experience from reforms that were already implemented in a similar context. This East-East collaboration that OSI supported throughout the 1990s is noteworthy and should be viewed as a precursor to South-South collaboration, advanced a few years later by UNDP and UNESCO. South-South collaboration is generously funded by a few bilateral donors, notably the government of Japan. The cases of Kyrgyzstan and Tajikistan, presented in this book, illustrate two concrete examples of the supportive role of the national foundations.

The Soros Foundation–Kyrgyzstan and the Foundation for Support of Educational Initiatives (a Kyrgyz NGO) assisted the regional department of education in implementing a voucher system for teacher training. The pilot project in the Issyk-Kul region began in 2005 and ended in 2007. It pursued several objectives: enhancing the quality and quantity of in-service teacher training, enabling NGOs to provide it, and giving choice to teachers to select courses they find relevant for their work. Different from most case studies in this book, where the national foundation is at the same time the donor and the implementer of a project, the voucher project was funded as part of the USAID project PEAKS, and the implementer was the regional department of education. The integration of the pilot into existing government structures was a key feature of the project. The regional department of education agreed to "de-monopolize" in-service teacher training and permitted NGOs and other organizations to serve as training providers. Furthermore, the training facilities were provided for free, and the transportation costs for teachers were to be covered by government funds. There was also a hand-over planned with regard to financing the project. The original agreement was that the department of education would not need to contribute any funds in 2005, would pay 40 percent of the project cost in 2006, and would fully cover all costs in 2007.

The Tulip revolution and other political changes in 2005 ended with a replacement of senior government officials throughout the country, and previous agreements were annulled. Regional education authorities only agreed to honor and fund the popular voucher pilot in 2007 after massive public pressure. As the authors of the case study Alexander Ivanov and Valentin Deichman convincingly point out (Chapter 6), the voucher financing mechanism is demanding from a management perspective. It requires that the centralist government, represented at the regional level, coordinate, facilitate, and negotiate. None of these practices is familiar to Kyrgyz government officials. Even though the pilot project was financed in the end with government funds, for the time being management of the pilot, both in the Issyk-Kul region and possibly in new regions as well, relies on support from NGOs.

The case study on Tajikistan also stands as an example in which NGOs cooperated with the government. After the end of the civil war in 1997 the government of Tajikistan finally adopted reforms that had already been implemented in neighboring countries. International donors poured in as soon as the country received "security clearance." OSIAF-Tajikistan observed with great concern as Tajik experts were reduced to project implementers, rather than acting as sector reviewers or designers and analysts of reforms. OSIAF-Tajikistan agreed to support the Ministry of Education in formulating country-specific needs for donors and international organizations by creating a national policy unit—ERSU. From a group of twenty-eight applicants, seven experts were hired and given extensive training in policy analysis. Funded by OSIAF-Tajikistan, ERSU was supposed to become the policy analysis unit of the Ministry of Education. Even though collaboration between ERSU and the Ministry of Education remained strong, the integration of ERSU into the institutional structure of the ministry failed. The author of the case study, Tatiana Abdushukurova (chapter 8), provides a detailed analysis of factors that hindered the successful integration of ERSU into the Ministry of Education. ERSU was eventually reorganized as an independent local NGO and registered under the name of PULSE. It now functions as a think tank conducting research on behalf of different organizations. The employees of PULSE continue to advise government officials on educational reform, but the collaboration is based on interpersonal contacts rather than on institutional agreements.

In reviewing the types of government-led educational reforms that the national foundations of the Soros Network have supported, one is at first surprised to find controversial reforms imported from Europe, North America, Australia, and New Zealand. The Soros Network has supported voucher schemes, standardized testing, and OBE, to list just a few, that were originally both ardently supported and vehemently opposed in their countries of origin. A closer examination, however, reveals that these reforms are reinterpreted, modified, and altered once they have been transferred into the postsocialist context.

The introduction of vouchers in in-service teacher training in Kyrgyzstan, for example, is seen as a "bottom-up" reform, offering practitioners a choice. Vouchers replace a system in which government officials and school principals determined what was good and necessary for teachers. Standardized university entrance exams, now spreading like wildfire throughout the region, are expected to curb private tutoring and replace bribes given to university lecturers and administrators for a place at a prestigious university. Finally, OBE is a method for finding public consensus on what students are supposed to learn, and then systematically translating the outcome into pedagogically useful tools. OBE in the post-socialist context replaces curriculum revision carried out at the desk of one or two government officials, whose task it is to replace one abstract document with another in order to provide proof to international donors that curriculum reform has been checked off. Development banks have channeled millions of dollars into this type of "top-down" curricula development over the past ten years. However, the revised curricula are shelved in technical reports written in English—and never make it into schools. What comes across as an outburst of neoliberal educational reform often has a different connotation in post-socialist contexts. In the three examples mentioned above, the reforms supported by the Soros Network attempted to support bottom-up reform, curb corruption, create more transparency, and generate public consent on educational reform.

Another well-studied phenomenon in educational transfer research is discursive borrowing, whereby only the label of a reform is adopted to attain an international "stamp of approval" for the introduction of a measure that would otherwise be contested. The association with reforms implemented elsewhere sends a positive signal that functions as a "flag of convenience" (Lynch 1998) to secure external funding. Once funding is attained, however, the project sails under a different flag, with a purpose entirely unrelated to what was stated in the original grant or loan proposal. To date, studies on the following "flags of convenience" have been conducted and published: multiculturalism (Silova 2006), vouchers (Steiner-Khamsi 2005), and OBE (Steiner-Khamsi, Silova, and Johnson 2006).

The surrogate role of NGOs

Almost two decades after revolutionary change swept through the region, individuals and institutions have taken a critical, perhaps cynical, stance toward the idea of transition. No doubt the early stage of transformation was characterized more by chaos than by anything else. However, the new "age of the market" (Sneath 2002) has created values and practices that are likely to remain. The "new entrepreneurship," for example, has become an object of admiration for some and of ridicule for others. Caroline Humphrey and Ruth Mandel comment on how the New Russians, New Armenians, and so forth—many of them members of the former Party and State *nomenklatura*—came to prominence:

> Their entrepreneurial success derives not from hard work, but from the social capital accumulated during the Soviet period—their already existing networks and connections. . . . In some regions of the former Soviet Union, this practice has been cynically termed *prikhvatizatsia* (from the Russian word *prikhvait,* "to grab"), a play on the Russian word for privatization, *privatizatsia.* (Humphrey and Mandel 2002, 6)

In research literature the term *transition* was used indiscriminately to capture all that was taking place during the period of transformation. The explanatory power of the concept became visibly flat as countries developed in different directions economically, politically, and socially. Yet, as Christian Giordano and Dobrinka Kostova cynically note, the "orphans of transitology" have moved on to study "democratic consolidation" as the step that presumably follows the transition period (2002, 74). The limitations of such abstract stage models become immediately apparent when one compares them with the realities of centralist governments discussed in this book. In addition, the case studies on Turkmenistan and Uzbekistan represent strategies of the Soros Network under regimes that are not only centralist but also authoritarian. In these two countries the initiatives substitute for reforms that have either been annulled (Uzbekistan) or never targeted (Turkmenistan).

The Soros Network has never been granted entry into Turkmenistan. The authors of the case study, Erika Dailey and Iveta Silova (Chapter 9), point out that international organizations based in Turkmenistan have two options: accept government-approved and government-controlled educational initiatives, or operate covertly by implementing alternative educational projects beyond government oversight. In Turkmenistan, the Soros Network operates *in absentia.* It provides scholarships for Turkmen citizens to study abroad, including in neighboring Kyrgyzstan, and sponsors national initiatives that promote open society values, such as youth seminars, from afar. Clearly, the scope of activities is limited, and the Soros Network is extremely cautious not to create a situation in which its local counterparts or project beneficiaries are subsequently harassed or black listed by government officials.

In Uzbekistan, international NGOs were able to operate until 2004, albeit under an oppressive centralist government. Jacqueline Ashrafi (Chapter 10) documents how OSIAF–Uzbekistan coped during its years of existence with two diametrically opposed expectations: to help create an open society and to abide by the rules of an authoritarian government. In a fascinating account of the regulations in textbook publishing, she focuses on the foundation's support for textbook development in civics and economics. The project was funded by OSIAF-Uzbekistan, but Ministry of Education approval was required for distribution in schools. In other words, the textbooks had to comply with two divergent objectives. On the one hand, Ashrafi writes, they needed to "encourage critical thinking, raise awareness of legal rights, and promote a sense of citizenship among students." Not only did the content of the textbook have to reflect these values, but the process of development had to fulfill the rigorous requirements of OSIAF-Uzbekistan: democratic selection procedures, involvement of teachers in piloting new textbooks, and transparent evaluation criteria. On the other hand, the textbook had to follow the rules of the Ministry of Education. Each law or civic-education textbook had to include at least fourteen direct quotations from presidential speeches and make frequent references to the work of President Karimov. Ashrafi remarks, "Generally, state authorities would be more likely to approve a school textbook if it strictly complied with or—better yet—exceeded the official quotas."

Political schizophrenia is a term used in the post-socialist region to describe the creative ways in which citizens coped in their daily lives with an over-controlling center under communist rule. It was common to insert "official knowledge" in strategic passages that the state censors were most likely to read, typically the first and last few pages of an article, dissertation, or a book. The rest of the document consisted of passages that reflected the author's own opinion, oftentimes conveyed in a coded manner. With the government shut-down of OSIAF-Uzbekistan in 2004, the Soros Network stopped operating in Uzbekistan. It left behind textbooks and other resources, as well as staff, who now work in other organizations. These individuals bide their time in the current era of non-reform, hoping for a future transformation of the education sector.

Even though the strategies used in Turkmenistan and Uzbekistan represent an extreme of how NGOs must operate under a centralist, authoritarian government, their methods for coping reflect legacies from the communist past. Applying a post-socialist perspective that moves beyond the transition period of the early 1990s enables us to see how organizations and individuals dealt with oppressive regimes. In her 1998 analysis of personal networks Alena Ledeneva focuses on economic aspects of the Soviet period and highlights the importance of the informal economy, which existed side by side with the "command economy." She identifies the practice of using personal network to get things done as one of the pillars of socialist governments. Personal networks were used to "obtain goods and services in short supply and to find a way around formal procedures" (Ledeneva 1998, 1), The informal economy of exchange networks was "the 'reverse side' of an over-controlling centre, a reaction of ordinary people to the structural constraints of the socialist system of distribution—a series of practices which enabled the Soviet system to function and made it tolerable, but also subverted it" (Ledeneva 1998, 3).

Arguably, residents of post-socialist countries with a centralist and authoritarian government have become masters in dealing with the reverse side of an over-controlling center. Similarly, NGOs identify niches that are beyond strict government control by supporting progressive national initiatives from outside the country or by undermining rules and regulations in subtle and creative ways.

Scaling up by scaling down?

Educational programs in the post-socialist region of the Soros Network are at an interesting crossroads: the OSI board scaled down the budget for educational projects considerably and at the same established education policy centers that are expected to scale up the political impact of the Soros Network. But organizational expansion represents only one form of scaling up.

Throughout the 1990s and until 2003 the educational programs of the Soros Network expanded organizationally within the post-socialist region. As mentioned before, the geographical expansion was eastward, with the MFOS constituting the furthest border of the initial post-socialist Soros Network. Geographic expansion was within the same world system: the post-socialist region, from Budapest to Ulaanbaatar, composed of educational systems that were similar or even, in the case of the fifteen republics of the former Soviet Union, identical. This allowed for meaningful East-East cooperation, where national foundations from one country learned from the experiences of others. Geographic concentration also had a positive impact on individual national foundations. Speaking in one voice to propel open society values across a huge territory, they were regarded as a (post-socialist) network, spanning over thirty countries, rather than as an individual NGO based in one.

The leverage for correcting or complementing ongoing educational reforms in ways that comply with the mission of the network should not be underestimated. In most countries of the region the Soros Network represented the first and financially the largest international NGO operating in education throughout the 1990s and the first few years of the new millennium. Several case studies presented in this book document the moment when the government "changed sides," typically as soon as a larger donor appeared on the scene. In donor-dependent countries, governments tend to side with those with the deepest pockets. In development studies, we criticize large donors, particularly development banks, for imposing their portfolio of best practices on low-income governments (for example, Jones 2004). They attach programmatic "strings"; that is, they transfer reform packages along with loans and grants. The inverse also applies: governments only subscribe to the mission of an external donor if the donor takes full charge of funding and, in some cases, implementing the proposed reform. Thus, scaling down geographically and organizationally risks diminishing the leverage that an organization has for educational change in countries with a centralist and donor-dependent government.

There exists a series of scaling up strategies besides those which are organizational or quantitative. Peter Uvin and David Miller (1996) mention functional and political scaling up of NGOs, which in the case of the Soros Network have been closely related. Functional scaling up occurs when an NGO expands its scope of activities within a sector, or when it expands the number of sectors in which it operates. Political scaling up captures the attempts made by an NGO to become a political actor and influence policymaking. This is how functional and political scaling was targeted in the Soros Network; the network moved away from pure project work in education and established policy centers that operate in a wide array of sectors (education sector, health sector, legal sector, media sector, etc.). The expectation of the OSI board is that the newly established policy centers, operating as think tanks, advocacy centers, and resource centers, would have a larger impact on policymaking than pilot and demonstration projects funded under the previous project-based OSI strategy.

In another article Peter Uvin, Pankaj Jain, and David Brown remind us that "scaling up is about 'expanding impact' and not about 'becoming large,' the latter being only one possible way to achieve the former" (Uvin, Jain, and Brown 2000, 1409). They analyze the four stages by which NGOs typically increase their impact. First, they expand coverage. Second, they scale up functionally by diversifying their activities. Third, they broaden their indirect impact by means of advocacy, knowledge sharing, and technical assistance or advice. This third stage often implies political scaling up. And finally, NGOs attempt to enhance organizational sustainability by securing for themselves a permanent place within the sector of civil society organizations, or the third sector. Arguably, the fourth stage does not apply for the Soros Network, since Soros believes that not only projects but also national foundations should have a limited lifespan. Uvin, Jain, and Brown contend that small NGOs can have a large impact, and challenge the "old paradigm" whereby scaling up is often confused with an NGO becoming larger and more professionally managed. Their proposed "new paradigm" for scaling up impact builds on "multiplication and mainstreaming through spinning off organizations, letting go of innovations, creating alternative knowledge, and influencing other social actors" (Uvin, Jain, and Brown 2000, 1417). The authors conclude:

> In the new paradigm, the extent to which an NGO successfully scales up can be judged not only in terms of its size, but also in terms of the number of spin-offs it created, the

number of projects that have been taken over by other actors, and the degree to which it contributed to the social and intellectual diversity of civil society. (Uvin, Jain, and Brown 2000, 1417)

The eight national foundations of the Soros Network presented in this book have spun off dozens of local NGOs in the region that continue to contribute, in one way or the other, to educational reform. They also piloted projects and best practices that were subsequently borrowed by other actors in the nongovernmental sector or mainstreamed into government structures. Even though the Soros Network moved on to policy and advocacy work in the form of policy centers, the educational programs of the national foundations left behind material resources. They also left behind human capital—individuals who continue either to correct or to support ongoing educational reforms, depending on the values they promote. It remains to be seen, probably in the next ten years, whether scaling up political impact in the post-socialist region has worked under the condition of scaling down projects and funding in education.

References

Anderson, Kathryn, and Steven Heyneman. 2005. Education and social policy in Central Asia: The next stage of the transition. *Social Policy and Administration* 39(4), 361–80.

Appadurai, Arjun. 2000. Grassroots globalization and the research imagination. *Public Culture* 12(1): 1–19.

ADB (Asian Development Bank). 2000. *Country assistance plan (2001–2003)—Mongolia.* Manila, Philippines: ADB.

———. 2004. *Governance: Progress and challenges in Mongolia.* Manila, Philippines: ADB.

Benavot, Aaron. 2005. A global study of intended instructional time and official school curricula, 1980–2000. Background paper for the EFA Global Monitoring Report 2005, *The quality imperative.* Paris: UNESCO.

Bologna Process Secretariat. 2005a. *From Berlin to Bergen: General report of the Bologna follow-up group to the conference of European ministers responsible for higher education, Bergen, 19–20 May 2005.* Oslo, Norway: Bologna Process Secretariat at the Ministry of Education and Research.

———. 2005b. *Applications for participation in the Bologna Process.* Oslo, Norway: Bologna Process Secretariat at the Ministry of Education and Research.

Crighton, Johanna. 2001. *OSI-Azerbaijan world history textbook project.* Evaluation report submitted to OSIAF-Azerbaijan. Cambridge, UK: Cambridge Assessment and Development in Education (CADE).

Fisher, William. 1997. Doing good: The politics and antipolitics of NGO practices. *Annual Review of Anthropology* 26: 439–64.

Giordano, Christian, and Dobrinka Kostova. 2002. The social production of mistrust. In *Postsocialism: Ideals, ideologies, and practices in Eurasia,* ed. Chris Hann, 74–91. London: Routledge.

Heyneman, Steven. 2006. Videorecorded interview. In *Comparatively speaking: The first 50 years of the Comparative and International Education Society,* produced by Gita Steiner-Khamsi and Eric Johnson. New York: Teachers College, Columbia University, and CIES.

Howlett, Michael, and M. Ramesh. 2003. *Studying public policy: Policy cycles and policy subsystems.* Oxford: Oxford University Press.

Humphrey, Caroline, and Ruth Mandel. 2002. The market in everyday life: Ethnographies of postsocialism. In *Markets and moralities: Ethnographies of postsocialism,* ed. Ruth Mandel and Caroline Humphrey, 1–16. Oxford, UK: Berg.

Jones, Phillip W. 2004. Taking the credit: Financing and policy linkages in the education portfolio of the World Bank. In *The global politics of policy borrowing and lending,* ed. Gita Steiner-Khamsi, 188–200. New York: Teachers College Press.

Kingdon, John. 2003. *Agendas, alternatives, and public policies.* New York: Longman. First published in 1984.

Ledeneva, Alena. 1998. Russia's economy of favours: *Blat,* networking and informal exchange. Cambridge, UK: Cambridge University Press.

Lynch, James. 1998. The international transfer of dysfunctional paradigms. In *Learning and teaching in an international context: Research, theory, and practice,* ed. D. Johnson, B. Smith, and M. Crossley, 7–33. Bristol: University of Bristol, Center for International Studies in Education.

Migration Policy Institute. 2006. Tajikistan: From refugee sender to labor exporter. Press release. Available online.

Mundy, Karen, and Lynn Murphy. 2000. Transnational advocacy, global civil society? Emerging evidence from the field of education. *Comparative Education Review* 45(1): 85–126.

Najam, Adil. 2000. The four-C's of third-sector government relations: Cooperation, confrontation, complementary, and co-optation. *Nonprofit Management and Leadership* 10(4): 375–96.

Nóvoa, Antonio, and Martin Lawn. 2002. Introduction. In *Fabricating Europe: The formation of an education space,* ed. Antonio Nóvoa and Martin Lawn, 1–13. Dordrecht: Kluwer.

OSI (Open Society Institute). 2006. *Education in a hidden marketplace: Monitoring of private tutoring.* Edited by Iveta Silova, Virginija Budiene, and Mark Bray. Available online.

Rathmann, Lothar, and Hans-Peter Vietze. 1978. Die Bedeutung des revolutionären Weges der MVR zum Sozialismus für die internationale Klassenauseinandersetzung [the importance of the revolutionary path of the MPR toward socialism for the international class struggle]. In *Der revolutionäre Weg der Mongolischen Volksrepublik zum Sozialismus. Probleme der Umgehung des kapitalistischen Entwicklungsstadiums* ed. Hans-Peter Vietze, 325–57. Berlin: Akademie-Verlag.

Rostiashvili, Ketevan. 2004. *Corruption in the higher education system of Georgia*. Tbilisi: American University's Transnational Crime and Corruption Center Georgia Office, Starr Foundation, and IREX.

Sabatier, Paul, and Hank Jenkins-Smith. 1993. *Policy change and learning: An advocacy coalition approach*. Boulder, CO: Westview.

Shirendyb, Bazaryn. 1981. A historic choice. In *The sixtieth anniversary of People's Mongolia*. Ulaanbaatar: Unen Editorial Board; Moscow: Novosti Press Agency Publishing House.

Silova, Iveta. 2006. *From sites of occupation to symbols of multiculturalism: Transfer of global discourse and the metamorphosis of Russian schools in post-Soviet Latvia*. Greenwich, CT: Information Age Publishing.

Sneath, David. 2002. Mongolia in the "Age of the Market": Pastoral land-use and the development discourse. In *Markets and moralities: Ethnographies of postsocialism*, ed. Ruth Mandel and Caroline Humphrey, 191–210. Oxford, UK: Berg.

Soros, George. 1998. Toward a global open society. *Atlantic Monthly* (January), 20–24, 32.

Steiner-Khamsi, Gita. 2005. Vouchers for teacher education (non) reform in Mongolia: Transitional, postsocialist, or antisocialist explanations? *Comparative Education Review* 49(2): 148–72.

————. 2007. *The stavka system in Tajikistan: Background, challenges and recommendations for teacher salary reform*. Dushanbe: Education Modernization Project Management Unit: Washington DC: World Bank.

Steiner-Khamsi, Gita, and Ines Stolpe. 2006. *Educational import. Local encounters with global forces in Mongolia*. New York: Palgrave Macmillan.

Steiner-Khamsi, Gita, Ines Stolpe, and Amgabaazar Gerelmaa. 2004. *Rural School Development Project in Mongolia. Evaluation report*. Ulaanbaatar and Copenhagen: Danish Mongolia Society and Mongolian Association for Primary and Secondary School Development in collaboration with Copenhagen International Centre for Educational Development and Mongolian State University of Education.

Steiner-Khamsi, Gita, Iveta Silova, and Eric Johnson. 2006. Neoliberalism liberally applied: Educational policy borrowing in Central Asia. In *2006 World Yearbook on Education,* ed. David Coulby, Jenny Ozga, Terri Seddon, and Thomas Popkewitz, 217–45. London: Routledge.

UNDP (United Nations Development Programme). 2005. The potential role of remittances in achieving the Millennium Development Goals—an exploration. Round table on remittances and the MDGs background note. October 10. New York: UNDP.

Uvin, Peter, and David Miller. 1996. Paths to scaling-up: Alternative strategies for local nongovernmental organizations. *Human Organization* 55(3): 344–49.

Uvin, Peter, Pankaj S. Jain, and L. David Brown. 2000. Think large and act small: Toward a new paradigms for NGO scaling up. *World Development* 28(8): 1409–19.

World Bank. 2004. *Memorandum of the president of the International Development Association to the executive directors on a country assistance strategy of the World Bank Group for Mongolia.* April 5, 2004. Washington DC: World Bank, Southeast Asia, and Mongolia Country Unit, East Asia and Pacific Region.

———. 2005. *Tajikistan: Civil and public service wage note.* Washington DC: World Bank, Poverty Reduction and Economic Management Unit, Europe and Central Asia Region.

———. 2006. *Mongolia: Public financing of education: Equity and efficiency implications.* Human Development Sector Report, East Asia and the Pacific Region. Washington DC: World Bank.

———. 2007. *Governance matters 2007. Worldwide governance indicators, 1996–2006.* Washington DC: World Bank Institute/World Bank Development Economics Research Group.

About the Contributors

Tatiana Abdushukurova holds a Ph.D. from the Institute of Philosophy and Law at the Tajik Academy of Sciences. She was a Fulbright Scholar in the Department of Near Middle Eastern Languages and Civilization of the University of Washington (1996), and a visiting professor at the University of New Mexico (1999). From 1989 to 2000, Tatiana Abdushukurova was an associate professor in the Department of Political Science at the Tajik State National University. Currently, she is an education program director of OSI-Tajikistan. Her research focuses on the issues of social stratification and social mobility, political culture, gender equity, and civic education in Tajikistan.

Jacqueline Ashrafi (a pseudonym) is an expert in the field of education in Central Asia. Her real name is withheld to avoid the possibility of reprisals for the views expressed herein.

Erika Dailey is founding director of the OSI's Turkmenistan Project, which was launched in 2002 as part of OSI's Central Eurasia Project. Since 2002 she has administered the division's grants-and-advocacy programs targeting the South Caucasus and Central Asia. She was researcher and Moscow office director at Human Rights Watch (1992–98) and has worked and consulted for numerous other rights-based organizations in the region. She has an M.A. in Central Asian studies from Columbia University and has traveled extensively in the USSR and the former Soviet states.

Valentin Deichman graduated from the Kyrgyz National State University and earned an M.A. degree in education policy at the Moscow School of Social and Economic Sciences in Russia. Valentin has worked at the Soros Foundation–Kyrgyztsan for over seven years and is currently directing a mega project in basic education reform, funded by USAID. He also works as a consultant for the Education Support Program of the OSI (London).

Natsagdorj Enkhtuya has an M.A. in education studies from Mongolian State University of Education. She has worked as an education development program coordinator in the MFOS for over six years (1998–2004). She currently works as executive director of the NGO Mongolian Education Alliance.

Alexander Ivanov is the chairman of the board of Education Initiatives Support, a foundation in Bishkek, Kyrgyzstan. He graduated from Tashkent State University in Uzbekistan with an undergraduate degree in psychology and earned an M.A. degree in education policy at the Moscow School of Social and Economic Sciences in Russia. He worked as a program coordinator at the Soros Foundation Kyrgyzstan for five years (1995–2000) and is currently overseeing implementation of various education reform projects funded by the ADB, World Bank, UNICEF, USAID, and other international agencies in Kyrgyzstan.

Saule Kalikova is a director of the Educational Policy Analysis Center at the Educational Center "Bilim—Central Asia" and a former director of educational programs at the Soros Foundation in Almaty, Kazakhstan. Saule Kalikova has a graduate degree from Kazakh National University. Before joining the NGO sector in the mid-1990s, she worked as a leading specialist at the Ministry of Education and Science and as an education adviser at the Parliament of the Republic of Kazakhstan. During the 1990s she worked extensively with local NGOs and international organizations, including the World Bank, the ADB, and United Nations organizations.

Elmina Kazimzade graduated from the Department of Psychology at Moscow State University and holds a Ph.D. from the Psychology Research Institute of Ukraine. She teaches at the Department of Psychology and Social Sciences at Baku State University and acts as education adviser of OSIAF–Azerbaijan. Elmina Kazimzade worked as education director and deputy director of OSIAF for eight years. She implemented various education projects in cooperation with state institutions, such as the Ministry of Education and Ministry of Youth and Sport, and international organizations, such as the World Bank, the ADB, and the Council of Europe.

Anna Matiashvili has an M.A. degree in economics and education policy from Teachers College, Columbia University, and a M.S.

in management from the Robert F. Wagner Graduate School of Public Service at New York University. She has worked for various international NGOs in Georgia and New York. She was a Manager of the Education Decentralization and the Management Development Program at the Open Society Georgia Foundation, and a director of regional programs at the International Institute for Education Policy, Planning, and Management in Tbilisi, Georgia. She also worked for the Education Development Center, World Education Services, and the World Association of Non-Governmental Organizations in New York City. She currently resides in New York City and works for the Inwood House—a social services agency working on teenage pregnancy and HIV/AIDS prevention, sexuality education, and youth development.

Iveta Silova is an assistant professor of transcultural, comparative, and international education at the College of Education, Lehigh University. Her research and publications cover a range of issues critical to understanding post-socialist education transformation processes, including gender equity trends in Eastern/Central Europe and Central Asia, minority/multicultural education policies in the former Soviet Union, as well as the scope, nature, and implications of private tutoring in a cross-national perspective. She is the author of *From Sites of Occupation to Symbols of Multiculturalism: Re-conceptualizing Minority Education in Post-Soviet Latvia* (Information Age Publishing, 2006) and coeditor (with Mark Bray and Virginija Budiene) of *Education in a Hidden Marketplace: Monitoring of Private Tutoring* (OSI, 2006).

Gita Steiner-Khamsi has been professor of comparative and international education at Teachers College, Columbia University, New York since 1995. She has been a guest professor at Humboldt University, Berlin; Stanford University; the University of Toronto; and the University of London Institute of Education. She is 2009 president-elect of CIES–United States and committee member of the World Congress of Comparative Education Societies. She has published four books and numerous journal articles and book chapters. Her two most recent publications are *The Global Politics of Educational Borrowing and Lending* (Teachers College Press, 2004) and, with Ines Stolpe, *Educational Import: Local Encounter with Global Forces in Mongolia* (Palgrave Macmillan, 2006). She does analytical work and applied research in Mongolia, Central Asia, and Europe.

Armenuhi Tadevosyan graduated from the Department of Literature and Linguistics at the Yerevan State University. She works as a coordinator of education and women's programs at OSIAF-Armenia. Her responsibilities include administration of projects that support policy analysis in the field of both general and higher education, and curriculum development in the areas of social sciences and humanities, women's human rights, violence against women, and gender education.

Index

ACCELS. *See* American Councils for International Education

ADB. *See* Asian Development Bank

Africa: educational development in, 13–14; Samoff on education reviews in, 17–18

Alesina, Alberto, 7

Alexander, Tom, 147

American Councils for International Education (ACCELS), xiii

Analytical Group, the : composition of, 147–48; founding of, 147; Kazakhstan, OBE introduced by, 151–52; Kazakhstan, SFK partnering with, 148, 151

Anderson-Levitt, Kathryn, 29–30

Appadurai, Arjun, 270

Armenia: community schools roles/responsibilities in, 88–89; Community TeleCenters potential success in, 91, 264–65; donor similarities with community participation in, 97–99; educational reform, community participation in, 86–88; education crisis in, 84–85; education loans for, 22; education workforce downsizing in, 24; Eritsian on educational reform in, 86; Eritsian on education crisis in, 84; OSIAF, community schools in, 83, 89–91, 263–65; OSIAF, ICT integration in, 90–91; OSIAF, Project Harmony, World Bank, community schools models in, 94–96; World Bank aiding educational reform in, 86–88; World Bank report on education crisis in, 85. *See also* Armenia School Connectivity Program

Armenia School Connectivity Program: community schools entering, 92; Project Harmony starting, 91–92

Asian Development Bank (ADB), xiii; Caucasus, Central Asia, education loans from, 21–23; donor logic of, 5–6; MOECS, funding priorities of, 14; Mongolia, focus of, 259, 265; Uzbekistan, textbook development aid from, 240

Azerbaijan: education law in, 113; education loans for, 22; Hunt and Read on textbook publishing liberalization in, 110; Jones, Annabel, textbook author training in, 103; Mardanov on textbook policy of, 113; OSIAF, textbook development process in, 108–9; OSIAF, World Bank aiding textbook publishing liberalization in, 111–12; OSIAF, World Bank, textbook reform principals in, 106–7, 115–16, 265; teacher opinions on textbook authorship in, 107–8; textbook finance policy in, 113–14; textbook publishing liberalization in, 110–12; textbook reform challenges in, 106, 114–16; World Bank, textbook quality goals in, 108, 265

Balci, Bayram, 221

Berdymukhamedov, Gurbanguly, 211; Niyazov, service of, 228n–229n; Turkmenistan, donor relations under, 223; Turkmenistan, educational reform advancement of, 227–28; Turkmenistan, educational reform, higher learning of, 216–17

Also from Kumarian Press...

Civil Society and Governance

The Charity of Nations: Humanitarian Action in a Calculating World
Ian Smillie and Larry Minear

Nation-Building Unraveled? Aid, Peace and Justice in Afghanistan
Edited by Antonio Donini, Norah Niland and Karin Wermester

CIVICUS Global Survey of the State of Civil Society, Volume 2:
Comparative Perspectives
Edited by V. Finn Heinrich and Lorenzo Fioramonti

New and Forthcoming:

The World Bank and the Gods of Lending
Steve Berkman

Mobilizing for Human Rights in Latin America
Edward Cleary

Surrogates of the State: NGOs, Development and Ujamaa in Tanzania
Michael Jennings

Building an Inclusive Development Community: A Manual on Including
People with Disabilities in International Development Programs
Edited by Karen Heinicke-Motsch and Susan Sygall

Visit Kumarian Press at **www.kpbooks.com** or
call **toll-free 800.289.2664** for a complete catalog.

green press
INITIATIVE

Kumarian Press, Inc. is committed to preserving ancient forests and natural resources. We elected to print *How NGOs React* on 30% post consumer recycled paper, processed chlorine free. As a result, for this printing, we have saved:

4 Trees (40' tall and 6-8" diameter)
1,705 Gallons of Waste Water
686 Kilowatt Hours of Electricity
188 Pounds of Solid Waste
369 Pounds of Greenhouse Gases

Kumarian Press, Inc. made this paper choice because our printer, Thomson-Shore, Inc., is a member of Green Press Initiative, a nonprofit program dedicated to supporting authors, publishers, and suppliers in their efforts to reduce their use of fiber obtained from endangered forests.

For more information, visit www.greenpressinitiative.org

Kumarian Press, located in Bloomfield, Connecticut, is a forward-looking, scholarly press that promotes active international engagement and an awareness of global connectedness.